PERSONAL BUSINESS

Victorian Literature and Culture Series

JEROME J. MCGANN AND HERBERT F. TUCKER,
EDITORS

PERSONAL BUSINESS

CHARACTER AND COMMERCE
IN VICTORIAN LITERATURE AND CULTURE

Aeron Hunt

University of Virginia Press
CHARLOTTESVILLE AND LONDON

University of Virginia Press
© 2014 by the Rector and Visitors of the University of Virginia
All rights reserved
Printed in the United States of America on acid-free paper

First published 2014

1 3 5 7 9 8 6 4 2

LIBRARY OF CONGRESS CATALOGING-IN-PUBLICATION DATA
Hunt, Aeron, 1969–
Personal business : character and commerce in Victorian literature and culture /
Aeron Hunt.
pages cm. — (Victorian Literature and Culture Series)
Includes bibliographical references and index.
ISBN 978-0-8139-3631-4 (cloth : acid-free paper) —
ISBN 978-0-8139-3632-1 (e-book)
1. English literature—19th century—History and criticism. 2. Economics and
literature—Great Britain—History—19th century. 3. Literature and society—
Great Britain—History—19th century. 4. Finance, Personal—Great Britain—
History. 5. Economics in literature. 6. Business in literature. I. Title.
PR468.E36H86 2014
820.9'3553—dc23

2014004407

For Andrew

Contents

Acknowledgments

WRITING THIS BOOK HAS NOT BEEN A SOLO ENDEAVOR, AND I'M delighted to have the chance to take care of the personal business that acknowledgments represent. My first thanks go to my readers at the University of Chicago. Elaine Hadley has been an inspiring model of critical engagement; her faith in this project from the start and her advice over the long haul have helped me through many transitions. Elizabeth Helsinger and Larry Rothfield gave generous and rigorous attention to the manuscript in its early stages. Financial support from the Rosenthal fellowship made the initial research possible.

At the University of New Mexico (UNM) it has been my great fortune to have Gail Houston as a colleague. Her critical acumen, scholarly dedication, and remarkable energy help me to remember what is best about my profession. Gary Harrison has offered gracious and incisive mentorship. Marissa Greenberg, Greg Martin, and Carmen Nocentelli have inspired me with their intelligence and boosted my spirits. I thank other New Mexico colleagues for their valuable suggestions and support of all kinds, especially Jesse Alemán, Pamela Cheek, David Jones, Michelle Hall Kells, Dan Mueller, Anita Obermeier, Mary Power, Scott Sanders, Kathleen Washburn, and Carolyn Woodward, as well as the wonderful staff and students of the English Department. Grants from the Research Allocations Committee at UNM enabled crucial research trips. I am also extremely grateful for comments and encouragement from scholars elsewhere, especially Tanya Agathocleous, Tim Alborn, Gordon Bigelow, Dan Bivona, Lana Dalley, Nancy Henry, Jen Hill, Deanna Kreisel, George Levine, Pericles Lewis, Stefanie Markovits, Linda Peterson, Mary Poovey, Jill Rappoport, Talia Schaffer, Marlene Tromp, and Ruth Yeazell.

Friends in many locations have lived through this project with me and kept me going. I especially thank Margaret Keller, a wonderful interlocutor and even better roommate. I learned so much from everyone at *Critical In-*

quiry, in particular Jay Williams, who proved that a workplace can be professional, pedagogical, and a space for true and lasting friendship. Zarena Aslami makes it fun to be a Victorianist. Ken Shadlen and Susan Martin put me up in London and offered moral support along the way. Marcus Kurtz provided valuable guidance about the publishing process. I am so happy to have shared the writing of this book with Dora Calott Wang and Julie Heinrich, great girlfriends and generous playdate hosts. Emily Harmon and Arand Pierce endured my grumbling and brought me out of it with their warm friendship and the occasional dance-off. Thanks also to Durwood Ball, Christy Coch, Christine Cooney, Charley Davis, Rebecca DeRoo, Dovya Friedman, Paul Gilmore, Jolisa Gracewood, Dan Graff, Martin Heinrich, Tina Kachele, Nicole MacLaughlin, Brendan Mathews, Jamil Mustafa, Jennifer Peterson, Alison Pollet, Will Pritchard, and Paige Reynolds.

Librarians at my home institutions and at the British Library and the Guildhall Library were exceptionally helpful: thank you all. I am grateful to the Guildhall Library and Standard Chartered Bank for permission to reprint images and to Suzie Andrews and Duncan Campbell-Smith for their assistance. Portions of chapter 3 were previously published as "The Authoritative Medium: George Eliot, Ruin, and the Rationalized Market," *Journal of Victorian Culture* 17, no. 2 (June 2012): 164–82.

The excellent insights and careful attention of the editors of Virginia's Victorian Literature and Culture series, as well as the anonymous readers of the manuscript, have helped make this a much stronger book. Cathie Brettschneider has shepherded me through publication with professional grace and exemplary patience; my thanks also to Raennah Mitchell and Mark Mones for their thoroughness and willingness to field my questions and to Carol Sickman-Garner for her careful editorial eye.

My family encouraged my love of reading and my curiosity about other histories and places right from the start. I thank my parents, Alan and Bernadette Hunt, Vanessa Hunt and Matt Godbolt, and all the extended Hunt and Belanger families—those who are here and those who are no longer—for their love and care over the years. I am grateful for the warm welcome I received from Maryanne Schrank and a new extended family; thanks especially to Kitty and Vince Hartigan, who is much missed, and to Trip Hartigan and Page Heslin, for making Chicago and New Haven feel like home.

My children, Sylvan and Sadie, have patiently put up with my distraction and brightened every day. I don't know where to begin to thank Andrew Schrank. This project would never have been completed without his confidence and endurance, his enthusiasm and intelligence, and his willingness to read . . . and reread. He has been the book's best friend and its author's. Thank you for everything.

PERSONAL BUSINESS

Introduction

IN CHARLES DICKENS'S 1847 NOVEL *DEALINGS WITH THE FIRM OF DOMbey and Son: Wholesale, Retail, and for Exportation,* Uncle Sol, the proprietor of a small shop selling maritime instruments—or, rather, not selling, since the shop transacts exactly no business over the novel's many hundreds of pages—bemoans his sense of being out of step with the new commercial world. "Tradesmen are not the same as they used to be," he complains. "Apprentices are not the same, business is not the same, business commodities are not the same. Seven-eighths of my stock is old-fashioned. I am an old-fashioned man in an old-fashioned shop, in a street that is not the same as I remember it. I have fallen behind the time, and am too old to catch it again. Even the noise it makes a long way ahead, confuses me."[1] Uncle Sol's emphasis on the dramatic change that overwhelms him does not lack for company in Victorian fictions featuring economic subjects. From technological revolution and conflict between industrial employers and workers; to grandiose commercial and speculative frauds, enabled by the joint-stock corporate form and the limited liability company; to international investment schemes and imperial trade ventures; to new commodities and dazzling commercial displays and advertising, the novels of the period vividly depict a social and economic life characterized by extreme instability and rapid transformation.

Within this fictional context it is significant, albeit not surprising, that Dickens's lament for a passing way of life is voiced by a small business owner, an individual identified with his shop and liable for its successes and failures. Uncle Sol's sense of his own outdatedness seems to confirm even as it establishes our impression that Victorian capitalism is most typified by—and most interesting for—its rapid changes. Perhaps chief among these, in terms of the critical attention they have attracted, are those larger and more complex corporate organizations and forms of investment and exchange that severed the links between businesses and their identifiable, responsible, personal agents. Uncle Sol and his business model are left in the dust, in this view, as the Victorian economy follows a path of depersonalization and abstraction toward the heady reaches of finance capitalism.[2]

Compare Uncle Sol's account of loss with the nostalgic glow suffusing this 1956 speech by the chairman of the Ottoman Bank—offices in London, Paris, and Istanbul—on the centenary of the bank's establishment in the City of London:

> I happened to glance, just for interest, at the very first Report and Balance Sheet of the Imperial Ottoman Bank and was interested and touched to see among the names of the Committee those of Hottinguer, Mallet, Pillet-Will and Stern, which figure on the Report and Balance Sheet we passed at our meeting this morning. This continuity, from generation to generation, which is also reflected in the Management and in the Staff of the Bank, is all part of that "esprit de famille" which we value very highly indeed.[3]

Far from heady and impersonal, finance capital here feels downright cozy. But we don't need to accept at face value the chairman's avowals of emotion and his celebration of the familial spirit and makeup of the company (an international, joint-stock, limited liability affair) in order to find a counterpoint to the narrative animated by Dickens. In the first place, the continuity of the firm's representatives from the mid-Victorian establishment of the bank to the mid-twentieth century suggests an empirical difference from the picture of increasing abstraction and impersonality: it may not be the whole story, but at least in some ways the company has maintained an identity associated with particular family representatives. And what's more, this is something that the chairman highlights: if his affect is exaggerated, or the familial continuity relatively incidental, it becomes all the more significant that they inform so strongly the rhetoric chosen to shape the company's public image and its self-image. Furthermore, the chairman goes on to celebrate the way that twentieth-century technological developments have helped keep the company as close-knit as a local branch bank: "Thanks to the aeroplane, no branch of the Bank is more than a day or so's travel from London or Paris. The Directors and Management today enjoy, therefore, a more real close and personal knowledge of the Bank's affairs than ever before."[4] No one would mistake these directors and managers for Uncle Sol, the small businessman, but the practical and rhetorical value of "real close and personal knowledge" is assumed in the language of both the fictional Victorian shop owner and the chairman of an international bank one century later—even if the balance between practice and rhetoric has altered.

I excerpt this example of a twentieth-century business speech not to deny the truth (of which it hardly needs saying there is a great deal) in an account of Victorian capitalism that emphasizes change and a tendency to complexity, abstraction, and impersonality. What I suggest, instead, is that even in a case that exemplifies many of the elements that we might associate strongly with those qualities—finance (as opposed to industrial production), an international scope, and limited liability, for instance—there are more points of resemblance to what business historians have called "personal capitalism" than tend to be acknowledged in recent cultural studies.[5] The speech suggests that empirical details about the organization of business (for example, the persistence of families and individuals identified with their firms) might cause us to revise our tendency to assume that Victorian business *was* most characteristically complex, abstract, and impersonal—and that it was experienced as such by those who participated in it. But it also highlights the way personal knowledge, oversight, and connections continued to be ideologically and rhetorically prioritized as businessmen imagined the ideal workings of enterprise and as they represented this ideal to others.

This study therefore aims to refocus attention on what I call the personal business of Victorian commercial culture and its literary manifestations: the persistent, if shifting, complex of ways in which businesses, business writing, and writing about business invoked and engaged the personal. The term *personal business* implies, first, a historical and social reality: the interpersonal networks and relationships through which commercial transactions and interactions occurred, in contexts ranging from small family firms to large and complex organizations and in relationships with customers and coworkers, credit seekers and lenders, bosses and subordinates, bank chairmen and board members, and so forth. Though its contexts and terms may have changed, personal business persists to this day, encompassing aspects of commercial life that run the gamut from benign, to positive, to decidedly negative. Job networking associations, or a decision by a business to use one contractor over another because longstanding association provides grounds for confidence: these are arguably productive aspects of personal business, generating efficiencies and stability. But in recent years the dark side of personal business has been just as strongly in evidence. The Ottoman Bank chairman's "esprit de famille" finds a perverse updating in a scene from December 2008, in the conference room of Bernard L. Madoff Investment Securities LLC, where the operator of the largest Ponzi scheme in history—international in its reach but enacted on more intimate stages, from the Palm Beach Country Club to the local school—sits at a board meeting for a charity foundation surrounded by family members and friends from "every decade of [his] life," conscious that these associates and others, drawn in through religious, social, and familial networks, are about to be wiped out.[6]

The persistence of personal business suggests that its Victorian instantiation should not be viewed as an anachronistic, antimodern holdover in an otherwise modernizing age. Nor should it be taken simply as the stable material and embodied foundation from which economic relations spiraled away toward the ever more purely "symbolic."[7] Instead this study insists that personal business was a dynamic and inescapable feature of Victorian economic life, one that was actively constructed throughout the period and shaped the form of its modernity. An analysis that takes this insight as a point of departure generates a new perspective on the problems of representation not only in the Victorian economy but in the writing, literary and nonliterary, that engaged and helped to produce it. This perspective centers on character: the social, performative, and textual form through which the personal emerges in practice and discourse as a crucial vector of power within economic life. More specifically, repositioning personal business at the heart of Victorian economic life requires a focus on what I call *transactional character*, a phrase that yokes together two senses of *transaction*—its economic sense as well as the more general implication of interactive exchanges between people (and between people and texts)—to capture what emerges in situations where character must be represented or interpreted in a business context.

The renovation that these terms contribute to Victorian literary and cultural studies can best be introduced by acknowledging my argument's critical debts. After all, the claim that character and commerce are intimately related in the capitalist culture of eighteenth- and nineteenth-century Britain has a distinguished pedigree in historical and literary studies, especially in the history of the novel. It also has found inspiration in the rich body of scholarship, guided by the principle that literary and economic writing be read together as part of a broadly constituted discursive field, that has come to be known as the new economic criticism, which has emerged in recent years as one of the most fruitful areas within Victorian studies.[8]

But the robustness of these critical traditions has led them to a crucial juncture, as the connections they posit among literary writing, readers, and economic writing and practices have come to appear as near orthodoxy, assumed rather than explained or evidenced. The time is thus ripe for reexaminations. And that process has begun, most notably with Mary Poovey's probing, self-reflective—and strongly skeptical—challenge to the assumption that the concept of the discursive field justifies yoking together disparate texts and genres.[9] To advance understanding of the relation of literary writing to economic cultures, in history, this challenge must be addressed,

and the grounds for connections must be explored and specified. This entails, I suggest, a move away from the focus on broad conceptual categories
or theoretical issues—the economy, capitalism, or market culture; political
economy and the semiotics of money—that has shaped much of the significant work in both the new economic criticism and the history of the novel,
at the expense of attention to the material, embodied, and socially embedded
interactions that constitute much of economic life. What a focus on personal
business contributes is a crucial level of mediation, a more grounded picture
of economic activity that does not diminish the significance of abstract philosophical questions but seeks a wider range of concrete actions and situations in which they come to life.

I argue that attention to the everyday relations of personal business suggests that common ground between literature and economic practice is not
merely critical convention (or invention) and that character provides the
connection: at once vitally economic and importantly (though not exclusively) literary, textual, and performative, mobilized continually through
representations and interpretations that draw on multiple sources. In the
frame of personal business concrete genres and examples of character as a
transactional form become visible, available for analysis of how they mediated encounters and exchanges while simultaneously eliciting epistemological concerns. Novels and other character narratives joined with the representational practices of business to find the genres and forms that would manage
these problems and navigate the representation of truth and the discernment
of value in the transactions of a competitive and volatile market.

For Victorian authors and businesspeople alike, character became the
form on which hopes for a disciplined, moralized economy were pinned.
Skill in character interpretation joined the encouragement of good character
as the economic safeguard of choice, a means to moralize the marketplace
through individual actions and responsibility. But as it was transacted, character exerted a power that exceeded—and even countered—these reformist
aims, as character narratives and performances were used to generate income
and credit and as character forms were created that mediated new commercial practices and organizations. The tension between these two possibilities
conditions character's distinctive modes of power in Victorian economic culture. These were constituted by the dynamic interplay among the sometimes
overlapping, sometimes antagonistic forms and representations of character
summoned in everyday commercial texts and encounters and imagined in
narratives—forms and representations that might appeal just as much to
conventions of storytelling as to factual truth. Because the personal was not
separate but rather radically embedded in economic representation and prac-

tice, it functioned more as an amoral medium than as an opportunity for precise analysis and ethical reform through the instrument of character.[10] As character proliferated in concrete situations, it could never be the dependably stabilizing technology that observers hoped; instead, character enabled modes of power and authority that were, finally, profoundly ambivalent.

This emphasis on the concrete and the everyday has thus guided my choice of terminology, cases, and texts. "Business," for instance, is a capacious concept, one that might reasonably seem to call for disaggregation.[11] But in employing this term and the more expansive framework it entails, I intend to invoke the obsolete meaning that lingers in the word: busyness, in the sense of activity or engagement. We speak of "doing business" to describe commercial, or work-related, transactions. Shops, banks, and firms of all sorts have "business hours," during which activities with customers, coworkers, and clients occur—often, though not always, at their "place of business." In emphasizing activity, as these examples suggest, the term also invokes social and interpersonal relations, reminding us that commercial activity is not— no matter how abstract its components may become—a purely abstract field, in which constructed figures like *homo economicus* or entities such as limited liability companies pursue their calculable interests in the idealized grid of a perfect market by exchanging symbols of wealth. Thomas Carlyle, in *Past and Present,* complained of the "delusion" that "any man . . . can keep himself apart from men, have 'no business' with them, except a cash-account 'business.'"[12] Carlyle's critique suggests the tension within the term—the "cash-account" propensities of capitalism that define business as asocial and depersonalizing crowding out the social exchanges that it also invokes. By insisting on the social—and emphasizing that even a "cash-account" business necessarily involves people having business and doing business with each other—we expand our definition of the historical and empirical field that writing about commerce engaged and avoid reinforcing the abstracting tendencies that Carlyle condemned.

My focus on everyday personal business has shaped a set of cases based in a complex of relationships, roles, interactions, and transactions that have gone un- or underexplored: managers and owners; creditors, debtors, and bankruptcy court officials; company promoters, investors, and investment advisers; coworkers; customers; supervisors; lines of succession, and so forth. Family businesses and private partnerships and the particular negotiations and stresses that they involve become as interesting as joint-stock and limited liability corporate forms, sites of dynamism in their own right—and therefore more promising sites of analysis—rather than frozen, static background. Furthermore, within the new, apparently more impersonal business organizations, and in the culture of investment that expanded along with them, new puzzles emerge about how the personal is represented or obscured in everyday transactions and what relations it forges or forecloses. What, for instance, are the conditions of meaningfulness for the names "Hottinguer, Mallet, Pillet-Will and Stern" in the Ottoman Bank in 1956, and what were they over the course of the firm's hundred-year history to that point? And what registers of meaning would those names—those invocations of the personal—imply for those who dealt with the company's officers, or its stocks, or its promotional materials?

Business writing represents a vast and diffuse archive, especially when everyday communications are considered. I have, therefore, focused on written materials and reading practices that highlight transactional character: the information books kept by firms (ledgers with notations about associates, potential associates, and customers); company annual reports and investment prospectuses; character certificates for bankrupts; business advice manuals; business biographies and histories; financial journalism and trade publications; parliamentary debates; legal cases; scientific treatises; and, finally, novels. This principle of textual selection has introduced limits: I have drawn on a range of commercial sites and sources, with attention to different sizes and structures of business and to different aspects of business practice; however, within that range the relationships and hierarchies that emerged as most central tend to be somewhat class restricted, extending mostly through the gradients of lower- to upper-middle classes. The implications of the personal business framework for industrial novels and other Victorian representations of relationships between working- and middle-class subjects receive less attention here, as they raise historical and archival issues distinct enough and vast enough to deserve a book of their own.

From a different perspective, after all, my textual archive is characterized not by limitation but by expansiveness, especially in the variety of genres it incorporates. How to evaluate and address the distinctness of genres has been an active question in recent years, especially with the new formalist challenge to interdisciplinary and new historicist critical practices.[13] My argument suggests that recognizing genre differences does not nullify the value of examining character across a broad textual field. Because this field is unified, to a degree, by common transactional aspects, patterns may be traced, and shared—and divergent—representational and interpretive modes may be compared. As these different texts proffered, revised, and questioned models of character and character interpretation, they claimed authority and power to address the challenges of economic life alongside the increasingly privileged discipline of professional economics, whose ascendancy Poovey has traced. Neglecting or downplaying the way character was imagined and practiced within business not only leads us to ascribe an overly comprehensive authority to professional economics but also risks repeating a Victorian binary: either pinning naive hopes on the disciplinary possibilities of character or viewing character as at best ancillary to an economy in which rational calculation is the dominant knowledge mode. In assuming that character and its various representations and narratives are not already crucially embedded in the economy, both these positions obscure the forms of power that character continues to exert not only in Victorian business culture but also in the practice of business today. And in restoring character to its place in the picture, we may reassert the value of reading across genres, across fields, embedded in history.

Modernizing, Personal: Perspectives on Victorian Business

In studies of the economic culture of Victorian Britain, the personal is a vexed concept. On the one hand, several theoretical, historical, and critical traditions have sought to understand the experience of the personal—indeed our very concept of the personal, emerging from and relating to the privatized, subjective individual—as a historically specific formation, produced by and transformed within the changing conditions of capitalism. From Marx's analysis of the way that "man as a bourgeois"—a "partial," private being defined through economic activities and property relationships—had been naturalized into "the *true* and *authentic* man," to Foucault's account of the formation of the modern disciplinary subject, this has been fertile ground for critics seeking to investigate how literary narratives shaped and were shaped by the intersection of capitalist modernity and the personal.[14] Classic accounts of the history of the novel by Ian Watt, Michael McKeon, and Nancy Armstrong, for example, have written that history as an aspect of the social changes wrought by capitalism, in which the novel is a function of the emergence of bourgeois, mercantile culture and its self-reflexive orientation toward everyday and individual experience (Watt); or constitutes itself as a genre through negotiating the epistemological and social-ethical questions raised by the early modern movement away from an aristocratic ideal (McKeon); or constructs personal virtue, grounded in deep subjectivity and desire, as the standard of value for the new socioeconomic order (Armstrong).[15]

Many foundational texts of the new economic criticism approached the relationship between literature and economics from a different theoretical angle. Influential analyses of money as a signifying system—even as the paradigm for modern and postmodern understandings of representation and value—by critics and theorists such as Marc Shell and Jean-Joseph Goux

were predisposed toward abstraction: focused on the philosophical problems evoked by coins as symbolic tokens, or the theoretical significance of
the passage from metal to paper money to electronic flows, and so forth.
In Shell's *The Economy of Literature*, for instance, the textuality of money
is foregrounded and analyzed transhistorically, from ancient Greece to
nineteenth-century Britain; "character" is discussed primarily in relation to
its numismatic meaning—the varieties of inscriptions on coins in contrast
to the material value the coin apparently contains.[16] The historical macro-
economic, monetary questions that captured critical attention also kept the
focus trained on money as a representational problem.[17]

Recent critical turns have refocused on the personal, first, by building on
Marxist, Foucauldian, and psychoanalytic insights into the forms of subjectivity generated under capitalism; and, second, by working within an intellectual history paradigm to expand understanding of the specific logics of
capitalism, in particular the various models of economic man produced in
classical and neoclassical political economy. In these works the subjective experience of the individual comes into focus, especially in explorations of the
emotional and affective impulses that accompany economic decisions and
the narrative forms that helped give shape to the subjectivities of participants
in the capitalist market.[18] Their understanding of economic relationships as
more than mere calculation stands as the point of connection to literary writing. Novels (realist, Gothic, sensational, adventure) and theater (its melodramatic and sensational varieties, in particular) are understood to mediate the
individual's subjective and even somatic incorporation of risk, panic, mania,
and other phenomena experienced at the community or mass level.[19] But
the focus on individual subjective experience still captures only part of what
the personal might be taken to encompass. Without understanding the interpersonal interactions and transactions in which the social form character
develops, our account of economic experience and modern subjectivity risks
being skewed.

Furthermore, when literary critics come to put descriptive flesh onto
the broad conceptual and historical outline of "Victorian capitalism," the
business world they depict often feels like a very impersonal place. By this
I do not mean so much that they highlight a pattern of alienation. (Such a
focus would, of course, be very much centered on the personal, constituting
its fundamental characteristic in terms of alienation, loss, or lack.) Instead,
I mean that the institutions and practices that generate attention tend to
hover (in their representation, at least) at a level of abstraction above the
most immediate forms of human production, exchange, and interaction. The
stock market and finance, for instance, have been fertile subjects for critics, as

have those forms of ownership, investment, and incorporation that seemed
to disassociate the practice of business from individual, identifiable, morally
and financially responsible agents—in particular joint-stock ownership and
limited liability.[20]

One obvious reason for this critical focus is that new forms of corporate organization loomed large in the popular imagination. Victorian literary writing participated in the debates over joint-stock and limited liability, and many of the most memorable businesses and business characters in
fiction are associated with these corporate models, from *Martin Chuzzle-
wit*'s Anglo-Bengalee Disinterested Loan and Life Assurance Company to
Melmotte and his South Central Pacific and Mexican Railway in Anthony
Trollope's *The Way We Live Now*. Writers were fascinated by the challenges
to norms of responsibility and individual agency that these corporate forms
entailed, but part of their interest may stem from a representational bias toward novelty and change. Joint-stock ownership was not a Victorian invention, but its availability was extended in 1826 and then opened to all in the
1844 Company Acts. Limited liability, introduced in 1855, presents perhaps
a more striking turning point. As Boyd Hilton and P. L. Cottrell have noted,
after long-held resistance to the principle, English company law underwent
a thorough renovation in just a few years following the passage of limited
liability legislation.[21] These corporate forms were widely blamed for the instability that was a key feature of the nineteenth-century economy as Britain
endured financial and economic crises decade after decade from the 1820s on
and thus remained a live issue for writers and commentators alike.

Later critics, therefore, may reproduce a bias toward novelty generated
by their primary materials. But the critical readiness to adopt this empirical focus on certain kinds of commercial organization rather than others,
as well as the particular emphasis their analysis often takes, may also be explained by the way that joint-stock and limited liability, as "impersonal"
forms, mesh easily with the emphasis on abstraction that is central to many
of the most potent theoretical accounts of modernization in general and economic modernization in particular, from Marx's analysis of class relations,
fetishism, and alienation, to Weber's discussion of rationalization, specialization, and bureaucratization—not to mention the representational over-
drive theorized in postmodernism. These paradigms also powerfully shape
a conception of the experience of the personal—one that has maintained
popular and scholarly purchase—in which business is figured as the site of
the loss of personal identity in the service of the corporate body and its profit
requirements. Even in the boom periods of recent decades, when tales of su-
perstar CEOs and rebellious, individualistic startup entrepreneurs provided

a counternarrative of business as a hyperpersonalized zone of self-realization, the mid-twentieth-century specters of the Organization Man and the Man in the Gray Flannel Suit, their individuality subsumed in their companies' service, haunted representations of drones isolated in cubicles in suburban office parks.[22]

This combination of theoretical factors has meant that variations on the theme of abstraction, complexity, and impersonality structure many of the assumptions in literary criticism and cultural studies of the period, crowding out of the picture the personalized experiences and interpersonal relationships that persist. Two examples may serve to illustrate this pattern. First, to take a classic and subtle instance, Raymond Williams's *The Country and the City* locates the source of Dickens's originality in his play with abstraction and concreteness: his ability to make visible cultural change by dramatizing "those social institutions and consequences which are not accessible to ordinary physical observation," presenting them "as if they were persons or natural phenomena." "The law, the civil service, the stock exchange, the finance houses, the trading houses, come through, in these ways, as the 'impersonal forces'—the alienated human forces—that they are."[23] The scare quotes and qualifying appositives of Williams's last sentence register the way in which "impersonal forces" are not, ultimately, impersonal, but rather generated by human actors who convey the effect of abstraction as they are alienated in modern institutions and systems. But despite this subtlety, the effect of abstraction finally dominates Williams's own analysis: the passage's general presumption is that what Dickens is representing *is* ultimately abstract— something "not accessible to ordinary physical observation," something that must be *made* to take on physical shape through Dickens's words "*as if*" in the bodies of persons or representative institutions. Of course, stock exchanges and finance houses have brokers, jobbers, bankers, customers, and so forth, but these become empirically invisible in Williams's formulation, their concrete interpersonal relationships subservient to the "abstract forces" where, he implies, the real analytical interest lies. And, witness to the way this presumption becomes a kind of ground for Williams, the phrase "impersonal forces" recurs elsewhere in the book minus the problematizing scare quotes.[24]

Another example, from a widely used recent reference work on the period, Blackwell's *Companion to Victorian Literature and Culture*, puts the presumption of abstraction and impersonality even more strikingly on display. The Victorian financial system is described as one in which "interpersonal credibility" was being "overtaken by impersonal exchanges over greater and greater distances" and in which economic relations and transactions, mediated by different forms of paper—from Bank of England notes, to bills of sale, to checks—were becoming ever more "complex, distant, and anony-mous."[25] In the industrial realm, the introduction of limited liability is said to lead quickly to an organizational revolution in which "ownership of a fac-tory and mill by a single master gave way to ownership by a corporation." In this account, "the entrepreneurial vigor of the independent capitalist whose fortune was one with his firm" is displaced either by a corporation or by a depersonalized person—a "figure, corporate or managerial man," who is detached from workers and the processes of production.[26] Even in an essay that carefully traces the varieties of Victorian commerce—from "the village baker" to large mercantile firms to "the public lecture-tour manager"—the "modern market" is identified as being, fundamentally, "invisible, anony-mous, abstract."[27]

Business and economic historians tend to paint a different picture. In their view, notwithstanding profound changes in company law and the emer-gence of a number of noteworthy large joint-stock corporations, the Victo-rian economy in Britain is most strongly marked by personal capitalism: the survival of the family firm and the congruence—rather than decoupling—of ownership and control (in the sense of day-to-day management).[28] Through-out the nineteenth century most British businesses were either individually owned or owned by partnerships: they might be family firms composed of partners from a single family with continuity over generations, or they might be short-lived ventures started by an individual only to fail or be quickly sold; they might involve large factories and hundreds of workers, or they might consist simply of a couple of family workers; but the general pattern was far from a wholesale midcentury transformation in which identifiable, respon-sible owners vanished from the scene. To the contrary, there was no rush to adopt limited liability; it made slow advances until the 1880s, and even in the middle of that decade private family partnerships remained the most common form.[29] Furthermore, when limited liability was adopted, it by no means meant the end of family identification; as late as 1914, Mary B. Rose notes, "four-fifths of registered joint stock companies were private," "pre-dominantly one-time partnerships, availing themselves of limited liability."[30] That same year, the three largest companies in Britain, J&P Coats, Imperial Tobacco, and Watney Combe Reid, were family firms run by the families that had founded them, testifying to the persistence of businesses associated with identifiable, personal representatives.[31]

In fact, a remarkable feature of British business is the degree to which families and individuals maintained control not only over ownership but also over the practical management of their enterprises, through the nine-teenth century and beyond. This characteristic was not limited to small family firms but extended even to larger publicly held companies, as families maintained control through concentrating ownership of stock.[32] Though a class of managers did exist, particularly in industries such as railways that posed complex organizational problems, more commonly management remained in the hands of family members. The majority of business owners, William Lazonick has noted, "brought their sons and sons-in-law to manage their businesses, thus perpetuating the integration of family ownership and control."[33] Family control remained a priority in the mergers and acquisitions of the late nineteenth and early twentieth centuries, guiding the arrangement of loose federations of relatively autonomous companies and giving a distinctive aspect to the big businesses that emerged.[34] Finally, as Alfred Chandler has suggested, this managerial control was often passed on from one generation to another, sometimes with little heed to the interests or aptitudes of those on the receiving end; businesses were seen "in personal rather than organizational terms, as family estates to be nurtured and passed on to heirs."[35]

And so we find stories like this, from John Francis's 1849 *Chronicles and Characters of the Stock Exchange*, describing the deathbed scene of a figure from the world of high finance, Sir Francis Baring, the head of a bank that retained its national and global power long past the end of the Victorian era: "In 1805, this gentleman ... retired from business with a princely fortune, and shortly afterwards died, full of years and honours. A green old age, a career closed at the pinnacle of prosperity, and a death-bed surrounded by sons and daughters, whom the descendant of the German weaver had lived to place in splendid independence, was his enviable lot. The great commercial house which he had raised to so proud a position was continued by his sons, and may be considered the most important mercantile establishment in the empire."[36] Or the account in the *Bankers' Magazine* of the 1879 retirement party of Mr. William Haig Miller, chief of the Advance Department at the National Provincial Bank of England, a "pleasant meeting" attended by many guests (named in the article) who had known Miller for thirty or forty years, at which he was given a gift of a "Library Table," chair, book, and inkstand—Miller was a man of "literary pursuits," as an author and editor of *Leisure Hour*, as well as a man of "high character" and "business capacity," the inscription on the book reads.[37] This is one of a number of such stories that join obituaries and notices of personnel changes amid the tables of figures and balance sheets (jokingly referred to as "dry bank statistics") to create a sense that in this trade publication the community of bankers is an object of representational interest, not just cold, hard numbers.[38] An abstract market, a carefully tended patrimony, an impersonal field in which individual figures like Baring and Miller not only stand out but are propagated as characters in textual representations. Our understanding of Victorian business—even Victorian "big business"—must be flexible enough to comprehend the uneven, constantly transforming patterns of impersonality and abstraction, personalization and embeddedness, that coexisted in tension in representations and in economic practice.

To place literary accounts of Victorian business within a history that takes into consideration the empirical continuity and rhetorical power of personal business is to join a critical and theoretical conversation that eschews idealizing formulations—whether celebratory or critical—of the market. The abstract market, as Albert Hirschman reminds us, featuring perfect "allocative efficiency and all-round welfare maximization," "involving large numbers of price-taking anonymous buyers and sellers supplied with perfect information," and functioning "without any prolonged human or social contact among or between the parties," exists nowhere but in the formal models of economists. Such a market would have "no room for bargaining, negotiation, remonstration or mutual adjustment"; there would be no "recurrent or continuing relationships" between market actors, no formation of social and business ties. But these " 'lapses' from the ideal competitive model . . . are exceedingly frequent and important."[39] In other words, these so-called market imperfections are not the exception but the rule, playing a decisive role in governing economic behavior. Though there were (and are) strong tendencies toward abstraction, rationalization, and impersonality in capitalist social relations, economic behavior was (and is) nonetheless—and necessarily—circumscribed by the irrationalities of the psyche, as well as the social bonds and subjective formations of family, kinship, ethnicity, gender, national and local identity, friendship, and enmity. Analyzing the literary manifestations of personal business through transactional character forms contributes to our understanding of how this economy took shape during a period when there were strong pressures to embed society in the market rather than the other way around and to make questions of community, relationship, responsibility, and individual moral character subservient to abstract economic "laws."[40]

In her richly researched *Genres of the Credit Economy*, Poovey traces the emergence of disciplinary specialization and distinctions between kinds of writing that help to create the imaginative, representational possibility of the abstract market and its formal models.[41] Spanning the seventeenth through the nineteenth centuries and exploring the various genres of writing that developed inside and alongside the modern credit economy—from bank notes, bills of exchange, and checks, to financial journalism, economic theory, and novels—Poovey describes a gradual but profound divergence between genres and the disciplines that constitute fields of knowledge around them. At the start of the period, she argues, the categorical distinctions between different kinds of writing, say, a bank note and a narrative by Daniel Defoe, were unclear. They existed on a "continuum" that featured no clear divide between fact and fiction; furthermore both, she argues, would have *felt like writing,* with the bank note's representational qualities not yet naturalized into invisibility. But by the nineteenth century, "the continuum of generic kinds—along with the continuum that linked fact and fiction—was decisively broken up into . . . separate genres." Though hybrids existed, "writers and publishers increasingly insisted that all publications were not alike, that informational writing was different from Literary writing, and that Literary writing differed, in crucial (if not universally agreed-on) ways," from what was "disdainfully called 'reading for the million.'"[42] The new distinction leads, in her account, to a fundamental separation between "Literary" writing and the discipline of criticism that takes it as object, and economic writing and experience and the discipline of economics that established itself as the credit economy's hegemonic expert knowledge mode. On both sides of the divide, the process involves increasing formalism: from Jane Austen forward, she suggests, literature is formalist, self-referential, aestheticizing. Novels are enclosed in an inward-looking system that might purport to gesture to a real extraliterary world but does not really convey information about that world—nor would it be taken to do so. Her history of nineteenth-century political economic thought, winding up with the 1870s Marginalist Revolution, leaves the discipline poised for the flowering of mathematical modeling, having developed a "mode . . . whose referential capacity was arguably less important than its formal coherence."[43]

The arguments are provocative and challenging. The endpoint of Poovey's history of disciplinary specialization and divergence may not appear altogether surprising, with professional economics positioned as the expert voice on matters economic, and literature and literary criticism seen as having no particularly privileged insight into or purchase on economic truth. But the defamiliarizing work of the early part of the history, in which this trajectory was not predetermined, casts that endpoint in a new light. To new historicist critics who have made reading across disciplines and genres a fundamental practice, Poovey's insistence on the need to respect the differences that genre makes—and to resist dismissing those differences as merely theoretically benighted conventional wisdom—is likely to resonate, not least because of her admirable self-examination in questioning the grounds for claims about how literary writing shapes history through readers' responses. Moreover, this emphasis on recognizing distinctions unsettles the historical narrative that constructs the novel as a genre deeply implicated in capitalist economic relations, as both formal coherence and deep subjectivity are reinterpreted as markers of the separation of genres rather than points of connection between literary form and economic system.

My account concurs with Poovey's that there were significant points of divergence between literary genres and the genres of business writing during the nineteenth century; however, it finally argues for a more fluid sense of exchange between literary and business domains, grounded in the empirical realities and practical exigencies of personal business. Because both business and literary writing grappled with the problem of reading and representing the personal, shared preoccupations and shared practices can be discerned by expanding the range of business genres studied to incorporate not only the paper financial instruments, journalism, and economic theory that are Poovey's primary focus but also everyday forms of writing that businesses and businesspeople produced and engaged. These shifts in focus, I suggest, help us arrive at a more satisfying account of how texts, genres, and formal categories might have *operated* in the lived, interpersonal experience of a credit economy. A closer attention to concrete representational and interpretive practices, especially the forms of transactional character, may go at least some way toward addressing Poovey's concerns that the modes of connection among literary writing, readers, and economics are too often assumed or filled in through anachronistic styles of reading that would require nineteenth-century readers to adopt the techniques of literary critics trained in poststructuralist theory.

The first step in specifying these connections, I suggest, is to recognize that the claim that novels help to construct a modern subject for a capitalist world has often been generated with little reference to a vast and essential arena of capitalist activity: compare, for instance, the number of brilliant and convincing accounts of the novel's development of character through courtship and domestic life to the number centered on everyday business.[44] While I certainly do not wish to reinstate a divide between the private and the economic that has been justly deconstructed by feminist critics especially—this would be a strange move indeed in a book titled *Personal Business*—I suggest that the elision of business scenes and genres has left a significant gap in arguments claiming the association of novelistic character, subjectivity, and bourgeois capitalist culture: just *how* does this mode of character *work* in that sphere of activity that is, almost by definition, fundamental to that culture? The gap becomes most palpable, perhaps, in Deidre Lynch's superb *The Economy of Character: Novels, Market Culture, and the Business of Inner Meaning.* Lynch addresses the question, positing a *"pragmatics* of character" in analyzing the way eighteenth- and early-nineteenth-century readers "used characters ... to renegotiate social relations in their changed, commercialized world."[45] But the "business" invoked in the subtitle remains somewhat metaphorical in the analysis, where negotiation by and large occurs between readers and written characters in fictions, or readers and money or commodities; the interpersonal transactions of business are a social context that drops out of the picture of "market culture." Excavating the ways character was subject to transaction in practical relations between people in Victorian business gives a more specific content to the association of the novel with middle-class culture, a more nuanced historical description of how particular modes of character (such as deep psychology) and genres of representation (such as realism) were and were not incorporated into economic life.[46]

To raise the issue of use entails large questions: about how readers engage narratives; how they differentiate fictional characters from persons they encounter in their everyday lives; how fantasies animated in narrative forms address, assuage, or exacerbate particular epistemological and ideological challenges. It is precisely around such questions, I suggest, that the co-implication of literary and economic genres and practices becomes most evident and the value of studying them in conjunction most apparent. To emphasize generic distinction, as Poovey's history-of-the-disciplines argument does, focusing on the emergence and hardening of a division between informational and fictional genres, tends to prioritize a narrow model of "use" for genres of fiction. Thus, discussing Trollope's *The Last Chronicle of Barset* (1867), she suggests that the novel's economic plots are used "to elaborate the complex relationship between imaginative fictions like this one and the actual operations of the credit economy" that the novel "seems to, but does not, help readers understand."[47] This "not understanding" relates, in her view, to the way Trollope seems uninterested in the particular details his economic plot devices might conjure for the reader (the way a check works in the real world and the scandalous collapse of the discount house Overend, Gurney and Company), except insofar as they allow him to construct a new, aestheticized model of character, as the reader pieces together an understanding of the novel's confused protagonist, Reverend Crawley, who may or may not have stolen and cashed a check.

The novel does not inform about the economy in the manner of a factual guidebook; no reader would mistake its accounts for informational reference. But that does not mean that a reader could *only* experience its plots, its details, and its characters as utterly removed, existing in a purely aesthetic, formal plane; as Thomas Pavel has suggested, "literary artifacts often are not projected into fictional distance just to be neutrally beheld" but rather "vividly bear upon the beholder's world," through what he terms a "principle of relevance."[48] That principle extends to the exploration and modeling of character that the novel performs (and that Poovey brilliantly illuminates), to the experience of character and the difficulty ascertaining it that it constructs, and to the fantasies about character that it animates—which, if they are more formalist or aestheticized, may therefore be relevant in new ways. In other words, a move to a formalist construction of character may represent not a *dis*engagement from problems of knowledge in the credit economy, but rather a new angle on a central aspect of that economy. The "distended, displaced" version of character as "a function of relationship" that Poovey finds in her reading of the novel's secondary City plot—like the Reverend Crawley's character, as she notes—does not lose its economic meaningfulness because the novel does not "systematically or explicitly expose" the social underpinnings of credit; these were as often as not part of conscious experience, not requiring exposure.[49] Because character remained an essential—if vexed—component of Victorian business practice and thinking, the revisions of character that literary writing elaborates and grapples with must be viewed as important potential contributions to the reader's understanding of economic life—just as important, indeed, as any strictly factual depiction of the crash of Overend, Gurney.

As recent accounts have insisted, fictional characters are particularly charged sites for the routine acts of cognitive and affective translation between textual and actual worlds that ordinary readers perform. Relating to characters, trusting or distrusting them, finding them plausible according to expectations of consistency: such habits have histories of which business character practices are a part.[50] Even theories that insist on character as a textual artifact often imagine it as a hinge point between writing and actual experience. Perhaps most significantly for the nineteenth century, character representations offered a repertoire of fantasies and imaginative play that addressed the information gaps that everyday life entailed. It does not seem coincidental that many of the puzzles tackled by narratological theorists concerned to distinguish the forms of fiction and the worlds fiction creates—puzzles about coherence and completeness of information, referentiality, probability, and credibility—find analogues in the mental exercises demanded in business, prompted by the textual forms and reading practices that character transactions elicit.[51] In a context in which networks were fundamental, the distribution of attention among major and minor players was a demand in daily life as well as in the "character-system" of the nineteenth-century novel.[52] Where uncertainty was the norm, the cognitive processes and fantasy formations sparked by character narratives were newly charged.

In the chapters to come, my analysis of the formal, narrative, and interpretive experiments undertaken by Victorian literary writers and Victorian business writing and practice suggests that they were engaged in navigating a common—though not congruent—cultural terrain. For businessmen and novelists alike, the field of the personal represented an epistemological and representational challenge with a compelling, though uncertain, balance of risk and reward. I turn now to detail some of the ways writers and readers in and out of business took up this challenge, drawing connections and marking distinctions between representational practices and the kinds of profits they promised.

Reading and Writing Commercial Character

In the late 1870s or 1880s a young man entering a commercial career might have invested sixpence in a slim handbook bearing the weighty title *How to Read the Character by the Actions, Manner, and Speech, According to the Observations and Maxims of the Most Eminent Philosophers, Poets, Statesmen, Men of Business, Etc.* The pamphlet's cover quotes the popular moralist and advice writer Sir Arthur Helps to address its desired audience: "A man of business requires a great knowledge of character." Interspersed with maxims from statesmen, physiognomists, business writers, and political economists, and with the interventions of a sage, anonymous editor who comments instructively on the miscellany, a wide array of literary writers and philosophers are marshaled to give the businessman the training he needs: Addison, Carlyle, Coleridge, De Staël, Emerson, Hazlitt, Herbert, Horace, Johnson (and Jonson), LaRochefoucauld, Locke, Longfellow, Milton, Montesquieu, Hannah More, Sidney, Southey, Shakespeare, Smollett, and Sterne.

In its selections from the works of these writers, the pamphlet presents models or descriptions of character and the problems it presents, rather than offering the busy businessman practical training in discovering character through close reading. Nonetheless, reading is emphatically the metaphor through which the process of understanding character is represented, and if close reading is not actively elicited by textual examples, its interpretive techniques are sketched. On the very first page, for instance, Lord Chesterfield recommends not only "reading men" but "studying all the various editions of them," in order to "discern the shades and gradations that distinguish characters seemingly alike."[53] These "shades and gradations" point to the depth model of character that the pamphlet continually evokes, in which the "continent of undiscovered character" within becomes readable through surface detail; these depths likewise gain a temporal dimension as, Emerson counsels, details of "look, and gait, and behaviour" enable the keen eye to "read . . . all your private history."[54] Literary selections highlight the presence of these depths: Milton reminds the businessman of the need to watch for hypocrisy, which "neither man nor angel can discern"—though the editorial voice reassures that it "may often be detected if you have observation and patience."[55] Some idea of the degree to which the resulting discriminations of character might then play into the activity of business may be suggested by reference to pocket guides to commercial correspondence that attempted to model the "customary phraseology and courteous expressions" necessary to commercial life.[56] Though the proportion varies, letters pertaining to character—testimonials, requests for references, applications for credit or employment, and so forth—make up a large part of the correspondence modeled. In one handbook, printed around 1880, of forty-eight sample letters at least twenty address issues of character.[57]

In this section, I will discuss the historical circumstances that helped make the notion of character specifically, and the personal more generally, into features of business interest. In particular, I will sketch the career of business character, examining the models of character that were proposed and employed, the transformations that they underwent, and the formal strategies that businesses used to try to harness character's potential to discipline and manipulate the market. Alongside this, I trace the intersections and divergences of literary models of character with the culture of personal business. Narratives of character participated in constructing the personal business culture of Victorian Britain, sometimes by setting the terms through which character could be enacted or interpreted in business settings, sometimes by disseminating or contesting representations of business character. And their conceptions and constructions were influenced by the expectations that were placed on character within the commercial world, as well as the challenges that commercial practice and character representation posed to each other.

The Victorian history of business character begins in crisis. In the late 1830s a rash of bank failures swept Britain and the United States. In the panic that followed and its aftermath, a great deal of blame was levied against the new joint-stock banks that had recently started to displace British private bankers. Because they separated operational control (by a group of directors) from their dispersed investor owners, the joint-stock banks seemed to present an intangible—and illegible—structure of responsibility. This illegibility preoccupied skeptical commentators. To J. R. McCulloch, for instance, the joint-stock banks felt elusive, seductive rather than straightforward, appearing to the public "all ... dressed up in the most captivating manner."[58] His feminized trope suggested a potentially dangerous discord between appearance and substance that translated into an even more dangerous opacity of class, social position, and property: in joint-stock banks, the public had "no accurate knowledge of the parties with whom they [were] dealing," who might be "men of straw or *millionaires*."[59] In contrast, the private banker Mr. Pearie in a *Blackwood's* short story of the time is a model of masculine forthrightness. The visual signs of Pearie's body represent property directly and accurately, his "plump expression of body and feature" telling of his prosperity "as plainly as words could have done," such that "an eye with any speculation in it, could see at a glance that one hundred thousand pounds at least were written in the swell of his waistcoat."[60] Pearie poses no interpretive challenge: the speculative eye meets with the happy—and, in commercial tales such as this, unusual—result that its perceptions are accurate and immediate, able to bypass the gap between signifiers and their referents.

It is tempting to take this fantasy of representational self-evidence for granted; after all, who wouldn't feel more secure trusting their commercial affairs to someone whose probity and property were clear to see? But in fact the 1830s valorization of the private banker as a figure who offered more direct access to the truth by embodying property in a human form, subject to examination, demonstrated a kind of willful longing. Private banks were not exempt from volatility; indeed, the severe crisis of 1825, whose memory haunted Britons with each successive commercial crisis, had demonstrated that private banks were just as liable to fail and leave clients destitute as their joint-stock competitors. There was no *necessary* reason to imagine that personalism would render them less risky and therefore no necessary reason for images and rhetorics of personalism to take on the function of reassurance that they did. To solve the representational problem of joint-stock banks, McCulloch recommends personal information: publishing the names and addresses of all company directors. Remedies such as transparent accounting were not enough for the critics of joint-stock banks; open account books, even displays of stacks of gold, were seen as inadequate, subject to manipulation and fraud.[61] Of course, so were names and addresses: the same article anxiously repeats the rumor of a "person without a shilling" who, by taking "a house looking into ____Park," manages to establish both respectability and a bank.[62]

Though there was nothing foreordained about the early Victorian prioritization of the personal, the move had a history with effects that endured. In part the history is an intellectual one: Adam Smith's political economic

theory, for instance, tended to take the individual as its primary agent, privileging private businesses (with circumscribed, personally responsible ownership) above joint-stock not only because they were more easily analyzed
within this principal framework of self-interest but also because they had a
discernibly personal aspect that could be subjected to scrutiny. For McCulloch, the popularizer of political economy, a chain of personal responsibility, self-interest, and character would discipline the market: owners liable to
the extent of their fortunes would be more likely to "seek out and appoint
managers of character and ability," while the public, who had no privileged
insight into the actual affairs of the concern, would be placed on safer ground
by trusting to "the character and responsibility of the partners."[63] Attention
to the personal and to character, then, could uphold laissez-faire principles
and bypass the necessity of legal reforms and regulations. As the *Economist*
pronounced in an 1849 article, "It must always be impressed on traders of all
kinds, that no law can so effectually guard them against losses and serve the
best interests of society as their own care, vigilance, and intimate knowledge
of the character of those they trust."[64] This note was sounded in the journal over the decades in discussions of other controversies over commercial
matters, for instance company law reform and limited liability legislation.
Character knowledge was positioned as a way to manage risk and to preserve
commercial morality, a solution to potential excesses that allowed the market
to function properly and freely.

　　As a result of this emphasis, opportunities for representing, performing,
and examining character abounded in Victorian business. In private life or
at the bank, in the workplace or in the bankruptcy court, at the shareholders' or board meeting or on the company cricket team, businessmen encountered the scrutiny of lenders, employers, coworkers, partners, investors, and
so forth.[65] The disciplinary effect that occurred through the Victorian examination of character was not, as Lauren Goodlad reminds us, a panop-
tic Foucauldian model. However, in the transactional exchanges of business
neither was it tantamount to the later Foucauldian notion of pastorship, the
character-driven interpersonal model with which Goodlad replaces the pan-
optic, bureaucratic eye.[66] Instead, personal business sought to tame the volatile economic landscape by aligning the antimaterialist, sometimes religious
(or at least moral), sometimes liberal concept of character with the incentives
of self-interest. Reform could be achieved and risk could be managed privately by impressing on participants "the pecuniary value of a good moral
character."[67]

　　But though writers were quick to suggest that character had a value, just
what that value represented in practice was more elusive. In fact, character

remained stubbornly difficult to define even in those texts that took that task as their specific aim. Was it a thing or a possession? An internal quality or capacity? Was it a process, constructed by the repetition of habits and actions? Or was it a social artifact, established only through the testimony of others? What was its relationship to property? To family? All these questions and others bedeviled the representation of character in business language and business writing. I focus here on modes of writing that give a broad perspective on the constitution of business character and the transactions through which it emerged: correspondence, especially letters seeking credit or positions; and information books (also called character books), which recorded testimonials, hearsay, and observational notes about local and foreign business clients and associates, especially potential ones.[68]

As the phrase "the pecuniary value of a good moral character" suggests, character and money were often difficult to disentangle. The editorial counsel of *How to Read the Character* sums up one prominent perspective *dis*articulating the two, suggesting that "a man who is not worth a dollar, is frequently more worthy of credit than another who has the nominal possession of thousands. Losses almost always occur in trusting to property and reports, and not to men."[69] But if character and property were detached from each other, in this view—that is, you didn't need to have property to have character—character simultaneously came to represent a parallel value as a source of credit. In a sample letter refusing to fill an order until references are supplied, for instance, character testimonials stand in for money, as the writer reminds his correspondent "that it is customary in all cases of a first order being given, to furnish satisfactory references or to forward cash; and as we have not had the pleasure of transacting business with you, and have, indeed, no knowledge of you, we must beg of you to furnish us with the names of some two or three respectable firms with whom you are in the habit of doing business"— or to express willingness to pay ready money.[70]

Similarly, in an information book kept by the company, a correspondent of Antony Gibbs and Sons, Ltd., a London merchant banking firm with interests on several continents, remarks in 1877 of Ernst Niebuhr Jr., a potential associate in Hamburg, that he is "thoroughly respectable + trustworthy. We may do business with him with perfect confidence—money considerations included—more on acct of his thorough respectability + prudence than of what may be his personal means." A later annotation following Niebuhr's death suggests that the bank should reconsider its relation to his business, as Niebuhr's "*personal* abilities were what made him recommendable for us." Now that a former clerk is in charge, the capacity of character to stand in for property—and thus to generate money for Niebuhr's firm through credit—

vanishes.[71] Conversely, the possession of property is not enough to make up for a deficit in the character ledger. In an 1863 entry about the business of John Hoyle, of Trujillo and Lima, Peru, the correspondent notes, "from what we have heard we fear that the father is given to intemperance + does not take the same active part in the management of his business, he used to do formerly." Though the correspondent "can bring no positive charge against" the son, he "does not inspire us with much confidence." Therefore "though the old man must be possessed of a good deal of property we think some caution in your transactions with his firm would be desirable." Robert Kayser of Hamburg is dismissed more concisely with the notation, "plenty of money but rather slippery."[72]

The delicacy and the ad hoc, case-by-case quality with which these information books juggle the terms of money and character suggest the way the market within which business was performed was more than a framework of economic laws. Today we would use the metaphor of the network; in Victorian terms we might (with some caution) characterize the effect produced by the books' accretions of notes through the Eliotesque figure of the web.[73] Connections are elaborately, variously, and particularly traced. An entry from 1882 on Bosanquet and Co. of Colombo notes not only that "Mr. Bosanquet is most respectable, careful, + of good business capacity, but not of very large means," but also that "he is first cousin to the London Bankers of that name."[74] Marriage relationships are noted, as are details about what they signify in property terms (Carlos van der Heyde, of Lima, it is observed, has "since his marriage . . . insisted on his wife's portion . . . being handed over to him to employ in business on his own account"). Ever more particularistic connections are logged: "Haynes' boys' schooling paid through him," an entry on a connection at Frères Monod of Geneva notes parenthetically.[75]

Above all, what emerges from the books is the effort to render businesses and businessmen in Lima, Santiago, Hamburg, and Colombo as concrete as if they operated around the corner in the City, available to the same degree of character scrutiny and personal knowledge. The sources or conduits of information are generally specified: the bankers, agents, correspondents, and so forth who serve as nodes in the web and whose capacity to serve that function is similarly bound by expectations of trust and reciprocity. The language used in the notations, in fact, often seems to strain to achieve the flavor of the real voice of the correspondent. Eruptions of the foreign language in which he speaks are common: the local correspondent splutters, in a note on Safatti, of Venice, that he is "in difficulties, no means, poco respettabile!"[76] The (intentionally ethnicizing?) exclamation point here is joined by underlining elsewhere, as a means of suggesting the emphases and intonations of direct speech: an 1868 conversation on the subject of P. Sainte Marie, for instance, is recorded to give a sense of the hedging that accompanied the conversation. As the (named) correspondent "verbally confirms" his "good opinion . . . as regards [Sainte Marie's] integrity," he expresses concern about "making any advances for which we have not ample cover," following with the reassurance that he "does not think Sainte Marie would *ask* for large advance," because of his limited means."" The language, in other words, is not always dry accountant speak; if the books of this global company don't rise to the level of novelistic realism, they nonetheless share an interest in making the world they describe mimetically concrete.[78]

Thus, though Victorian realist novels often feel frustratingly vague when it comes to describing and engaging commercial activity, the culture of personal business meant that the two discourses shared assumptions about the importance of character, about how to analyze it and develop it, and about the desirability of representational concreteness.[79] In a volatile, competitive business culture marked by fraud and scandal, the promise to get at the real held strong appeal, and the realist, mimetic impulse therefore was in dialogue with business practice as it was elaborated and formalized during the Victorian period—even if the forms it takes, in genres as disparate as information books and three-decker novels, varied widely. In fact, business emerges at some key moments in which theories of realism were codified or where self-conscious reflection on realist technique and characterization occurs. George Eliot's essay "The Natural History of German Life," for instance, opens its illustration of realist doctrine with an account juxtaposing the perspectives of a man with little experience of railways beyond his local station and track lines and a man who has "had successively the experience of a 'navvy,' an engineer, a traveller, a railway director and shareholder, and a landed proprietor in treaty with a railway company"—rendering business a prime example of realist necessity and technique. The man with little experience, she suggests, may "entertain very expanded views as to the multiplication of railways in the abstract, and their ultimate function in civilization. He may talk of a vast net-work of railways stretching over the globe, of future 'lines' in Madagascar, and elegant refreshment-rooms in the Sandwich Islands, with none the less glibness because his distinct conceptions on the subject do not extend beyond his one station and his indefinite length of tram-road." But, she continues, "if we want a railway to be made, or its affairs to be managed, this man of wide views and narrow observation will not serve our purpose."[80] The concreteness of realist vision is linked to practi-

cal business success, and business is used as a way of clarifying realist objec-
tives, implying the costs to adopting an idealized method not drawn from
real observation. Eliot's appeal shows the power of the fantasy linking realist
perspectives and descriptions to a "safe" economic culture in which projects
such as railways—within recent memory an example of rampant speculation
and fraud—can be grounded, trustworthy, and profitable.[81]

In this essay Eliot doesn't develop the implications of the realist perspective described with the railway metaphor for character representation and
interpretation. But its emphasis on accurate observation and eschewing the
ideal recurs in the famous, quasi-programmatic statement of realist character
aesthetics in chapter 17 of *Adam Bede*. Its model of character built out of
cumulative and seemingly inconsequential detail, purporting to be bound
by no codes or formulas other than fidelity to the real and representing non-
idealized, ordinary individuals as opposed to grand or heroic figures, was
also echoed in business biographies, prescriptive business writing, and journalistic representations of business character, particularly in the early and
mid-Victorian period, though the mode persisted into later decades as well.
But along the way, as character knowledge was elevated to a privileged position as a practical business matter and as a means of minimizing risk, character itself became more transactionally valuable. Character representations
proliferated, borrowing from the languages of romance, enchantment, and
science to construct new versions of personal business that sought to establish the truth and power of character on different terms.

But the relationship among business, narrative, and character had never
been as tidy or uncomplicated as the fantasy of effective market discipline
through character suggested. In fact, for business the narrative aspect of
character always represented both a source of value and a poison pill. As the
potential to constantly manage and expand the character accounts in information books suggested, with actual, embodied persons character was always
under construction and elusive. Even if it *could* be documented scrupulously
and comprehensively, with the kind of thorough access to motivations and
tendencies that an omniscient narrator could provide—which of course it
could not—with a living, temporal person past history could be no guarantee of future results.

Thus, an entry on one associate, described in warm terms as deserving
"a very good credit," being "honest, intelligent, and rich" and possessing appropriate social connections through a marriage "to daughter of old Chas
Latham," is revisited, with a comment added: "N.B. in our subsequent dealings with him found him any thing but 'loyal'—very tricky."[82] The informa-

tion books of the banking firm Kleinwort, Sons, and Co. contain an 1893 notation about the firm R. Steel and Co. of Calcutta. The initial entry states that the firm came recommended by a Mr. Patterson and provides details of who has contributed what capital—£8,000 from a Duff Gordon, for example. Information accumulates, literally exceeding the pages of the ledger: a memo on the stationery of the brokers Cox, Patterson and Co. is fastened into the book, specifying, "Duff Gordon is brother-in-law of [Roger?] Cunliffe + son-in-law of [?] Hammerley of Coutts," the well-known London bank. But if this additive form—more testimony, more specificity—reassures, it also unsettles: the following year the broker tells the Kleinwort's writer that "the first season has not been a good one for the Cpy but the reports that they had lost their capital are untrue."[83] As updates, memos, and extra notes are added, the rhetoric of concreteness that access to the personal was meant to convey is undercut by the books' boundless narrative temporality and their testimonial addenda. The temporality within which literary characters were constructed through narrative, in contrast, was by and large circumscribed by the imaginations of authors, the arc of a plot, and the not-unlimited patience of readers and publishers. Even though a literary character was, as Ruth Ronen has suggested, "incomplete" when measured against a hypothetical real-world referent, that character's position within a narrative "neutralized" its incompleteness; narrative created the terms of "sufficiency" through which the literary character might come to feel knowable.[84] For the business writer, working to capture a character with an independent existence in a story that remained in process, the fantasy that character could provide a solid, knowable foundation was always liable to unravel around the prospect of narrative.

Thus, as character flourished and morphed within business culture, even into nearly unrecognizable versions of itself, a parallel track sought to protect business from these risks by making character and its vagaries subject to market devices. Suretyships attached a price to trust, though they also bound private individuals (often friends or relatives) closely in a relationship of responsibility. Guarantee societies invoked the impersonal power of the market to relieve people of the "ever attendant anxiety" of private surety and allowed employers to apply the principles of insurance to the "contingencies... of human frailty" no less than to fire.[85] But despite such steps, the dialectic between market and character representations was ongoing. Both nonprofessional economic writing and the practical experience of commercial life insistently invoked character—even, at times, as they radically transformed the concept. And character narratives were just as insistent in engaging and transforming the terms through which business character was understood, the transactions in which it was mobilized, and the fantasies that it enabled and the responses it foreclosed in the risky world of Victorian capitalism.

My argument is organized around particular cases of personal business and the character problems they raised that emerged at specific historical moments between the late 1830s and 1890, the end of a decade in which British business finally begins to adopt in greater numbers larger-scale, more complex forms. The two chapters in part 1, "Reading Character across Business Contexts," examine scenes of transactional character reading—an intimate one within the setting of the family firm and the more variable situations of the investment milieu—that reflect how the personal inheres in business even as contexts of interpretation and models of character change. Chapter 1 investigates an instance in which the knowledge of personal character was imagined to temper the risks of the marketplace: the effort to codify business trust—specifically, trust between employers and employees—that preoccupied observers in the 1840s and 1850s, including Charles Dickens in his novel *Dombey and Son*. Chapter 2 is situated in the investment culture of the 1850s–1880s and focuses on biographical representations of businessmen, tracing the emergence of routinized charisma, whose navigation of personal and impersonal qualities shaped a powerful mode of business personhood. I illustrate the challenge that it posed to the realist character representations privileged in literary writing, analyzing Anthony Trollope's response to this new mode of business character in his autobiography and fiction, in particular his 1875 novel *The Way We Live Now*.

Part 2, "Locating Character in Commercial Representation," centers on efforts to fix and locate business character: in histories, in testimonials, in networks, in families, and in the body. Chapter 3 examines the bankruptcy reform debates of the 1850s and early 1860s, which focused attention on the perspective through which character could best become known and communicated: whether the disinterested observations of a state apparatus and a classificatory system or the interested, embedded position of creditors. I read George Eliot's *The Mill on the Floss* in relation to this concern with how to locate and narrate character; the novel's exploration of disinterested and embedded perspectives on characters and their histories and obligations asserts the realist novelist's superior purchase on character even as it highlights the inevitable failure of character to meet market expectations. Chapter 4 continues this focus on novelists' responses to changing character terms, examining Margaret Oliphant's novel *Hester* (1883) in light of the turn to the scientific language of heredity to construct and intensify the representation of the personal in business. In particular, I suggest that Oliphant's attention to gender as she maps the vagaries of hereditary talent challenges readers to reevaluate contemporary concepts of business character, along with the narratives available to everyday people who might hope to become characters in their own story of a life in business.

PART I

READING CHARACTER ACROSS BUSINESS CONTEXTS

1

The Trusty Agent

PROBLEMS OF CONFIDENCE
IN DICKENS'S FAMILY FIRM

AT THE END OF JUNE 1846, CHARLES DICKENS SENT A LETTER FROM Lausanne to his friend John Forster, bearing the good news that he had commenced work on his first long novel in two years:

> I have not been idle since I have been here. . . . I had a good deal to write for Lord John about the Ragged schools. I set to work and did that. A good deal for Miss Coutts, in reference to her charitable projects. I set to work and did *that*. Half of the children's New Testament to write, or pretty nearly. I set to work and did *that*. Next I cleared off the greater part of such correspondence as I had rashly pledged myself to; and then . . .
> BEGAN DOMBEY!¹

A few days later he set to work and wrote a rather less exuberant letter to Thomas Chapman, senior partner in the mercantile firm John Chapman and Co.:

> My Dear Sir
> It was a very considerate and friendly act of you to time your communication on the most painful subject of the breach of confidence in your house, as you did, and to make it to me yourself. Accept my thanks for this proof of your regard among many others: and with them the assurance of my friendship and esteem.
> I have been perfectly horrified by the whole Story. I could hardly name a man in London whom I should have thought less likely to stand so committed, than he. Not that I had any intimate knowledge of his pursuits, or any close acquaintance with himself or his usual mode of thinking and proceeding—but I had an idea of his great steadiness and reliability, and a conviction of his great respect and

regard for you. God help him, I believe, even now, that he was sincere
in the latter feeling, and was overcome and swept away by the by the
tide of circumstances on which he had madly cast himself.[2]

Dickens's subject was the theft, through "forgery and peculation,"[3] of
£10,000 by Thomas Powell, a managing clerk in Chapman's company and—
the letter's disavowal of "intimate knowledge" and "close acquaintance" notwithstanding—a sometime author with whom Dickens had been on friendly
terms. Dickens's letters to Powell himself are familiar and jocular, at times ap-
proaching the intimacy here denied.[4] Powell had dined at Dickens's house; a
few months before the discovery of his crimes he and his wife had been Dickens's guests at a benefit performance in which the novelist was acting.[5] And
there was more to draw Dickens and Powell together in Chapman's mind
and thus to defend against in this note. A couple of years earlier Dickens
had written to Chapman hoping to obtain a situation for his seventeen-year-
old brother Augustus: "He is quick and clever; has never given any trouble
to anybody; and has been well brought up. Above all, I have no reason to
suppose that he is addicted to authorship, or any bad habits of that nature."[6]
The petition was granted, and Augustus was dispatched to Powell to begin
work, a situation that he continued to hold through the discovery of the
crimes. Dickens's task, then, was to reassure Chapman of the faith that he
and Augustus had maintained with the merchant and of their ignorance of
the deeds of a friend and coworker who, it turned out, *had* harbored an un-
healthy addiction to authorship, which Dickens assumed supplied the motive for his crime. "It has often awakened great wonder within me how all
those publishing expences . . . were defrayed," he suggested. "But whenever I
have sounded Augustus on the subject; which I have done once or twice; he
always hinted at a Rich Uncle, and some unknown share in some unknown
business, which of course I could not gainsay. He told the tale as it was told
to him, and had every reason to believe it. Indeed, I suppose you and your
partners laboured under the like delusion?"[7] Dickens and Augustus harbored
no ill intent, in other words; they simply took the stories of their friend and
coworker on trust, in the same way that the partners in the firm must have
done. If the novelist and his brother had misread Powell's character, the failure wasn't theirs alone.

Concerned for the welfare of Powell's wife and children, Chapman declined to prosecute his managing clerk but did dismiss him from his post.
Two years later a warrant was issued for Powell's arrest on new charges of
forgery. He never actually faced these charges; instead, Powell was committed to an insane asylum, perhaps to evade prosecution, and left for New

York early in 1849. From across the Atlantic he continued to torment his London connections, publishing a biographical sketch of Dickens in which he accused the novelist of breaching the trust of his friend and the employer of his brother, "grossly libelling and caricaturing" Chapman by taking him as the model for the cold, proud, and callous merchant Mr. Dombey in the novel that Dickens was undertaking at the moment Powell's first crimes were revealed.[8]

Once again Dickens was obliged to set matters right with his City friend. Powell's charge prompted a new letter from Dickens, reassuring Chapman that he would add a preface to the upcoming reprint of his *American Notes* to denounce the absconded former manager as an "unmitigated villain."[9] Under these circumstances, Dickens's closing "Believe me[,] Faithfully Yours always" seems more than mere epistolary formula. Clearly dismayed by the threat posed to his own standing by a past connection to a forger and thief, as well as by the calumny that he judged Powell to be spreading, Dickens reaffirms his loyalty to the merchant and proceeds to engage him in a project of mutual defense, soliciting statements for a booklet testifying to Powell's criminal character. "I am much obliged to you for the enclosed," Dickens writes to the merchant in mid-December. "I have dispatched matter, by the steamer, enough (in any country but America) to beat this unutterable scoundrel into dust."[10]

The tangle of business, friendship, and family ties evidenced in the Dickens-Powell-Chapman extended episode; the management of emotions and reactions that the letters themselves work to accomplish; the recognition of character as a significant and vulnerable element of commercial and social connection: all these are aspects of personal business that demonstrate its immediacy and its vitality in everyday practice. The transactions of character in this case address the specific problem of trust: obtaining it, maintaining it, rebuilding it. Powell's own breach of the trust that his employer placed in him in his role as managing clerk is only the start. Did Charles or Augustus Dickens know anything about Powell's character and activities, criminal or otherwise, that they should have communicated to his employer? Most likely not, but we—and Chapman—have only their word for it. Did Dickens in fact base the character of the selfish, abusive, unfeeling merchant in *Dombey and Son* on that of his friend—thoughtlessly and perfidiously, if not absolutely falsely, as Powell claimed? Did Chapman hire Augustus on his brother's recommendation, only to have the young employee pass along information and impressions that contributed to the novelist's unflattering portrait? Dickens strenuously denied the connection, and we don't know much about Chapman's behavior at the firm or about what Augustus may have said. However, circumstances seem to tell against Dickens: we know from his letters that the real-life breach of confidence in a mercantile and shipping firm was on his mind as he began to compose his novel, and Dombey's mercantile and shipping firm is, after all, brought down by the machinations of his own "trusty agent," the manager Carker.[11]

Dickens's correspondence surrounding this episode, with its information disclosures, its performances of emotion, and its efforts to manage reactions, neatly illustrates the intensely interpersonal labor that Anthony Giddens suggests represents a distinctively modern variant of trust. In circumstances in which the risks and relationships of commerce are defined both globally and locally, through contract as well as informal connection, and often incorporating increasingly specialized knowledge, the older criteria of "kinship, social duty, or traditional obligation" were no longer adequate to inspire trust or to compel loyalty. Modern trust, in Giddens's account, has taken two forms, one associated with systems such as expert credentialing and the other a function of what he calls the "pure relationship," purged of the traditional modes of connection mentioned above and "mobilised . . . by a process of mutual disclosure" and intimacy that is "reflexively controlled over the long term."[12] While the purity of these relationships seems debatable—certainly elements such as kinship, friendship, and ethnic and religious connection continue to affect the ways trust is determined—nonetheless, Giddens's formula captures what is novel in Dickens's negotiation of this crisis. The personal business of trust in this episode did not merely depend on the preexistence of ties of family and friendship. Instead for Dickens, Powell, Chapman, and Augustus it was a function of transactional character: trust emerged and was maintained (or failed) through ongoing interpersonal exchanges centered on the performance and management of character.

In this chapter I examine one particular category of such exchanges: the negotiation of trust between managers and employer-owners, focusing especially on the years between 1840 and 1860 when, as Dickens and Chapman were to discover, the question of such trust seemed to be of special concern. My choice of focus is motivated in part by the way managers typify the ambivalence that conditions Victorian personal business: as for-hire figures they are taken to represent more purely economic relationships to their employers and their firms; at the same time, their legal and practical function is specifically defined by its closeness to owners and employers. Even more significantly, however, during the period I discuss this relationship was conceived as a problem of interpretation—reading, in fact—that highlights connections between representational and interpretive practices across cultural domains. By tracing the intersections and divergences between modes of interpretation in different genres—advice manuals, journalism, and Dickens's novel of (mis)management, *Dealings with the Firm of Dombey and Son: Wholesale, Retail, and for Exportation*—I suggest that the co-implication of representational concerns in commercial and literary practice was very much a live question, animating and vexing Dickens as he pressed forward his aesthetic and social agendas.

Because the category "manager" is fairly broad, some further explanation of my terminology is necessary. The pages of Victorian business manuals, economic texts, journals, and novels are populated by managers, managing clerks, directors, confidential agents, confidential managers, confidential clerks, and so forth. (Dombey and Son's Carker is called variously a "confidential" or "trusty agent," as well as a capital-M "Manager," for example.) In using *manager* I risk trading some subtlety for conciseness, especially with respect to distinctions of status and responsibilities among the different occupations that the term encompasses: the bank clerk, the manager of a large mercantile firm, and the director of a joint-stock company, for instance, are all examples discussed by historians and eighteenth- and nineteenth-century writers in terms of their managerial functions. However, two inextricably linked qualities consolidate the category for my purposes: first, that managers by definition are considered to hold positions of trust; and second, that these different "managerial" positions share the characteristic of requiring their holders to work as agents enacting business on behalf of another who holds the principal interest in the concern—the bank clerk for the bank owner, the manager for the owner of the firm, the joint-stock company director for shareholders.

The proper fulfillment of managerial trust, therefore, centered on the need for the manager to know his employer's interest and make it guide his behavior. This was clearly felt to be a matter of some delicacy. The pull of self-interest was always imagined to be exerting itself, necessitating constant vigilance against fraud, theft, or a simple lack of dedication attendant on nonownership. A wide variety of tactics were advised. From one side came efforts to harness the motivations of self-interest, using market or legal mechanisms. In addition to the penalties that law prescribed, sureties or guarantees to cover the cost of any misdeeds were required of friends or families of employees, and public guarantee societies emerged offering opportunities to insure against breaches of trust without recourse to private connections. Compensation through devices such as partnership, profit sharing, and commissions was designed to render congruent the self-interest of employees and employers—or at least to persuade employees of that congruence. Other recommendations worked through the nexus of personal relationships, for instance, the encouragement of employers to cultivate ties of affection and social interaction with their employees.

Most important, however, was the advice given to businessmen to seek out good character in their employees as a guarantor of trustworthiness. In fact, character was defined as a more significant managerial qualification than any technical or commercial expertise; as an 1844 manual for the owners of ironworks put it, "In the choice of your subordinates . . . character is the first requisite, cleverness and skill in his craft the second."[13] Implying a combination of intelligence, moral probity, and a disinterestedness of mind that would allow the employee both to develop necessary skills and to work honestly for the benefit of the firm, not directly for himself, character would provide the foundation for trust between employers and the managers on whom they relied. Thus the managerial scene was conceptualized as a process of mutual interpretation, in which managers read owners' characters and owners read managers' in order to ensure that the trust managers were charged with was carried out.

But the very flexibility of interest that was inherent to trust in managerial positions rendered them a site of considerable conceptual stress. The ideal of character that was intended to ground the trust placed in the manager depended on his capacity to subsume his own self-interest; in the words of a firm whose business it was to evaluate trust, the agent who was "engaged in business on his own account" was a suspect figure and could not be guaranteed.[14] However, in order to execute the terms of his trust, the manager must go a step further: suppressing his own interest, he must take on the character of his employer, imagining and interpreting his interest in order to carry it out in the employer's place. In other words, the proper exercise of the manager's responsibilities demanded an act of imaginative and practical imposture, requiring him not to demonstrate thoroughgoing *firmness* of character, but rather a lability that undermined the foundation that character was asked to provide. Furthermore, the imaginative, interpretive act on which this imposture was based threatened, in more ways than one, the distinction between manager and employer, requiring the manager to consult his own understanding of self-interest in order to properly understand his employer's interest. This act of reading, shuttling between self and other, pulled the manager back to what he was supposed to lay aside. If he didn't already have a well-developed sense of self-interest, imaginatively occupying the employer's position would be likely to develop it.

These internally contradictory expectations of management and character account for the degree of attention that the figure of the trusty employee attracts in midcentury writings about business, where he emerges again and again as a treasure to be prized, a problem to be solved, or a criminal cipher lurking in the heart of the capitalist enterprise. It is testimony to the persistence of this anxiety that Dickens followed up his representation of the untrustworthy manager Carker, who not only takes down his employer's business but also seems to want to take it and his family over, with a strikingly similar replay of this structure and plot in the machinations of Uriah Heep within the Wickfield family in *David Copperfield*.

Business advice writers proposed that employers address the interpretive problem that the manager represented with a method of reading and a model of character that itself had a great deal in common with the manager's own practice. Like managerial reading, this method shuttled between self-analysis—looking inward to scrutinize and consult one's own interests and motives—and the close observation of the employee's "surface" behavioral details, which were interpreted as indicative of deep character and analyzed with reference to the depths one had discerned within the self. Several implications followed from this back-and-forth process. First, the presence of acts of sympathetic imagination on the part of both manager and employer meant that the imaginative boundaries between the two were continually dissolving and reforming. Rae Greiner has suggested that the cognitive practice of sympathy, defined as " 'going along with' the historically embedded mentalities of others" much in the manner of readers of realist novels, both implied a condition of "fellow-feeling" and reminded its practitioners of their individual distinctness.[15] The "fellow-feeling" that one needed to experience in the context of business management—feeling and understanding another's interest—was not necessarily the sort to promote sociable cohesion among the members of a firm; instead, the individualizing tendencies of the practice held a disruptive potential whose energies were liable to undo the firm's original hierarchies and boundaries. Second, as these processes of interpreting character focused on internal, even psychological qualities—a combination of impulse, affect, interest, and motive percolating under the surface of peoples' countenances, words, and deeds—they made these business relationships into sites that at once helped to *produce* a model of "deep" character and made those inward depths commercially significant. Names, addresses, lists of personal and familial connections—modes of representing the personal that were called on to ground commercial practices during earlier upheavals, such as the 1830s joint-stock banking crisis—might still be useful, but they could not be wholly adequate as character representations. There was more to know in one's associates, competitors, supervisors, and underlings than met the eye.

In the scene of management and in its written representations, therefore,

we can see how a particular model of character assumed a business value
and demanded a particular interpretive skill that was at once imaginative,
cognitive, psychological, and aesthetic. Because this aesthetic, grounded in
attention to surface detail and the movement from surface detail to characterological depth, had a parallel in the kind of interpretive practice that was
increasingly demanded of novel readers, management represents a case study
establishing in business practice a link between market culture and a form of
subjectivity imagined through literary writing.[16] But even though it promised to offer reassurance, this link was troubling precisely because its representational problematic was foregrounded in a business culture in which
character reading was being promoted as a key to managing the problem of
trust. Fictional characters, with their bounded textual existence—in which
they were equal to their representation—offered a comparatively secure, log-
ically and experientially sufficient set of signs and problems to interpret.[17]
Thus, even as fictional characters engaged the reader in a process of interpretation that developed a model of character as something that needed to be
painstakingly sought, chased from surface sign to deep truth, they offered a
fantasy of comprehensibility that real characters—with their comparatively
opaque consciousnesses, their historical referentiality countered by an openness to change—would never match. The twinning of fullness and elusive-
ness highlighted the potential for representation to mislead.

This tension made the aesthetics of representation especially charged in
discussions of trust. Crimes against trust were frequently given an aesthetic
component or cast: the breaker of trust was represented as a more skilled
reader than his victims and was often pictured as having literary, artistic, or
theatrical tastes and aspirations. As Dickens explored the issue of commercial
confidence through the trusty and untrustworthy agents of *Dombey and Son,*
aesthetics came to the fore. Dickens's experiments in this novel, which forged
a new path for his fictional practice, mixed the character expectations and
modes of interpretation of psychological realism, with surface signs pointing
to inward depths, with the antirealist figures of romance—uneasily engaging
through this generic flux the aesthetic questions raised as the human and intimate transactions of readers and characters were implicated in the process
it was hoped they could protect.

Character and Confidence in Management

By the 1840s the role played by trust in the operations of capitalism had
long been acknowledged. Trust was an essential element of credit decisions,
banking operations, local and international mercantile and financial transactions, and so forth; indeed, the degree of commercial confidence in Britain

and the empire was recognized as a primary aspect of the prosperity that the nation was enjoying and deemed nothing short of a wonder. As the Reverend Thomas Chalmers wrote in 1820, it was a "sublime homage . . . to the honourable and high-minded principles of our nature" that a British merchant with "all, and more than all his property treasured in the warehouses of India" could "sleep with a bosom undisturbed" for its safety "because there he knows there is vigilance to defend it, and activity to dispose of it, and truth to account for it, and all those trusty virtues which ennoble the character of man to shield it from injury, and send it back again in an increasing tide of opulence to his door."[18] In Chalmers's example perfect trust cancels itself out to become knowledge: unspoken in this passage is the delicate process of weighing facts and faith that every act of commercial trust involved, as businessmen attempted to determine the limits of their knowledge and the risk that they would accept based upon it. This merchant slumbers peacefully because he simply "knows." Nearly four decades later, Samuel Smiles would cite approvingly Chalmers's encomium to the global operations of British commercial trust and remark further on the local relations whose path it smoothed:

> If we reflect but for a moment on the vast amount of wealth daily entrusted even to subordinate persons, who themselves probably earn but a bare competency—the loose cash which is constantly passing through the hands of shopmen, agents, brokers, and clerks in banking houses,—and note how comparatively few are the breaches of trust which occur amidst all this temptation, it will probably be admitted that this steady daily honesty of conduct is most honourable to human nature, if it do not even tempt us to be proud of it. The same trust and confidence reposed by men of business in each other, as implied by the system of Credit, which is mainly based upon the principle of honour, would be surprising if it were not so much a matter of ordinary practice in business transactions.[19]

Here there is no vaulting over the language of faith and credit to the language of knowing. Commercial trust is honorable, even (most remarkably) ordinary, but its place at the threshold of knowledge is granted.

The tensions in Smiles's claim—in which trust is simultaneously ordinary, remarkable, and surprising—have both conceptual and historical roots. The element of surprise represents an implicit recognition on Smiles's part of an insight that has shaped theories of trust for more than two centuries: that trust represents a mode of behavior that exceeds self-interest, pointing to the existence of other motivations guiding human interactions and sociability.[20] Eighteenth-century political economy sidestepped the conundrum by constructing a theory of trust's "ordinariness" grounded in the self-interested activities of commercial relations. For Adam Smith, for instance, the atmosphere of trust was a *product* of commercial exchange: "Whenever commerce is introduced into any country, probity and punctuality always accompany it." This probity was not the result of an innate individual or national tendency toward virtuous behavior, preexisting and enabling the introduction of commerce; rather, it was "far more reduceable to self interest, that general principle which regulates the actions of every man, and which leads men to act in a certain manner from views of advantage." Time and repetition were key: "A dealer is afraid of losing his character, and is scrupulous in observing every engagement. When a person makes perhaps 20 contracts in a day, he cannot gain so much by endeavouring to impose on his neighbours, as the very appearance of a cheat would make him lose." By rewarding trustworthy behavior and punishing faithlessness, market mechanisms would generate and enforce trust and thereby improve "the manners of a people."[21] But by grounding trust in a system of self-interest, reward, and punishment, this model redefined it into something unrecognizable as trust. Early nineteenth-century Christian political economists maintained this view of market-generated trust but recognized the uneasy fit between trust and self-interest in their view of economic activity as an arena of moral trial in which self-interest presented temptations, the overcoming of which forged and demonstrated one's character—defined and exemplified as trustworthiness. By this account, it was necessary to imagine an economic reward from self-interested behavior that would exceed the reward that probity would bring; without this possibility, the moral trial would be merely trivial. If this model finally ends at the same place as Smith imagined, with trust generating reputational rewards to self-interest, the recognition of these contradictory tendencies marks an important distinction.[22]

The relation of self-interest to trust is similarly put in question in eighteenth-century theories of how trust should be priced. This concern had particular significance for the discourse of management. For Smith, the degree of trust that a position necessitated figured into the price of its wages and was one of the causes of variation in compensation; the wages of a manager, for instance—to use Smith's terms, a "principal clerk," responsible for "the labour of inspection and direction" of an enterprise based on someone else's capital—were determined with reference "not only to his labour and skill, but to the trust which is reposed in him."[23] This payment, presumably, had to be enough to overcome the employee's self-interested incentive to dishonesty. However, calculating the value of an intangible such as trust—particularly one necessitated by risk, incomplete information, and the physical limits of individuals and geography—was different from pricing bolts of cloth, and the valuation was by no means standardized or agreed upon. David Hume's assertion that this was a matter of common sense—"It is a familiar rule in all business, that every man should be payed, in proportion to the trust reposed in him, and to the power, which he enjoys"—does not clarify what that proportion should be, and of course not everyone felt the market was doing a good job of determining it.[24] As one mid-nineteenth-century commentator complained, if the relative scarceness of fraud by shopmen, agents, brokers, and clerks redounded to their honor, it was "a dishonour to commercial nature, that, considering the profits made by merchants, the daily intercourse they hold with their clerks, and the trust they are compelled to place in them, they pay in so small, and work in so great a degree."[25]

Confidence in the probity of employees in positions of trust was shaken repeatedly during the 1840s and 1850s, as a number of incidents kept employee betrayals in the public eye, ranging from Thomas Powell's forgery and theft, to the 1850 scandal in the Globe Assurance Office centered on a thieving clerk named Walter Watts, to the 1857 sensation surrounding Leopold Redpath, the registrar in charge of stock transfers in the Great Northern Railway Company. Although it was acknowledged that "from time immemorial, clerks have been discovered embezzling the property of their employers," nonetheless many observers felt that "frauds of this kind" appeared to be "greatly on the increase."[26] Furthermore, these crimes seemed to have wider implications. Thefts involving breach of confidence were treated as more than "simple larceny" by the legal institutions that dealt with them; "servants of [a] company . . . placed in situations of trust" could be charged with the separate offense of "larceny as a servant."[27] As the judge pronouncing sentence on Redpath put it, "frauds committed by persons in situations of trust, with salaries which ought to enable them to live in a manner such as persons in their stations of life ought to do, are much aggravated by the relations which exist between the employer and the employed."[28] The judge's "oughts" signal the manifold assumptions that shaped contemporary views of employee betrayals, which represented not only crimes against property and the proper workings of self-interest but also crimes against beliefs about class propriety and the fantasy of socially based trust.

The dim view of employee managers that these well-publicized crimes helped to reinforce was largely implicit already in the work of early political economists. Smith, for instance, found little to commend as he surveyed the large, joint-stock, monopoly companies that in the late eighteenth century were most likely to afford insight into the operations of enterprises run by persons other than the owners. In an observation about the colonial trade, Smith suggests it could not be expected that clerks out of sight of their masters would "give up at once doing any sort of business upon their own account, abandon for ever all hopes of making a fortune, of which they have the means in their hands, and content themselves with the moderate salaries which those masters allow them."[29] And even if managers resisted these temptations, their lack of direct self-interest meant that they were less likely to work as hard or as well as an owner. "Being the managers rather of other people's money than of their own," he suggests, they "cannot well be expected" to exert "the same anxious vigilance" that partners in a private company would.[30] Smith's misgivings about joint-stock enterprises' reliance on employee managers set a tone that was to persist for decades, during which commercial failures were regularly blamed on incompetent, lackadaisical, or dishonest managers.[31] Doubt of the possibilities for success of *any* firm—joint-stock or private— that trusted its operation to someone other than the vigilant, self-interested owner persisted as well: as late as 1860 William Crawshay II wrote anxiously to his son, who was supposed to be superintending the family's ironworks, "I know what the Master's Eye is—nothing can go long without it and I dread the consequences of your longer continued inability to personally look after the large concern at Cyfarthfa."[32] The individual owner with direct, day-to-day control over his enterprise and a straightforward exercise of self-interest continued to be the ideal.

However, businesses were sometimes compelled to deviate from that ideal, particularly in sectors where the scale of an enterprise was especially large or complex. The number and size of managerial staffs still remained relatively small, but by the 1830s managerial work would have featured on the menu of career options, in industries ranging from joint-stock railways, where managers were common, to privately held mercantile firms like Dombey and Son.[33] The range of duties these employees were responsible for varied greatly, depending on the kind of business, but they might include such different tasks as supervising manual or lower-level clerical labor, keeping accounts, coordinating the stages of production or distribution of commodities, and so forth. The salaries and status of managers rose up until the 1830s or so, while lower-level clerks experienced declines; consequently, the distinction between the higher and lower echelons of staff within companies that employed managers grew during this period. Managers were often, though not always, drawn from the ranks of children, relatives, and friends of the owner, or they might marry into the family of the owner. It seemed logical to turn to family members, partly to provide for them, but perhaps even more importantly because it was thought that they would feel a mutual interest with and affection for the owner and would thus be more trustworthy than a stranger whose relationship was purely financial.[34] After years of service, managers might purchase or be rewarded with a partnership. As the demand for experienced, skilled men grew, managers might leave for other firms if raises, promotions, or partnerships were not proffered or might set themselves up in rival businesses with capital raised through new partners or their own savings.[35] But it was becoming less common to achieve the goal of working up to partnership, and many managers who did so ended up decidedly, and permanently, junior. In fact, the rise in salaries has been linked to the decreasing reliance on partnership as compensation, a shift that may have contributed to the view of managers as potentially unpredictable individualist elements within the corporate body.[36] Managers thus found themselves in a complicated situation in terms of status and mobility, experiencing a sense of possibility as their own positions grew in prestige and as a hierarchical ladder within business became more distinct but also often bumping up against social and familial blockages that severely limited their upward trajectory.

The terrain on which managers interacted with owners and subordinates could be overlaid, then, with numerous axes of connection and with different combinations of affection, loyalty, and resentment. All of these factors played roles in shaping the advice given to employers about how to foster and maintain trust in their employees: from the cultivation of sociable or (quasi) familial relationships with their managers, to the alignment of the manager's interest with that of the firm through different modes of compensation. Attachment to the idea that trust depended on the maintenance of affectionate relations between employer and employee persisted for quite some time, but it was often lauded in the breach. Reflecting in 1857 on the robbery of the South-Eastern Railway by one former and two current employees, Mr. Baron Martin regretted the increase in crimes, "very numerous of late," in which "the great joint-stock companies which have come into existence in such numbers within the last quarter of a century have been plundered by their confidential servants. It seems as though the feeling of attachment and fidelity, which ought to exist between clerk and employer, is wholly wanting in the case of these companies, and they appear to be regarded as a public spoil." On the following day at the trial of Redpath, a judge concurred with Martin's analysis of the reason for the increase: "It is that in these large companies servants are not brought into contact with their masters; they form no attachment for them; and they are not prevented, therefore, from any feeling of that kind from committing depredations." (Perhaps fearing the implications of this reasoning, he reverts to the logic of contract to assert that employees must nonetheless behave: "But that is no excuse for a servant, because persons who are not bound by the ties of attachment are equally bound with others to render honest service to those who employ them."[37]) The *Edinburgh Review* voices a similar concern that the environment of business has changed too much, in an "age that produces railroads which, for a few shillings, will convey a labourer and his family fifty miles to find work," for a return to traditional deferential and affectionate relations: "The deference which a man now pays to his 'brother of the earth,' merely because the one was born rich and the other poor is either hypocrisy or servility. Real attachment, a genuine feeling of subordination, must now be the result of personal qualities, and requires them on both sides equally."[38] The reviewer conflates "a genuine feeling of subordination" with "real attachment" to produce an affectionate and heartfelt acceptance of social inequality—this time based on the qualities of individual character rather than accidents of birth. But, returning to his explicitly free-market premises, he goes on to express skepticism over the effectiveness of changing the "personal demeanour" of individual employers and adopting the strategy of affectionate social intercourse with subordinates, since "the gratitude of men is for things unusual and unexpected," and if the mass of employers were to adopt such tactics they would lose all their value. Instead their "hope for healing the widening breach" lies in appealing to the self-interest of the employees.[39]

In arguing for this plan to reconstruct an environment of confidence, the review refers to "the wisdom," "universally recognised in theory," of "associating the interest of the agent with the end he is employed to attain." The place where this theory could be seen to be operating well in practice, the author points out, was in "the plan of remunerating subordinates in whom trust must be reposed, by a commission on the returns instead of only a fixed salary."[40] Proposals to guarantee trust by appealing directly to this self-interest, to the point of rendering alike the interests of the employee and the employer through devices such as commissions, partnerships, or shares in profits, were in a sense attempts to make an end run around the problem—to render trust itself unnecessary by removing the hypothetical from the precept that the trusty employee should "proceed...with that care and economy which would influence [him] if the whole of the work was [his] own."[41]

But these strategies were not always simple to enact, as they required investments of social capital, organizational changes, and institutional support. The recommendation that employers should learn to understand and evaluate the character of managers and potential managers, on the other hand, offered a relatively flexible response. In framing both the problem and the potential solution to managerial trust as one of character interpretation, Victorian business manuals picked up on an essential feature of the manager/

owner relationship: the structural and legal sense in which the roles of manager and owner were, literally, interpersonal. According to the law of principal and agent, which governed the employer-manager relationship, in most business situations in which an employee was entrusted with powers of management he would implicitly be understood to be acting legitimately as the employer's agent—fulfilling and enacting his superior's interests and wishes. This implicit identification went so far as to determine that employers could be held responsible for their employee's actions even in the absence of specific authorization: "if he is acting in the usual manner, in ordinary business affairs," the employee "will be able to bind his principal to third parties ignorant of his special instructions."[42] Though protections against grosser misdeeds, such as forgery, did exist, this left wide latitude within which an employer could be made to pay for both the genuine mistakes and the crooked actions of his employee.[43] This interpersonality comes sharply into focus in the Victorian texts, shaping their diagnoses and prescriptions. In the earlier models presented in *Wealth of Nations*, for instance, the interpersonal relation between managers and owners is implicit in Smith's assumptions about the difficulties managers were likely to present, as they were tasked with enacting through their labor the interest of those with an ownership stake. But it remains largely abstract, easily lost in his illustrative examples—the colonial managers and directors of large joint-stock companies, who are much less subject to interpersonal exchange with the owners they represent. A telling contrast is found in the suggestive image chosen by Sir Arthur Helps in his very successful advice manual, *Essays Written in the Intervals of Business*, to illustrate the particular importance of choosing agents with care: in making the selection, he cautions, "you have to choose persons for whose faults you are to be punished; to whom you are to be the whipping-boy."[44]

As Helps's vivid metaphor implies, the role-swapping relationship of manager and employer was not merely a legal construct but rather a viscerally (and financially) felt process, enacted every day between people in the workplace and in the imaginative practices which their labor entailed. In its intimate physicality the whipping-boy image contrasts sharply with Smith's more physically distanced examples, as well as with familiar later emblems of white-collar corporate alienation. The image of the Organization Man or the nameless "suit" fails to adequately capture the experience of the mid-Victorian manager who, as Helps's example makes clear, did not necessarily subsume his individuality to a large and faceless firm. Instead, in a personalized manager-owner relationship alienation might entail not the loss of the self in the larger corporate body, but rather a specific dynamic in which roles and identities were imaginatively and practically adopted and exchanged.

In this model manager and owner alike were subject to alienation, becoming vulnerable as their characters were transmuted from supposedly stable marks of personal qualities and identity to mere roles.[45] This mode of alienation, therefore, not only kept personal identity in view but took it as staging ground, proliferating and elaborating discourses and techniques of selfhood, character reading, and character development whether it was invoking character as a deep personal quality or as a part that one might play.

As advice manuals tackled the question of how to evaluate and develop character in business, the role-swapping model loomed large. The businessman needed to find, or nurture, someone who could act in his place. This presupposed a certain capacity for independent thought and judgment— enough to be able to imagine the owner's interests and motivations, which a merely mechanical manager would not be able to do. Thus Helps, for instance, describes responsiveness as a key component of an ideal business character; developing suppleness of mind rather than mastery of information is the crucial aim of a commercial education, in which the student "is not intended to become a learned man, but a man of business; not a 'full man,' but a 'ready man.'"[46] Helps recommends that the employer cultivate this readiness in his employees, taking care to promote "independence of character and action" and "spontaneous development." The employer should take as his example a "wise father," one who is not "unreasonably solicitous to assimilate his son's character or purposes to his own."[47] Thus two contrary pressures governed the question of managerial character in the role-swapping model of manager-owner relations: the first, to have or to develop a character independent enough to imagine *how* to act in the place of the owner (and even to act as a responsible source of difficult or unpopular advice); the second, to be willing to shed one's independence—to assimilate one's character—in order to act in the place of the owner.[48]

The catalog of qualities that define character in business advice books is not surprising. According to Smiles, character is composed of a mixture of moral virtues and practical habits, including "sense, industry, good principles, and a good heart," along with "self-respect, self-help, application," and a just exercise of power over subordinates.[49] Helps emphasizes "decision," "a vigorous but disciplined imagination," attention to detail, and openness to argument, as well as sympathy and "charity."[50] Every business writer stresses punctuality in general practice and in the payment of obligations: it is "the very essence of a business character" in the view of one 1864 advice manual.[51] Above all, character is defined by consistency: "Aim at a character which is not a piece of patchwork, but a garment of the same weft and warp throughout," motivated equally by morality and principle in all areas of life, acting correctly "whether in secret or in the sight of men."[52]

Mixing qualities and habits in their definitions, business writers emphasized the constructed, in-process nature of character, its formation day by day in "the repetition of little acts."[53] Smiles gives perhaps the most succinct expression of this tendency, suggesting that "as daylight can be seen through very small holes, so little things will illustrate a person's character. Indeed, character consists in little acts, well and honourably performed; daily life being the quarry from which we build it up, and rough-hew the habits which form it."[54] If character is continuously constructed and reconstructed in the "little acts" of everyday life, it must also be ceaselessly observed and interpreted if it is to maintain its value in smoothing out the problems of business trust. Knowledge of character is thus defined as a crucial commercial skill—one of the qualities that Smiles cites as justification for designating the Duke of Wellington (and Napoleon as well) "a first-rate man of business," for instance—and business writers set about to advise their readers how best to attain it.[55]

Helps, in particular, was loquacious on the subject, fashioning a method of interpretation shaped by the intimate, interpersonal relations of business. Grounded in self-scrutiny, sympathy, and the close observation and interpretation of details of behavior, Helps's mode of reading injected an element of psychological depth into the representation of business and business character. Helps begins his essay "On Our Judgments of Other Men" by referring the reader to his conception of his own self: "Who does not feel that to describe with fidelity the least portion of the entangled nature that is within him would be no easy matter?" But the complex and multilayered nature one envisions for one's own self is not granted to others: "the same man who feels this, and who, perhaps, would be ashamed of talking at hazard about the properties of a flower, of a weed, of some figure in geometry, will put forth his guesses about the character of his brother-man, as if he had the fullest authority for all that he was saying."[56] For Helps, in other words, the task of understanding characters—whether one's own or another's—is worthy of the same kind of sustained, probing, even scientific scrutiny that one might train on a botanical specimen or mathematical problem.

As a result, the businessman's understanding of character is notably self-reflexive and involved. In discussing the development of self-discipline, for example, Helps counsels an immediate and searching follow-up to the first "faint glimpse" of a problem that teaches the businessman his own character depths: "Let him not be contented with that small insight. His first step in self-discipline should be to attempt to have something like an adequate idea of the extent of the disorder. The deeper he goes in this matter the better: he must try to probe his own nature thoroughly."[57] This probing involves an effort to fit the pieces of information gleaned about the self into a pattern: a "habit of introspection" that scrutinizes each action "as if it were a thing by itself, independent and self-originating," is "too limited"; rather, introspection must be "both searching and progressive," aiming "not only to investigate instances, but to discover principles."[58]

This kind of self-reflexive examination of one's own character should become a part of the calculation in everyday business dealings with others, whether employees, partners, competitors, or customers. For instance, "in commenting on any error of an agent or dependant," Helps counsels, "beware of making your own vexation, and not the real offence, the measure of your blame," and suggests that the employer who hears falsehoods from his subordinates look to his own temper, reflecting "how fearful a part the angry man may have in the sin of those falsehoods which immoderate fear of him gives rise to."[59] Helps's exemplary businessman is constantly revisiting his actions and feelings to understand their sources and their place in the warp and weft of his character. Perhaps anticipating that readers might find such constant disciplinary introspection burdensome and enervating, Helps includes in *Essays Written in the Intervals of Business* a section, "Aids to Contentment," that aimed to provide "some antidotes against the manifold ingenuity of self-tormenting."[60]

A practice that threatens to shade toward self-tormenting does not easily fit our conception of model business procedure grounded in calculation and executive decisiveness (qualities that were also urged on Victorian businessmen). However, Helps claims a practical value for it. Self-scrutiny reminds the businessman that complexity and depth structure the character of others and teaches him to take superficial details as signs of deeper meanings. "It is well to be thoroughly impressed with a sense of the difficulty of judging about others," Helps notes,

> still, judge we must, and sometimes very hastily: the purposes of life require it. We have, however, more and better materials, sometimes, than we are aware of: we must not imagine that they are always deep-seated and recondite: they often lie upon the surface. Indeed, the primary character of a man is especially discernible in trifles: for then he acts, as it were, almost unconsciously. It is upon the method of observing and testing these things, that a just knowledge of individual men in great measure depends. You may learn more of a person even

by a little converse with him than by a faithful outline of his history. The most important of his actions may be anything but the most significant of the man: for they are likely to be the results of many things besides his nature. To understand that, I doubt whether you might not learn more from a good portrait of him, than from two or three of the most prominent actions of his life. Indeed, if men did not express much of their nature in their manners, appearance, and general bearing, we should be at a sad loss to make up our minds how to deal with each other.[61]

The character that one needs to find out, in this account, is unconscious, hidden, inadvertently revealed rather than willfully represented—but it is traceable in surface "trifles," for those who have taught themselves to read.

As he sketches daily activities of business, Helps emphasizes the need to attend to the little actions and details that are not intended to be communicative. Business "interviews" (a term that for Helps designates a wide range of business meetings) are particularly fertile, for example, despite the hazards that come with on-the-spot interaction: "The pen may be a surer, but the tongue is a nicer instrument. In talking, most men sooner or later show what is uppermost in their minds; and this gives a peculiar interest to verbal communications. Besides, there are looks, and tones and gestures, which form a significant language of their own."[62] In his everyday life, the businessman must be a creative reader, looking for the "language" of trifles that act as signs conveying the truths of strategies, desires, and character.

Such an approach to character and character reading also forms a practical business strategy, according to Helps, because it generates insight into actions and motivations that exceeds conventional business wisdom. "A little thing may make a great difference when we come to investigate motives," Helps argues, and thus may be the key to unraveling the character subject to a variety of impulses and concerns. Looking to self-interest, the standard explanation for commercial actions and bargaining, is inadequate, as "we have scarcely ever such a knowledge of the nature and fortunes of another, as to be able to decide what is his interest, much less what it may appear to him to be." Furthermore, he suggests, "a man's fancies, his envy, his wilfulness, every day interfere with, and over-ride his interests. He will know this himself, and will often try to conceal it by inventing motives of self-interest to account for his doing what he has a mind to do."[63] Overcoming this difficulty demands an act of sympathetic imagination. "Few people have imagination enough to enter into the delusions of others, or indeed to look at the actions of any other person with any prejudices but their own," Helps argues.[64] Those who

do have sufficiently developed sympathetic capacities have a leg up in understanding the undercurrents of will and fancy, as well as interest, that may be
at play in the interactions of business. And those who are thus able to comprehend the source of different reactions in their business associates may be
better able to make wise decisions, reaping balance-sheet benefits from their
interpretive skills.[65]

The interpersonal transactions of business for Helps, then, are occasions
for practicing a mode of interpreting character that closely resembles the
kind that was increasingly demanded of readers. Helps's counsel to notice
the "trifles" that "lie upon the surface" and move from them to discern a "primary character" defined as "deep-seated and recondite" mimics the model
suggested in Victorian literary criticism, for instance in David Masson's
praise of Laurence Sterne's "art of minute observation" and his skill in "giving
significance to the most evanescent minutiae in thought, feeling, look, and
gesture."[66] Novels, especially, offered the reader a wide variety of detail to
practice interpreting, from descriptions of "manners, appearance, and general bearing," to speeches and conversations whose precise terms could be
carefully analyzed.

The connection, in fact, was self-consciously made by many business
writers. Some, such as John Tulloch, in his advice manual *Beginning Life*,
recommend reading literature as a way of gaining experience with character transactions. In a chapter entitled "How to Read" Tulloch argues that
novels and other "fictitious or ideal representations of human life and character" may be a "true education" for the young man starting out in business,
a chance "to study human nature in the mimic scenes of the novelist or the
poet." Tulloch's insistence that novels may be a site for "study" makes the
reading of literary character an active and significant process, more like than
unlike the reading of more ostensibly serious genres such as history in developing the independent "capacity of looking for the truth—of sifting the
essential from the accidental . . . and piercing below the incrusted dogma of
popular narrative or description to the direct face of facts."[67]

I close this section by drawing attention to an enactment of this contemporary connection between reading texts and reading people. The financial
journalist David Morier Evans, who chronicled the major commercial crises of the mid-nineteenth century, pauses in the midst of his account of the
Crystal Palace Company frauds perpetrated by the employee William James
Robson, a sometime poet and dramatist, to cite and examine a couple of instances of the criminal's writing.[68] The first is an early poem, "The Dreams
of Youth," which Evans notes is "not very original in manner or in matter"
but which he reads nonetheless as bearing "internal evidence of having been

written at that age when the stern realities of life are beginning to destroy the unreasonable dreams of boyhood." That Evans draws this particular meaning from a two-stanza meditation on growing up ("We all have dreams in early youth, / Ere life hath gathered elder dross"; "We backward gaze in after years, / To view the scenes of early days") is perhaps not surprising.[69] More noteworthy is his identification of the "internal evidence" of a text as a manifestation of character, a detail that, though not necessarily produced to let the reader know something of the author, can be used by Evans to reconstruct the internal state that might have led the promising young man to criminal ends. The next example that Evans quotes at length (I excerpt it here) is a letter that Robson wrote to a friend, complaining of the sorry state of the literary marketplace: "Some institution is required, to be presided over by a paid council of intelligent literary men capable of separating the chaff from the wheat, and stamping their verdict on the work, somewhat after the fashion that true gold is marked at Goldsmith's Hall. If this system were instituted, there would be no flower born to blush unseen; works of worth and genius would be preserved to the public, and the authors of them saved from discourteous snubbings or polite falsehoods."[70]

In the midst of a piece of financial journalism, close reading breaks out. "The letter is chiefly valuable . . . as an index to character," Evans claims. "The writer incidentally manifests that vanity which was so strong an element in his composition. Doubtless he regarded himself as that oft-quoted 'flower' which is 'born to blush unseen.' "[71] Going so far in his exegesis as to refer to specific quotations as signs that "incidentally" reveal identity, Evans reads character in reading Robson's words—and leads his own reader to do the same. Although in these cases the character that the writing is taken to reveal is that of the writer himself, not that of a person presented within a narrative, Evans's interpretations suggest the extent to which the interpretation of significant trifles—a letter to a friend, a reference drawn within it—had come to be part of the interpretive toolkit of readers of texts and of people. A businessman who was skilled at both might hope to navigate the treacherous waters of commercial confidence, discerning the associates, customers, and employees who would best justify the trust it was necessary to place in them.

"Too Deep for a Partner"

When Dickens embarked on the writing of *Dombey and Son,* he was no stranger to the tensions inherent in managerial relationships. During his short-lived stint as editor of a start-up newspaper, the *Daily News,* he experienced them from both sides. As editor, Dickens was responsible for engaging and negotiating with staff and directing many aspects of the administration of the paper; as a key founding member he helped solicit capital, writing a prospectus and lending his name and fame to the project. However, he remained at the same time a (generously) salaried employee who needed, finally, to bow to the wishes of those who had invested even more, notably his publishers, Bradbury and Evans—and according to the terms of the contract he signed, they retained the right to hire and fire all their various employees, including their editor and anyone he had recommended. Dickens clashed with his publishers over a number of issues during his association with the newspaper, but employee matters were prominent in his complaints.[72] In particular, Dickens had advocated hiring John Powell as his subeditor, a position, Dickens noted in his initial letter negotiating terms with Bradbury and Evans, that needed to be filled by someone "to whom I can, with perfect confidence, hand over the practical management" of the paper "when I am not there, or after I have left the office."[73] The choice had not gone over well with the newspaper's publishers, and Dickens was outraged:

> You know that I recommended Mr. Powell to you, as the man, of all others in London, best qualified to act as one of the Sub Editors of an enterprising Paper. You know that I was very anxious to secure him, and considered it a very great point when he was engaged, and have always spoken of him with great confidence.
>
> One week after the starting of the Paper, you come to me, and give me to understand, on certain nameless authority (which you call "gatherings") that he is quite unfit for the place he holds! I wish to know from whom you learn this: and I consider myself justified in putting you upon your honor to withhold from me the name of no person with whom you have taken counsel on this subject.
>
> When I tell you, distinctly, that I shall leave the Paper immediately, if you do not give me this information, I think it but fair to add that it is extremely probable I shall leave it when you have done so. For it would be natural in any man, and is especially so in one in my position, to consider this, disrespectful, and quite unendurable. I am thoroughly disgusted, and shall act accordingly.[74]

Dickens was already unhappy in his editorship, but the questioning of his judgment, particularly over a matter so closely connected to himself as who would act in his stead, offered a perfect pretext for abandoning the enterprise.

The note of grievance struck in this letter suggests that Dickens's sense of insult, experienced in his capacity as subordinate, overwhelms the assumption that he shares with Bradbury and Evans in his capacity as superior: a manager needs to be someone who can be trusted to act in one's place. As his judgment is called into question, Dickens's experience highlights the way the managerial role produced a constant, chafing reminder both of one's independence—as someone who could be trusted to exercise judgment—and of the tenuousness of that independence. As the experience is transmuted in *Dombey and Son,* this tension structures Dickens's representation of commercial relations in the titular family firm. Anxiously working out its tale of a villainous manager and a self-centered owner, the novel is decidedly ambivalent about both the managerial role and the function of character and reading in guaranteeing business trust.

Dombey and Son is one of three primary economic sites in the novel, joined by the Wooden Midshipman, the small shop offering marine instruments, and the railway. This threefold division has prompted critics to propose a temporal schema in which Dombey and Son sits anomalously in between emblems of the old-fashioned way of business and of the disruptive, modernizing force of industrial capitalism. As a merchant family firm located in the City of London, Dombey and Son is ambiguously placed. It is taken to represent the dehumanizing tendencies of capitalist modernity, as Dombey treats his family as coin that can be invested (his son, Paul) or as base coin that cannot (his daughter, Florence, and his second wife, Edith). Simultaneously, however, it is taken to be "a relic of the past," as F. S. Schwarzbach has suggested, a backward-looking symbol of eighteenth-century mercantile capitalism, superseded by the vanguard form of industrial capital.[75] By this account, the firm's undoing is a result of its archaism, as patriarchal inheritance fails with the death of little Paul Dombey and as a new man enters the scene: Carker the manager, not drawn from the ranks of the family and emblematic of the cash-nexus relations of the capitalist labor market.[76]

But to read the collapse of Dombey and Son and the machinations of its manager as a clash between the forces of the future and of the past misses the way the novel engages its present. Viewed as an example of personal business, Dombey and Son appears profoundly Victorian, characteristic of a hybrid system and a fluid moment. Such a perspective, I suggest, allows a richer reading of one of the novel's strangest figures, Carker, to emerge and through this a deeper sense of the novel's conflicted encounter with contemporary capitalism, as it entered current debates about business trust that were themselves invoking novelists and the forms with which they worked.

From the start of the novel, Dickens foregrounds the tension that he himself experienced between the expression of individual agency and character in the workplace and the expression of the owner's wishes and interests. Initially, however, this tension emerges not through the novel's manager, but through the representation of Dombey and Son's Son, the sickly, bewildered, and otherworldly Paul, born into a sequence in which he cannot lay claim to any individual identity but can be merely, as the elder Dombey declares, "the present unworthy representative" of his family name and firm (106). Dombey, who "had risen, as his father had before him, in the course of life and death, from Son to Dombey," is delighted at the birth of this "new partner" and proceeds to rear his child as if he were an undifferentiated extension of himself, a Son who couldn't become Dombey quickly enough (2). Again and again as the father looks at his child, he aches to make time hurry up. "Would you like to begin to be Dombey and Son, now, and lend this money to young Gay's uncle?" he demands, as he prompts his five-year-old boy to make his first business decision, in response to a request by Walter Gay, nephew of Sol Gills, the owner of the Wooden Midshipman, for a loan to assist the floundering small businessman (112). Placing Paul in a "hothouse" school in preparation for his accession to the management of the firm, he notes to the schoolmistress that Paul's life is not to be governed by his own choice or by accident: "His way in life was clear and prepared, and marked out, before he existed" (119, 117).

As the Son of the firm, in other words, Paul is charged with learning to discern and enact a preexisting role. At times he seems to be mastering the elder Dombey's character, exhibiting, for example, an "abundant promise of being imperious" (76); at other moments he appears so closely connected to his father as to voice, as if telepathically, "the subject of Mr. Dombey's thoughts" (77). But Paul never manages to comfortably and completely enter the identity that his father represents. Wondering "Papa! what's money?" one night by the fireside, for instance, Paul begins in synch with his father's thoughts; however, his own independent perspective uncontrollably seeps through: if money is, as his father replies, "a good thing" that "can do anything," Paul responds with the impermissible, self-focused musing, "I wonder why it didn't save me my Mama" (77, 78). Rather than fitting smoothly into the pattern of generational substitution that is laid out for him, Paul becomes what those around him describe him as—an "odd child," "singular" (156, 155). With his own difference denied, but continually breaking out and preventing him from embodying the role that he was born to fill, Paul weakens, dashing his father's hopes by dying at the end of the book's fifth number.

As it invites and then crushes the reader's attachment to the beleaguered child, the novel builds an unimpeachable critique of Dombey's self-centered, familialist disregard for the individuality of those who are part of his firm. His insistence on perfectly reproducing himself has in fact been interpreted as a mark of Dombey and Son's archaism, an inability to adapt to a changing economy in which expansion, risk, and the incorporation of "other identities and activities than those in which it ordinarily consists" are necessary to business health.[77] But the novel is more ambivalent than such a reading suggests, precisely because the question of how to incorporate those "other identities" was neither straightforward nor settled; instead, it raised the thorny problem of intrafirm trust. As the novel reworks the pattern established by Dombey and Paul in its representation of Carker the manager—the other character given the task of understanding and reenacting Dombey—it continues, to a degree, the critique that is instantiated clearly in the depiction of Paul's short life. But at the same time this portrait suggests a profound discomfort, both with the form of individuality that Carker represents and with the responses offered to it in contemporary debates over business trust.

From the first scene in the offices of Dombey and Son, when Carker replies "I don't know that I need trouble you" to Dombey's query as to whether there is anything for him to attend to, Dombey cedes the entire management of his business to Carker (144). Even the lowliest messenger in the firm is able to report that the nominal head of the firm "does nothing without Mr. Carker, and leaves all to Mr. Carker, and acts according to Mr. Carker, and has Mr. Carker always at his elbow" (335–36). Dombey's style in domestic affairs is the same. In his early meetings with Edith Granger, the beautiful widow who becomes his second wife, Dombey delegates the niceties of courtship the way he would the negotiation of terms in a business deal. On an expedition to Warwick Castle and Kenilworth, for example, he leaves it to Carker to discourse upon the artworks as they tour a gallery, "thinking that his remarks, which were, as one might say, a branch of the parent establishment, might amuse Mrs. Granger" (329). Asked by Edith to choose a vantage point for her sketching, Dombey defers to Carker; when she offers him opportunities to be of service by sharpening her pencils and to uphold his portion of gallantry by praising her drawing, Dombey again gives his manager the tasks. Such demonstrations are not grounded in recognition of Carker's independent talents; instead, they are cast as examples of Dombey's arrogant confidence in the trusty agent's absolute fidelity to his interest and his failure to imagine that employees are anything but extensions of himself.

So striking is Dombey's supreme self-centeredness that it is made to stand for a particular relation of protagonist to minor characters in Alex Woloch's sociohistorically and formally astute account of what he calls the character-systems of nineteenth-century realist novels, as he quotes Dombey's incredulity that "these people . . . should be *necessary* to him." In Woloch's "labor theory of character," the formal relation of minor characters, *"the proletariat of the novel,*" to round, humanistic, psychologized protagonists may be mapped onto the "conjoined processes of social stratification." A dialectic is possible in which the functionality of minor characters—their reduction to thematic significance in the protagonist's story, for instance—may be unsettled by the "flash" of understanding of their power in defining the protagonist or by the sense that they, too, could be protagonists, if the story were told differently.[78]

The difficulty readers might have in seeing Carker as decisively minor speaks to the strength of Woloch's analysis: as Dombey attempts to literalize in Carker the functionalist, referential role of a minor character, the power Carker has grows, as does the potential for a critical political perspective on the process by which a human agent—a potential protagonist—may be transformed into a node in a network (narrative or commercial) overlaid with class hierarchy. Dombey's refusal to acknowledge Carker's separate feelings and interests becomes most pronounced, and comes in for nearly explicit criticism, in the scene in which he asks Carker to act as the enforcer of his domestic rule. When Dombey orders Carker to communicate to Edith "the very disagreeable necessity" that the manager will henceforth act as "the bearer of yet more unwelcome and explicit communications" if she refuses to behave, Carker's obsequious demeanor slips—momentarily, but enough to make even Dombey experience "some embarrassment"—as he subtly confronts his principal with the sense that in employing the manager as an instrument of humiliation, Dombey humiliates him (499, 500). Carker's complaint to Edith, "You may imagine how regardless of me, how obtuse to the possibility of my having any individual sentiment or opinion he is, when he tells me, openly, that I am so employed," not only feels justified; it also cements a parallel between shady manager and innocent son that highlights the novel's sympathy for the claims of independent, individualistic character (525).[79]

However, that same form of character is both the source and the means of Carker's breach of trust. As the novel contrasts the management styles of Carker and his counterpart, the old seaman Captain Cuttle, who runs the Wooden Midshipman in Sol Gills's absence, it suggests that the tension between the interests of employer and employee may not in fact be susceptible to resolution through the kind of character that business writers and Dickens himself, at moments, were looking to. To the degree that Carker represents a mastery of managerial character and character practices—his independent sensitivity to interest; his ability to read and analyze character and to enter into the character of another—their ability to guarantee trust is put in question. The constancy and commercial incompetence of the sea captain suggest that business trust may depend, not on finding Helps's "ready man" of "independence of character and action," but rather on finding a man with no self-interested depths and therefore no capacity to perform the self-referential, sympathetic imaginative act that defined the trusty agent.

If the advice given to early- to mid-nineteenth-century managers on fulfilling the trust placed in them was to act as if the business were their own, Carker takes it to a perverse conclusion. Imitating his principal's dress, deportment, and haughty way with subordinates, Carker's strategy is to efface the difference between himself and his employer—to show himself so able to anticipate any need, wish, or interest that Dombey could have that it is as if he is, in fact, a second Dombey. As Carker proceeds with his attempts to take over the interest of his principal in more concrete ways—contemplating using Florence, Dombey's neglected daughter, as a way to become another "Son"; and finally, when he runs away with Edith, attempting to take over Dombey's place with his own wife—his encroachments are cast in terms of sexual menace. This shift to a highly charged, sensational register suggests the threat implicit in a model of business that required employees to imagine and act as if they were the employer: that the employee will come to imagine himself actually *being* the employer, with all the danger to class distinction, hierarchy, and (notably, in the age of the family firm) family itself that such an eruption of desire and interest could imply. For Carker, a share in the profits is not enough to guarantee his trustworthiness by aligning his interest with the owner's. He already gets a *share:* he wants it all.

This picture is further complicated when Carker's fellow employee Mr. Morfin reveals the nature of the manager's ultimate crimes against the firm. These crimes are rather peculiar. In a conversation with Carker's sister Harriet, he informs her that her brother took no money from the firm, though he "oftener dealt and speculated to advantage for himself, than for the House he represented." But his "criminality," Morfin also reports, chiefly consists in a constant "ministration to [Dombey's] ruling passion." Carker has undertaken "possibly ... ruinous" projects "to swell the reputation of the House for vast resources, and to exhibit it in magnificent contrast to other merchants' houses." He has "pampered the vanity and ambition of his employer, when it was his duty to have held them in check" (627). Carker is censured, in other words, exactly *for* acting as his principal would—and as his principal continues to do: in his proud "infatuation" with the glory of the firm, Dombey maintains the practices that his manager has set up, refusing to "contract its enterprises by a hair's breadth," so that he bears the ultimate responsibility for the bankruptcy that results (680). The vexed situation of the manager, who must all at once act as himself (but not *too* himself) and as his employer (but not too much his employer, either), produces the criminal opportunity and even defines the crime itself.

Because his livelihood requires acts of imposture, both imaginative and practical, Carker's own character is slippery; he is a deeply interested individual who can affect to shed his own self at will and imagine himself fully in the place of another. Though this imaginative facility mirrors the sympathetic understanding that employers and employees alike were encouraged to develop and employ in day-to-day business, Dickens transforms it into something more sinister.[80] Carker's easy way of inhabiting others, a skill he has honed to perfection in his service to Dombey, lends him an almost mesmeric aspect that is experienced as mysterious and troubling. Uncannily injecting himself into the minds of those around him, Carker seems able to read and answer their thoughts without so much as opening his wide, toothy mouth. In an interaction with Florence, for example, he appears to divine her interest in the fate of her childhood friend Walter, presumed lost at sea on his way to Dombey and Son's office in Barbados. His apparently wordless communication, "there is no news of the ship," leaves Florence "confused, frightened, shrinking from him, and not even sure that he had said those words, for he seemed to have shown them to her in some extraordinary manner through his smile, instead of uttering them" (296). His assumption of "a confidence between himself and her" asserts an unsettling "power and authority" (336). The menace becomes even more pronounced in his relationship with Rob the Grinder, his terrorized servant, who feels as if he is in "the service of some powerful enchanter" who "engrossed his whole attention and exacted his most implicit submission and obedience"; he has "no more doubt that Mr. Carker read his secret thoughts, or that he could read them by the least exertion of his will if he were so inclined, than he had that Mr. Carker saw him when he looked at him" (492).

Carker's skill in reading—whether Rob's thoughts or the books, papers, and office correspondence of Dombey's firm—is a defining trait. Able to read multiple languages, able (as the eventual revelation of his misconduct reveals) to "explore the mysteries" of the firm's "books and papers, with the patient progress of a man who was dissecting the minutest nerves and fibres of his subject" and to make them say exactly what he needs them to say at any moment, Carker is also figured as able to read character through reading text (528). After finishing business correspondence, for instance, he turns to a letter from Dombey and peruses it "slowly: weighing the words as he went, and bringing every tooth he had in his head to bear upon them," going over it a second time to pick out passages whose specific language elucidates his employer's state of mind (252). In person, as well, Carker reads character as if it were text: Edith experiences the sensation at their first meeting, after which she announces to her mother that the manager "already knows us thoroughly, and reads us right," and she never loses the feeling "that he read her life as though it were a vile book, and fluttered the leaves before her in slight looks and tones of voice which no one else could detect" (334, 439). The manager's interpretive powers go astray when he asserts his self too much in the reading process, taking his own resentments as measure for the feelings of others, affirming to his good-hearted brother (and office subordinate), for instance, that he knows the "transparent secret" of the firm's employees—that each of them privately hates Dombey and would be "glad at heart to see his master humbled" (537, 536). As he plots his final vengeance, "pondering over the blackening grate, until he rose up like a man who had been absorbed in a book," the practice of reading shades ever darker (537).

In stark contrast, the novel's other manager, Captain Cuttle, is completely incapable of reading anything, whether person or text. In one early scene, for instance, he proposes to "sound Mr. Carker carefully" on the subject of Walter's prospects and to "say much or little, just as he read that gentleman's character"; discerning marks of favor in the manager's responses, the captain communicates the fantasy of Walter's marriage to Florence, which Carker later uses against the boy (195). Reading texts, similarly, is an act that brings confusion rather than understanding. When Rob the Grinder, who has been acting as Carker's spy in the Wooden Midshipman's household, leaves his service, the captain is staggered, having "believed in the false Rob," and "been glad to believe in him." When the boy departs, Cuttle takes up his newspaper "as if nothing unusual or unexpected had taken place, and went reading on with the greatest assiduity. But never a word did Captain Cuttle understand, though he read a vast number, for Rob the Grinder was scampering up one column and down another" (461).

Such uncomprehending reading is a regular practice for the captain, who judges books by the size of their covers: "he made it a point of duty to read none but very large books on a Sunday, as having a more staid appearance: and had bargained, years ago, for a prodigious volume at a book-stall, five lines of which utterly confounded him at any time, insomuch that he had not yet ascertained of what subject it treated" (595). His textual mantra, originating in the early pronouncement "Overhaul your catechism till you find that passage, and when found turn the leaf down" (35), represents a pattern in which words are seized, understood as definitively answering a preconceived need or narrative, but never grappled with in context for their richness of meaning. The Captain's confident textual mastery, when he reads of the sinking of Walter's vessel in the "Shipping Intelligence"—announcing, "This here fatal news is too correct. They don't romance, you see, on such pints. It's entered on the ship's log, and that's the truest book as a man can write"— turns out, happily, to be wrong in his surmise that the ship's loss means the death of Walter as well (389, 391).

If reading character has been figured in the business texts and Carker's practice, in particular in his conversation with his brother, as a shuttling process in which one understands the different layers and motivations of another character by reference to the depths one discerns in one's self, it is no surprise that Cuttle should fail so utterly at it. For Cuttle himself is a different kind of character from that represented in business handbooks and in the business-like world of the novel. He is, first of all, without depths. Trying to do "a little business for the young people," for instance, Cuttle leaves to meet Dombey to ask after his plans for Walter, believing himself endowed with a "surprising talent for deep-laid and unfathomable scheming." But even as he walks down the street, whatever motives he has come bursting to the surface in a nonstop series of winks, which bubble out automatically "as a vent for his superfluous sagacity" (192). When Carker accuses Cuttle, in their second meeting, of being "deep" and belonging to an "artful and audacious set of people," he fails to discern the essential dissimilarity between his own character, from which he takes his interpretive cues, and the sea captain's, which, far from deep and artful, is shallow and innocent, distinguished by "simplicity, credulity, and generous trustfulness" mingled with "an odd sort of romance, perfectly unimaginative, yet perfectly unreal" (394, 572). Cuttle is, furthermore, "subject to no considerations of worldly prudence or practicability"—that is, completely unmotivated by self-interest, as exemplified by his constant efforts to make over property to Walter and Florence and by his disinclination to take over ownership of the Wooden Midshipman even when it appears that Sol has died and left it to him. The good manager is not an employee, but a loving friend (572).

Cuttle's lack of self-interest and depth places him outside the interpretive framework used by Carker in his character reading; he has neither the economic motivation nor the psychological complexity that business handbooks encouraged readers to assume in their associates, through reference to their knowledge of themselves. Cuttle's form of character resists both being read and being a reading subject. But he is not therefore marked as untrustworthy. To the contrary, his steady faithfulness, uncoupled from the handbooks' character norms, stands as a rebuke to the model of character reading that was promoted in writings on employer-employee trust.[81] Captain Cuttle is ultimately rewarded for his perfect fidelity to the owner by being granted the managerial brass ring: a partnership. Golden letters announce the names "Gills and Cuttle" above the shop, and while the store still doesn't have much custom, Sol Gills's investments suddenly pay off to take care of any lingering financial concerns, leaving Cuttle happy enough with the fantasy "fiction of a business in [his] mind which is better than any reality" (731).

But even as the novel undercuts reading, it also alerts its readers to the process and even instructs them as to how to interpret the signs they see on the page. Take, for example, the scene of the dinner party at Dombey's house shortly after his marriage to Edith. In describing the party, the general chilliness of which typifies the coldness that has been emphasized as a key to Dombey's nature and his marriage, Dickens self-consciously draws attention to the literary device through which he advances that connection: "the long plateau of precious metal frosted, separating him from Mrs. Dombey, whereon frosted Cupids offered scentless flowers to each of them, was allegorical to see" (431). In case the reader misses the point, some moments into the dinner a cousin relates a joke about the wedding of a rich man and a beautiful poor woman whose punch line—"*She* is regularly bought, and you may take your oath *he* is as regularly sold!"—presents an interpretation of Edith and Dombey's marriage that everyone at the table recognizes with horror and that glosses its representation for the novel's own audience (432). At several other moments, Dickens highlights the way a reader might observe external details to discern the signs of character, constructing patterns and positing the inner truths to which they point. Though Dombey may "hide the world within him from the world without," following Edith's elopement, the marks of his humiliated pride—"hollow eyes and cheeks, a haggard forehead, and a moody, brooding air"—escape as "rebel traces" (600). As Carker plots his final breach, Dickens suggests that "everything that had been observable in him before, was observable now, but with a greater amount of concentration": a reminder that the signs have been there all along, for both Dombey and the reader to interpret (529). And though the "analysis of the character of P. Dombey" performed for Paul at school is laughable—in particular the resolution of the boy's character into numerically rated "first elements" ("Violence two. Selfishness two")—it does arrive at the term "old-fashioned," the adjective that the novel picks up and comes to associate with Paul (154, 155). Sharing the pedagogical task with its characters, *Dombey and Son* self-consciously highlights its own construction of a version of character as something that requires—indeed comes into being through—interpretation.

The ambivalent perspective on character reading in *Dombey and Son* can perhaps best be illustrated by the reading lessons that Dombey is made to undergo. The first instruction is forced on him by Carker. Introduced in the book as a figure who, in a sense, writes himself, the manager offers his character—especially his conviction that "there is no show of subservience compatible with the transaction of business between us, that I should think sufficient"—as if it were a transparently readable text: "If he had carried these words about with him printed on a placard, and had constantly offered it to Mr. Dombey's perusal on the breast of his coat, he could not have been more explicit than he was" (144). When he absconds, as if to demonstrate how grossly Dombey had been misdirected, Carker makes an effort to force him to read correctly, turning the "private books" of the firm into a primer, with "results so plain and clear" that they could be grasped, "numerous and varying as they are, with extraordinary ease." This final lesson focuses less on business strategy than on character, as Carker reveals the truth of his own duplicity and the truth of Dombey's nature as well, "as if he had resolved to show his employer at one broad view what has been brought upon him by ministration to his ruling passion" (627).[82] And the narrative itself continues Carker's pedagogy, giving Dombey numerous, insistent opportunities for re-medial reading. Dombey receives the news of Edith's flight in a letter: "He read that she was gone. He read that he was dishonoured. He read that she had fled, upon her shameful wedding-day, with the man whom he had cho-sen for her humiliation" (556). He is further forced to read the truth when he visits Good Mrs. Brown and her daughter Alice, earlier victims of Carker's depravity, in order to find out where his manager and wife have disappeared to. In a highly contrived scene, Dickens has Rob the Grinder spell out for Mrs. Brown, letter by letter, the place to where they have fled ("D.I.J.O.N.") while Dombey leans in to look, unobserved, over the boy's shoulder (617).

It matters, then, that Dombey be taught to read, enough that the plot strains to join forces with the devious manager to provide him instruction. But, importantly, the novel doesn't make these reading lessons into the oc-casion for Dombey's transformation. Instead, he persists in his proud ways, refusing to learn the lessons that Carker has written out for him, for a "whole year" until the firm is bankrupted (680). Only then does he recognize, after he has been stripped of both business interests and household goods, the im-portance of "that which he might have made so different in all the Past—which might have made the Past itself so different . . .—that which was his own work": his faithful, though despised, daughter, who returns to save him from suicide and restore him to the warmth of a new and loving home (701). Though the process of understanding Florence's worth begins with the re-ceipt of Walter's letter upon their marriage, reading it simply suggests value to Dombey insofar as it presents her as a lost object, "as something that might have been his, but was lost beyond redemption" (702). His transformation comes not through reading, but rather through memory, an internal process that finds external form as he reconciles with Florence and her new family. Returning to her fold, he retreats from the business world and devotes himself to her children—retreats, that is, from a world in which character is of a type that must be read to one in which character is unchanging and knowable, needing only to be apprehended and appreciated.[83]

Of course, in one fundamental characterological respect Carker and Cuttle share more with each other than with the reader: they are textual creatures, held within the pages of a book. As such, Carker and Cuttle are, in one sense, equally free from *real* depths, available to be fully understood through the narrative clues the text provides. Though Dombey may misread Carker, we do not. But to succumb to the fantasy of mastery that novelistic character permits, and to ground social trust in modes of character and reading that it exemplifies, misses the unpredictability set in motion by the novel's characterological pedagogy and the reader's interpretive energies and identifications. Dickens's novel is deeply ambivalent about the expectations placed on character in the culture of mid-Victorian capitalism. In its own practice it seeks to instruct readers in the process of discerning and piecing together the signs of character, expressing sympathy with independent individuality and encouraging the recognition and understanding of the distinctness of others. At the same time, the novel manifests a suspicion of the mode of character that is engaged and produced through this process of reading. Significantly, the political resonance of Captain Cuttle's flat characterization differs from that suggested by Woloch, who argues that Dickens's caricatures can reveal, in a radical flash, the deformations and distortions that capitalism inflicts on its human subjects.[84] Viewed through the lens of the contemporary theory and practice of management, *Dombey and Son* registers how deep character and the mode of reading that simultaneously plumbed, generated, and reinforced it were implicated in market subjectivity, through acts of sympathetic imagination that were as likely to undermine as to fortify the bonds of trust. Flatness, by this light, can signal preservation.

Thus the novel explodes its most conspicuous reader of character's depths and retreats to the consolations of romance and fairy tale, where character is on the surface, where Walter's marriage to the master's daughter is a Dick Whittington adventure rather than a hostile takeover, and where Florence the "wandering princess" and Cuttle the "good monster" can reap their just rewards (572). Romance is necessary in *Dombey and Son* not so much as a buffer of "human recognition" against "new social and economic forces," characterized by "impersonality," that are "grasped as global and inhuman in their scale," as Ian Duncan, through Raymond Williams, suggests.[85] Instead, occupied by figures whose lack of depths marks a difference from readerly subjectivity, it serves as a resistant, almost antihuman outpost in a cultural, economic, and literary field in which human recognition was profoundly, unsettlingly implicated.

High Art Crime

Ten years or so after the publication of *Dombey and Son,* a curious phrase makes its way into *Facts, Failures, and Frauds,* David Morier Evans's account of English business scandal. What the public had witnessed in the previous two decades, Evans argues, was the "inauguration, development, and rapid progress" of what he calls "'high art' crime," which had flourished while "'high arts' of a more innocent kind" had declined. Citing a list of recent commercial crimes, all but two of which involved an employee's breach of trust, Evans remarks on the "display of ingenuity, perseverance, and artistic skill" that characterized them.[86] The criminals in Evans's roster displayed artistic ambitions and inclinations: Walter Watts managed a theater; William James Robson wrote verse and drama and occasionally acted; Leopold Redpath "evinced good taste in artistic matters."[87] To this list one might add Dickens's friend Powell, the playwright, author, and thieving manager. The crimes themselves are represented as executed with a care and flair that make them aesthetic feats; Redpath, for instance, is "quite a connoisseur in the art of forgery."[88] But the defining aspect of high art crime, for Evans, is the way that all these criminals employ and manipulate "the elements of full mental culture, of position, and character" in perpetrating their frauds.[89] With their self-cultivation and their mastery of the norms of character—in its senses of deep personal identity and adoptable role—these untrustworthy managers unraveled its protective aura. In fact, they found in character itself the opportunity and means for their crimes, succeeding precisely because of their skill in constructing characters for themselves; reading the characters of those around them; and, as in the case of Powell and the "Rich Uncle, and some unknown share in some unknown business" that Dickens mentions in his letter to Chapman, inventing stories to cover their tracks.

It is this last element more than anything that binds the trust-breaking perpetrators of high art crimes, such as Powell, and writers of novels, both manipulating character and story with an eye to financial reward. Dickens himself was certainly not opposed to the practice of shaping and reshaping character depending on the perceived wishes of his audience and the relative chances of success; in writing *Dombey and Son,* for instance, he remained undecided as to whether Walter would go bad, as he originally planned, up through the writing of the third and fourth numbers. "Do you think it may be done, without making people angry?" he asks Forster, finally deciding some months later to "give that idea up" as it seems less attractive to carry out "after the interest [Walter] has acquired."[90] And the fortuitous resolution—the rich-uncle-and-good-luck-in-the-markets story with which Dickens made sense of Powell's implausibly robust finances—is hardly a rare occurrence in Victorian fiction: the sudden turn in Sol Gills's investments, for instance, an unlooked-for bit of fortune that enables *Dombey and Son* to arrive at a happy ending. As commercial crimes of trust become associated with the aesthetic and with notions of mental culture and character, the novelist's tricks of the trade may be tainted. In *Dombey and Son*, it is the novelist/narrator and the criminal Carker who are linked to each other in their capacity for giving reading lessons.

But, of course, mental culture and character, and the reading of character, might also be seen as tainted by having been pressed into commercial service by perfectly honest businessmen—especially to the extent that Dickens imagined his own trust with his audience as grounded in his willingness to play the critical role of the Uncommercial Traveller. Just how "high" Dickens's art is—how much he associated himself and his novelistic practice with "the elements of full mental culture . . . and character"—is a vexed question in his hybrid mixtures of high and low, character and caricature. The period around the writing of *Dombey and Son* has been construed as a turning point in Dickens's career, when his novels become more carefully shaped and unified, with more ambitious and acute representations of psychology and a heightened confidence in his own authorial powers.[91] (At the time the *Economist* praised Dickens's realism, describing his "hearty and healthy naturalness—great shrewdness, and minute and accurate observation."[92]) It seems noteworthy, then, that when Dickens returned to the problem of the untrustworthy manager in *David Copperfield*, he twinned the autobiographical writer figure, David, with the unctuous employee and character impostor, Uriah Heep, as if to give vent once more to an ambivalence about his own role as novelist in constructing characters that were "too deep for a partner."

In fact, Dickens's ambivalence about the trustworthiness of character lingers. In the preface to the 1858 cheap edition of *Dombey and Son*, Dickens once again felt compelled to give a new lesson in reading character, taking issue with a reviewer's complaint that Mr. Dombey's ultimate change of heart was less than believable. The reviewer's perspective on Dombey's final transformation, Dickens argues, is an instance of a more widespread deficiency in the skill of observing character, providing evidence of misreading in which the signs of the potential for transformation within the proud merchant's character had been overlooked. "The faculty (or the habit) of closely and carefully observing the characters of men is a rare one," he suggests. "I have not even found, within my experience, that the faculty (or the habit) of closely and carefully observing so much as the faces of men, is a general one by any means." But as he explains his construction of Dombey, it becomes apparent that observation alone would be insufficient to lead astute readers to the conclusions Dickens asserts. To interpret Dombey correctly, even to be able to discern the relevant surface signs, his claims suggest, one would need to be reading with the assumption of deep, complex, psychological character—a frame through which unacknowledged, even unconscious, and apparently contradictory motivations and behaviors can be understood: "Mr. Dombey undergoes no violent internal change, either in this book or in life. A sense of his injustice is within him all along. The more he represses it, the more unjust he necessarily is" (736).

Stung by the long-ago criticism, Dickens asserts not only his skill in constructing character but also the value of his novel's role in teaching the reading of it. But then he continues: "I began this book by the lake of Geneva, and went on with it for some months in France. The association between the writing and the place of writing is so curiously strong in my mind, that at this day, although I know every stair in the little Midshipman's house, and could swear to every pew in the church in which Florence was married, or to every young gentleman's bedstead in Doctor Blimber's establishment, I yet confusedly imagine Captain Cuttle as secluding himself from Mrs. Mac Stinger among the mountains of Switzerland" (736). Such a move to associate himself with the novel's least adept reader of character might appear strange, after the first part of the preface—especially alongside this aggrandizing reminder of the creator's supplemental knowledge (the details of beds, stairs, pews that remain in his imagination), a reminder that the reader's experience of a complete fictional world finally occurs in fantasy only. But what could be more evocative of Dickens's ambivalent practice in the novel than to follow the lesson in observation and interpretation of the depths that may lie within us and those around us—the lessons of Carker—with a representation of himself as the good Captain, seeking relief from the burdens and shadows of character in the clear mountain air of romance, with a "fiction of a business" in his mind "that is better than any reality"?

2

Routinized Charisma and the Romance of Trade

THE STORY OF COMMERCIAL
CHARACTER, 1850–1885

"IN A FEW DAYS MY BRIEF AND STORMY CAREER WILL FINALLY CLOSE," a weary voice proclaimed in the pages of the July 1876 *Blackwood's*. "I can calmly, and even thankfully, contemplate this premature extinction of an existence which has ruined reputations, shattered fortunes, and carried want and misery into hundreds of humble homes." The conventions of criminal autobiography are on full display in this opening: the penitential attitude; the promise to deliver excitement along with lessons in "the thrilling story of my life"; self-defensive gestures toward misbegotten origins and the influence of a corrupt society; and professions of fear that readers of imperfect virtue will make a how-to manual out of a cautionary tale. But these conventions look decidedly odd given the purported autobiographical subject: "a Joint-Stock Company (Limited)." The declaration by the essay's corporate subject that it is "reclining . . . at this moment in the arms of my official liquidator," for instance, is deathbed posturing with a twist.[1]

An autobiography of a joint-stock company (limited): even taking into account the tradition of it-narratives featuring adventurous bank notes and confessional shillings, the generic choice is odd, mixing a quintessentially personal form with a subject whose essence, notoriously, was its apparent impersonality. The essay's author, Laurence Oliphant, asserts that he has adopted the form to convey "valuable information" about backroom dealing and dishonesty in contemporary commercial life, which it would be otherwise "quite impossible" to obtain.[2] Oliphant tells the story of Albert Grant—"my Promoter," in the essay's first-person account—who during the 1860s and 1870s floated at least twenty companies, accumulated a fortune, and was elected to Parliament, before failing and retreating from public life.[3] But in turning away from a named subject to an anonymous, fictionalized autobiography that simultaneously personalizes (a corporate entity) and evacuates referentiality (to a specific promoter, Grant), the essay highlights form as much as it reveals content. The strain to repersonalize a corporation registers as a longing, a fantasy that biographical narrative might wrestle character back into a realm that seems to have cast it aside, so that it might serve, in Amanda Anderson's terms, as "the value-giving form of new and otherwise threateningly impersonal practices."[4]

If this was Oliphant's aim in invoking character, one could be forgiven for wondering at his choice of form. By the time this essay appeared, business biography was a well-established genre, published in great enough numbers in journalism, collections, and stand-alone volumes as to call into question the notion that what plagued the market was a deficiency of character stories. Joint-stock and limited liability corporations notwithstanding, the cultural representation of the economic scene was far from depopulated; instead, business biographies filled it with characters, often grand and heroic figures—a "galaxy of industrial knights," as a late collection put it, through which were scattered a great number of criminal darker stars.[5] And as the lionizing tone of this description suggests, the biographies' character offerings were not always likely to fulfill the disciplinary aims of a full, truthful accounting. Instead, their often strikingly repetitive accounts of capitalist virtues seem to demand a skeptical eye, as one after another of these tales of remarkable individuality winds up reflecting a narrative that is remarkably generic.

In this chapter, I treat seriously the purpose that Victorian business biographies avowed: providing "studies of character and energy" to serve as models of the personal qualities necessary to prosper in business.[6] To do so requires taking both the aim (and the longing it implies) and its frustration as a starting point for analyzing the modes of character that the biographies' textual representations construct. Given that business biographies often don't provide accounts that satisfy expectations for character that would have been present in novels, or even in the kinds of reading counseled in business practice—the advice given to employers discussed in chapter 1, for instance—what did they contribute to the discourse of business character?

I argue that the business biographies helped to construct a new mode of business character precisely through the tensions they evoke—between personal and impersonal, individual and generic, fact and fiction. The biographies' formal concentration on individuals and the terms in which they depict their subjects work to cast the economic sphere as a world of outsized personalities, in which the secret to business success rested firmly in the personal qualities of uniquely capable men. The exemplars of business character depicted by Samuel Smiles and other practitioners of the form are not simply placeholders filling a role within a rationalized system that might be filled by anyone else. And over the decades the subjects of business biographies come to be endowed with qualities that are even more personalized, constructed by an increasingly explicit rhetoric of heroism and romance that renders businessmen as geniuses, artists, even magicians. This heightened personalization invests them with charisma—in Max Weber's classic definition, a claim to authority and power that resides in "holders of specific gifts of the body and spirit."[7]

Charisma, however, holds an anomalous place within the economic sphere. Weber defines it as the antithesis of a modern rationality characterized by bureaucratic routine and institutional authority, in which business is discharged in an "objective" fashion, "according to *calculable rules* and 'without regard for persons.'"[8] Charisma's exorbitance also is antithetical to the economic rationality postulated by classical and neoclassical economics. Nonetheless, as Weber himself recognized, and as behavioral economists have noted, at different moments and in particular situations charisma has entered into the practice of capitalism.[9] The life stories of businessmen contributed to the formation of a charismatic mode in Victorian business by establishing charisma as a matter of narrative, even textuality. This narrative grounding helped negotiate the difficulty of routinization—incorporation into the everyday rationalities of modernity—that formed the most significant challenge for a mode whose essence emerges in the sacred or in the enchantments of magic, rather than the secular proving ground of profit maximization. Victorian business biographies suggest one manner in which the charismatic mode was integrated into economic activity that, theoretically at least, was inhospitable to it: the power of fictions to generate credit within the domain of transactional character, offering a means of simultaneously believing and not believing, grounding charisma in representations that were at once (and often self-consciously) full and empty.

The construction of charisma in Victorian business biographies thus presents a shift in perspective on the textual field of the Victorian economy. In particular, the biographies generated their new mode of charismatic business character precisely by playing with the relationship between fact and fiction, which was less a split than a productive ambiguity. Business biographies purported to trade in character truths, offering gestures toward the kind of personal knowledge that had long been held to be crucial information in the economy—hence Oliphant's fetishization of the life story form to address the depredations of the Joint-Stock Company, Ltd. At the same time, they built those character representations through techniques of characterization and narration familiar from literary writing, whether the accretion of incidental detail of realist writing or the more explicit codes of romance.

As a genre of biographies grew up, the informational claim remained but was often linked to a heightened forthrightness about the way their character knowledge was built through narrative formulas. Complicit with and dependent on storytelling that highlights itself, business biographies constructed charisma as the quality of embodying stories, exerting power in spite of the routine reappearance of the extraordinary tale or the clichéd motif that belied the claim to absolute individuality and in spite of the way belief in the stories was often qualified, cynically hedged, and a matter of convention. With the proliferation of texts purporting to offer personal knowledge, only to substitute an explicitly fictional content, business biographies constructed charismatic businessmen who carried great personal value, even as those who granted them this value were invited to be aware of its foundation in fictions.

Although business biographies were a significant publishing phenomenon and an important narrative form establishing modes of character, I am not suggesting that they alone transformed the concept of character in business. Nor was the version of charisma that they elaborated universal; other modes of representing character persisted. However, I argue that the shifts that the biographies register are instances of an emerging tendency in commercial attitudes to character and ways of reading character. By placing biographical accounts alongside materials such as investment manuals, prospectuses, annual reports, and finally a novel that explicitly invokes business biographies, I trace the transformation of a concept of character that helped shape an investment culture that can neither be fully comprehended according to models of rational calculation nor moralized through the reading of character and its depths. In the charismatic mode, character has instead become a new source of capitalist enchantment, a kind of "occult energy," to adapt Christopher Herbert's terminology, acting both as a force in economic life and as an explanatory horizon that leaves the real and its signs and interpretive impulses behind.[10]

"The Highest Romance of Real Life": Model Merchants and Industrial Knights

On April 29, 1851, Samuel Budgett, a Methodist proprietor of a grocery business headquartered in Bristol, died at his home in the nearby town of Kingswood. By the next year a biography had been written, William Arthur's *The Successful Merchant: Sketches of the Life of Mr. Samuel Budgett, Late of Kingswood Hill,* which would go through forty-three editions by 1877 (including "Welsh, Dutch, French, and German" translations) and three more by the time the Author's Uniform Edition was published in 1885.[11] The preface to this edition announces pride in having helped create "happy and useful men in business," who called the text "a principal instrument in shaping their character" as they engaged its lessons on the "practical morals of commerce."[12]

Arthur's opening chapter leads the reader through a landscape of contrasts, past "rough cottages," coal-stained laboring men, and women "in costume appropriate to other ages," toward "a few modern houses, aspiring towards respectability, a modern church, and modern chapels." The journey ends at a "substantial residence" at the top of Kingswood Hill, where bright lawns and fountains compete for attention with an aviary and a beautiful prospect over a rich valley and rolling hills (1, 2). The narrator directs the reader's imagined gaze to a "long column" of mourners, the funeral procession of Budgett, the village's "chief man" and the local agent of capitalist-driven improvement (3, 4). Although "a single glance" at the landscape is enough to comprehend the merchant's place in the community, this doesn't amount to a complete picture, Arthur suggests (3). What is missing is the intimate touch.

The subsequent account attempts to provide that intimacy in its reportage and its mode of address. Arthur recounts his interchanges with the common mourners, whose tender sentiments toward their master shine through their rough speech. He invites readers in as eyewitnesses to a present-tense account of the merchant's typical day—Budgett's drive through Bristol to his office; his prompt and methodical execution of the day's duties as laid out in his memorandum book; his gentle but firm dealings with clerks and commercial travelers. The narrative intimacy takes an expansive turn as, addressing the reader in the second person, Arthur leads a tour through an empire in miniature without leaving the bounty of Budgett's stock rooms, which encompass "a territory overgrown with tea-chests," "a colony of casks replenished with nutmegs, cassia, and all spicery," and "a vast and snowy region of flour" (11, 11–12, 12). This condensation of the glories of British commerce sets the stage for the next chapter's lament that despite such fertile materials there is no "great commercial epic" (22). And "what is far more wonderful," Arthur exclaims, "in 'a nation of shopkeepers,' we have no commercial biography. . . . With such a race in the midst of us, and such tokens of what they have been doing, we seek in vain for the Lives of the British Merchants" (28–29).

I have described the opening of Arthur's text at some length, first, to introduce and sketch common features of a popular Victorian genre that, apart from the works of its most famous practitioner, Samuel Smiles, is not particularly widely read. The account of Budgett's personal trajectory from humble (or at least humbler) beginnings to wealth, power, and prestige encapsulates many formulas that are reworked over the next decades as business "Lives" proliferated. Catalogs of exemplary humane actions are joined by catalogs of a more worldly sort, quantifying success from the account of the first shilling earned in childhood (a standard feature of most texts), through elaborately detailed tallies of factories, deals, and profits, through the size of the legacy left to heirs. Achievements outside the field of business are highlighted in accounts of public works, participation in scientific or trade associations, or careers in local or national politics.

More important, I highlight Arthur's text because of its self-consciousness about genre and about the relationship of literature to business. Biography's unwillingness to treat the details of business as anything other than "a dead weight" (30) represents a lost opportunity for both literature and business, he suggests: literature misses a chance to influence readers, most of whom (he imagines) are engaged in commercial pursuits, and also loses out on materials for exciting and instructive plots; business would benefit from literature's engagement of moral questions. Poetry, epic, biography: all are lacking, according to Arthur, and all would "find . . . materials" in the realm of commerce that would live up to generic expectations (28). However, as Arthur proceeds through his account another element is thrown into the mix: a realist approach that purports to convey the textures and complexities of a real life, one that requires the intimacy of a walk through the warehouse with a reader. The generic variety that *The Successful Merchant* invokes in the chapter that serves as its biographical manifesto—in particular the ever-shifting balance between realism and romance—continues to shape the tales that are told and the approaches to character in business biographies.

Realism is a tendency in Arthur's text rather than a consistently maintained mode; like most of the biographies that followed (and, of course, like many novels), in program and execution it is a hodgepodge of many different genres and styles. Arthur's construction of Budgett as an exemplar of Christian business conduct, which makes his character seem at times to exist as a pretext for the author's extended bouts of moralizing, certainly wouldn't lead anyone to confuse this biography with a high realist novel. Nonetheless, with generic and literary self-consciousness, Arthur recommends close engagement with commonplace experience and materials. Wordsworth's old Cumberland beggar, he notes, is a low subject. But the poem derives dignity and meaningfulness as it leads the reader to "almost count the nails in his footprint, and feel the dust from his meal-wallet" (34). The business biographer, Arthur suggests, must traffic in the everyday, acting simultaneously as a literary explorer who, in venturing into the "TERRA INCOGNITA" of business, discovers "the highest romance of real life" (35, 28); as a faithful painter of the dust of the warehouse; and as a thoughtful investigator of "the *morality of purchase and sale*" and "the effect of business upon character" (37).

Announcing his own approach, Arthur highlights the latter stances. In the preface, for instance, he asserts that his mode of characterization will be guided by realist, not hagiographic, intentions. Calling out biographers who "paint men as they ought to be" rather than representing "men as they are," he distinguishes himself from these untrustworthy portraitists, declaring that "in the picture you are asked to look upon, an effort has been made to insert, with a firm hand, every real scar. Some will say they are too slight; others will say they are too deep, and these they who most intimately knew the original" (ix). The true-to-life visual register, signified by flaws rather than idealized perfection, aligns Arthur's practice with the mid-nineteenth-century realist sense that "true" representations are ones that reproduce individuating details and imperfections.[13] The preface posits no simple equation of fault finding and truth seeking; in fact, Arthur's harshness in revealing imperfections is positioned as simply one facet of an effort to achieve an objective perspective on his subject's character, its dedication to this ideal only enhanced by the supposed objections of Budgett's interested acquaintances. Arthur's forthrightness about his method of collecting information through conversations with the merchant's connections is another strategy for constructing objectivity, as he alerts readers that some interlocutors were "aware and others not aware that a book was in contemplation" (viii). And finally, objectivity also requires a frank revelation of business success, covered by none of the misplaced modesty that the merchant's family supposedly requested: "A strong desire, indeed, was manifested to lay me under restraint as to anything which might be construed into business display; but my design required freedom to show what Mr. Budgett had attained, and that I was obliged to use" (viii). "Obliged" by the demands of accuracy to speak frankly of success, but unafraid to be "firm" in locating and depicting flaws, the biographer casts himself as both servant and champion of the real. While Arthur is, to say the least, no George Eliot, his declaration of obligation (to reveal success) almost prefigures her description of realist practice as being "obliged to creep servilely after nature and fact" (to represent decidedly nonideal characters).[14] Though the parentheses indicate an important refraction, the resemblance is nonetheless significant as an indication of the rhetorical power Arthur ascribes to realism's mimetic claims.

The strong distinction that the refraction marks—the exemplary quality of Arthur's narrative of Budgett as a model businessman—is, certainly, an insistent reminder of this biography's difference from the ideal of realist fiction. However, I draw attention to resemblances and echoes—subtle, partial, and, in some cases, as I shall suggest below, significantly abortive—to suggest what they reveal about the story of business character. In particular, two aspects of

Arthur's statements stand out. The first is the text's argument *through literary terms* for a vision of character that is complex and multifarious, in which the presence of true character (in business life and in the text representing it) is demonstrated by the degree to which character seems unconstrained by the demands of plot or literary convention. Thus, defending against skeptics of his claim that Budgett was all at once sensitive and thoughtful and capable of decisive action, he argues that although "critics sometimes censure writers of fiction for allowing their heroes to appear in aspects inconsistent one with the other . . . the actual men and women we meet here in this world of families, churches, markets, and amusements . . . are very far from being a rigidly symmetrical race. . . . Let the critics have it as they will, nothing is so natural in a man as contradictions" (68–69). In contrasting the messy contradictions of the "natural" with the clean lines of literary types, Arthur adopts a form of character established through a realist aesthetic, in which the codes that create the mimetic effect, structure character representations, and facilitate interpretation—such as contradictions or a failure to fit recognized literary types—are downplayed to the point of transparency.

Second, in his penultimate chapter, "The Inner Life," Arthur models a form of character that differentiates between the public and the inward, locating the essence of character firmly in the latter:

> There is a life the world sees, a life the neighbourhood sees, a life the family sees, a life God sees. These are often strangely inconsistent. It is pitiable when each succeeding enclosure you pass to reach the man introduces you to diminishing charms and growing blemishes. With Samuel Budgett it was not so: the merchant who only knew him as the unparalleled "buyer," the stranger who only heard of him from some men of business in Bristol, and many who saw but his outermost character, had no remarkable impression of his worth. But those who *knew* his works in his neighbourhood, beheld wondering; those who knew his home had a profound love of the man; those who knew his closet and his heart looked upon him with feelings which few men raise in the breasts of others. (386–87)

Inconsistency has shifted here from being an untidy indicator of "realness" to a marker of possible hypocrisy; as one follows the merchant through a series of enclosures, his public and private selves must correspond perfectly in order to exemplify good character. But significantly, this insists that true character is more likely to be found in the private enclosures, moving ever inward into the home, the "closet," and the heart of the man—evoking, as it does so, models of deep character that had received perhaps most elaboration and exploration in novels.[15]

However, a reader hoping to encounter the kinds of revelations of inner life that were provided by many midcentury novels would be disappointed by Budgett's biography and most others. Arthur provides no sustained *focus* on the private life of the businessman—the proclaimed locus of his true identity. No grieving wives, sons, or daughters appear amid the funeral crowd. In fact, though marriage and children are mentioned in passing within the narrative of Budgett's business affairs, it isn't until three hundred pages in, right before we follow the successful merchant to his deathbed, that Arthur devotes any sustained attention to these relationships. It is not uncommon in business biographies for events like marriage to be coolly narrated in terms of the capital the wife brings or for the existence of children to become known only when sons and sons-in-law become partners in the firm.[16] Thus, a later biography of the alpaca processor Titus Salt follows the narrative of his alpaca spinning discoveries and his 1848 election as mayor of Bradford with the apparent afterthought, "meanwhile, he had a young family growing up around him, having, as early as 1829, married Caroline, the daughter of Mr. George Whitlam of Grimsby. This lady bore Mr. Salt eleven children."[17] Nineteen years and eleven children are rhetorically—even grammatically—subordinated to the main story of the public life. Childhood generally receives more extensive treatment as the source of character development. But the narrative of *bildung* nonetheless fails to satisfy biographies' promise of engagement with characters who seem "actual" as well as "remarkable"—who seem, as Samuel Smiles put it in the epigraph (from Thackeray) to *Self-Help*, to be real companions whose "company" one might "frequent."[18]

As the origin of this epigraph suggests, the failure to deliver on this promise cannot be fully explained by reference to a generic difference between business biographies and the novel, in which one form was by definition interested in the public and the other in the private life. Not only do biographies' assertions of their aim to represent the "inner life" of their subjects complicate this division,[19] but the shared interest in reading practices grounded in the careful reading of incidental details of everyday life and behavior suggests that the discursive and characterological protocols of novels and business were not always as sharply differentiated as one might imagine. The existence of these interconnections makes the biographies' focus far from inevitable. As business biographies continued to promise what they do not deliver—a revelation of character and especially character as inner life—they helped alter the terms in which business writing treated character, simultaneously invoking and turning away from ways of writing character that had come to be conventions both in business writing and in novels.

It is such transformations in the *mode* of conceptualizing and conveying character that I wish to highlight here, rather than the specific content: the skimpy treatment of private life in business biographies is an instance of a larger pattern, rather than the key analytical feature of the change in mode. The change centers on what Herbert has called the "metaphorics of 'depth,'" one of the key registers of nineteenth-century selfhood in fields ranging from ethnography to Dissenting theology to (eventually) psychoanalysis—and including, as I have argued, discourses of management and business character.[20] From the 1850s to the 1880s business biographies engage their readers less and less in exercises developing and discovering "deep truths" of character. Instead, the business biographies of the mid- and later nineteenth century increasingly make "roundness" of character merely an element in an increasingly codified system. In Deidre Lynch's analysis of late-eighteenth- and early-nineteenth-century fiction and commerce, the counterparts to round or deep character are clichés and stereotypes; the notion of deep character develops in part in response to a perception of their inadequacy in a changing economic culture. Victorian business biographies reverse this pattern, as stereotypes and clichés come to gain significance in their own right as a powerful characterological mode. This change is effected largely through a shift in the balance between modes of characterization that derive from realism— the elaborated, multiple, and diverse systems of signs that conjure rich social and psychological worlds populated by characters that both prompt continual interpretation and feel alive and potentially familiar—and those derived from the more obvious and explicitly literary codes of other genres, especially those of the romance. As the balance tilts toward romance, the effort to mimetically convey realness shifts into acceptance of the compact conventions of story.

William Arthur's early biography calls for a commercial epic, a revelation of romance within everyday life, but it also starts and finishes with the stated aim of providing a true-to-life portrait of an individualized, flawed man with a depth of character that needs to be perceived in the full complex of his social activity and inward thought and feeling. Though the bulk of the biography certainly aims to construct its subject as a Christian business *hero,* in doing so it for the most part eschews the overtly literary language that its initial polemical chapter would suggest it adopt. Jump forward a generation to *Fortunes Made in Business,* a three-volume collection of biographies published in the mid-1880s, and the blend of realism and romance seems decisively altered. These biographies miss no opportunity to render their subjects not only heroes but (as the cliché goes) storybook heroes. The opening to the preface to the first volume immediately sets the tone, invoking "Aladdin" and "his Wonderful Lamp" as "a sort of prophetic mirror of many romantic incidents in the Modern Biography of Industry and Commerce."[21] "What is romance and what are knights-errant, and have we got either now?" one tale asks. To counter the "common belief" that the commercial preoccupations of England had made romance a relic—that "chivalry" and "knights and gentlemen were doomed by railways, and the last of these personages is on his way to the British Museum or Madame Tussaud's"—the volumes offer up their cornucopia of fabulous tales of businessmen and business families. Like Arthur, these authors strive to reveal the heroic in the everyday, to show how "the man in the black coat who but now passed us in the street" would be acknowledged a modern St. George if only we could "apprehend how he, at the peril of brain and life, has undergone privations and hardships and anxieties and disappointments; how he has passed through the wreckage of life in the contest with what are truly the monstrous powers of darkness, and has come forth, like the paladin of old, the hero of his country, and the benefactor of mankind."[22] But as the heightened drama of this quotation suggests, they follow this plan far more boldly than Arthur. Weaving literary and legendary references and language into their texts, they draw the subjects of the biographies out of the realm of the real, placing them firmly in a world of stories.

Immediately following the evocation of the archetypically everyday "man in the black coat," for instance, is this rather defensive endeavor to romanticize the particular man in question, Sir Henry Bessemer, inventor of the Bessemer steelmaking process, by comparing him to a modern-day Sir Lancelot: "some of our readers will here think we are leading them astray, as Sir Lancelot of the Lake is not expected to be found in a workshop; but this is quite a mistake, for a knight should be proficient in all arts useful to mankind, and necessarily in engineering."[23] The knights of industry and commerce, armed with industriousness and will, in addition to those all-important engineering skills, do battle with apathy and ignorance, government departments, and English law, as well as business crises and the competition of their rivals. Bessemer encounters "one of the imps of romance" in a lawyer who fails to support him in his quest to get compensation from the Stamp Office for use of one of his inventions (a stamp with moveable dates).[24] Mr. S. C. Lister, inventor of a process to reclaim silk waste, fights through the crisis of 1857, during which, while sustaining "loss upon loss," he "faced the brunt of the battle and carried himself gallantly through, not only bearing up against all this weight of misfortune, but against the enormously heavy expenditure which he was put to in regard to his silk inventions."[25] Quoting snippets of ballads, the biography places Lister's solution to the business problem of what to do with silk waste in the literary and romantic tradition of velvet- and silk-clad heroines. In providing luxury fabrics to a new generation of "enduring Grissell[s]" and "Lady Greensleeves," Lister becomes a latter-day Dick Whittington, who, the text notes, was also "a dealer in silks."[26] The world in which these businessmen operate is not merely governed by calculations of profit and loss and the transformation of material reality by human ingenuity; it is an enchanted world, where supernatural forces shape opportunities. Lister doesn't enter the church, his family's chosen path, because "the world was just then full of 'mighty workings,'" especially the revolutionary power of the "steam-god," and he feels drawn to join those new forces: transcendent and miraculous, but nonetheless conventional enough to be placed within quotation marks.[27] The dogged persistence demonstrated by one after another of the collection's heroes in navigating the ups and downs of commerce is matched only by their author's in his efforts to seize the power of narrative conventions to glorify his subjects.

Within this highly wrought mesh of allusions and conventions are infrequent gestures toward a deeper mode of character. But even these few remain, for the most part, gestures. A passage from the life of Bessemer is illustrative. The author claims to be presenting a kind of biography different from the usual "dry list" of works or discoveries, presenting "the personal revelations of Bessemer's struggles with life, such as are rarely made known, and which offer a picture of so much interest." These "revelations" center on "the expression of . . . feelings" of "all the bitterness of the long-smothered wrongs inflicted on him by the Government when he was but a defenseless boy."[28] This passage casts "personal revelations" and feelings and motivations as the center of interest in stories of individual lives; while the life that follows develops a character in which a unified psychology is shaped though narrative form, with an early source of bitterness (the government's failure to reward Bessemer appropriately for his invention used in the Stamp Office to prevent fraud) providing the key. Nonetheless, while Bessemer's biographer makes much of this rare offer of "the inner life," the representation doesn't live up to the promise, as the prevailing narrative mode in this as well as most other biographies in the collection creates little sense of interiority.[29] The "inner life" expressed in moments when the text adopts the point of view of its subject—as when Bessemer, finally succeeding in making crude iron into steel, "could . . . see in his mind's eye, at a glance, the great iron industry of the world crumbling away"—is in content and tone of a piece with the public narrative.[30]

The shift in the perspective on character can perhaps best be illustrated by a comparison of two moments in the collection in which interpretation is foregrounded. The first comes from the biography of Sir Josiah Mason, a manufacturer of steel pens. Having lost his job and prospects when an uncle decides to sell the business where he was manager, Mason is urged by a member of his church to contact another manufacturer, Mr. Harrison. Harrison responds bluntly that he isn't sure: "'I have had a good many young men come here,' he said, 'but they were afraid of dirtying their fingers.'" "At this, Mason, who had kept silence, involuntarily opened his hands, looked at them, and, speaking to himself rather than to the others, said quietly, 'Are you ashamed of dirtying yourselves to get your own living?' It was an unstudied touch of nature; and Mr. Harrison, who had a keen insight into character, was instantly struck by it."[31] Mason gets the job and goes on to renown. But this moment is hardly a triumph of interpretation. The behavioral signs that Harrison reads are deemed unstudied and natural by both manufacturer and narrator—and yet it is difficult to imagine a less spontaneous action than talking out loud to one's own hands (or a less appropriate response, if the action *is* truly spontaneous, than hiring the talker). The signs that Mason gives are described and read idiosyncratically, if not incorrectly: a theatrical, performative moment is taken for the real. But the plot of the life story fails to register any disconnection between the true character of Mason and this apparent blunder: Mason's eventual success confirms the "insight" that here looks questionable. In this way the text highlights a certain *kind* of character reading that had long held a place in business writing. But it does not construct a plausible example of it.

In contrast, the biographies in *Fortunes Made in Business* are more self-conscious and more self-confident in drawing attention to the narrative formulas that they employ. Early in the biography of John Brown, a Sheffield steel manufacturer, for example, the author signals the narrative strategies that he will employ and preemptively directs the reader's response. Beginning with an extended meditation on Brown's common name, the author immediately situates his subject within a range of textual possibilities. The name is "not entirely undistinguished in the annals of remarkable men," and it has even occasionally been honored by the "lyric Muse," but in general, the author admits, it would seem most at home in realism, as "it requires . . . an effort of the imagination to lift it out of the dull inglorious company of Smith, Jones, and Robinson."[32] But this imaginative and generic shift is what the biography promises to effect by purveying a "story which traces the gradual mastery of the innate strength over the external barriers" in which "the sentimental reader will not fail to detect a strand of romance which imparts a poetical charm to even a tale of steel."[33] This promise models a different kind

of reading, alerting readers to look at its subject as a "story" rather than a figure sprung to life. We are told what moments to pay attention to (those displaying triumph over circumstances); we are told which genre's rules should
govern their interpretation (the romance); and we are encouraged to adopt
a certain response to the reading process (to feel the "poetical charm" rather
than the cold material reality). It seems particularly significant that this passage describes an ideal reader who is both extremely well acquainted with
stories (he "will not fail to detect" their key moments) and "sentimental"—in
other words, who is ready to respond to genre conventions, like those produced by sentimental novels, rather than attempting to get beyond the conventional to the real. "Sentimental," in this regard, is not an adjective that
neatly fits our standard concept of a businesslike approach to character, one
governed by the market imperative to know what people really are like or
risk being subject to fraud or undone by failure to provide the right human
capital in a competitive marketplace. These anomalies, then, highlight a shift
in approach: only when character refers to a fiction, rather than to a presumed real essence discernible through behavioral details, can a "sentimental" reader, sensitive to formulas and conventions, be deemed superior.[34]

    This trajectory seems to move far from Laurence Oliphant's notion
that biography, in its capacity to reveal character truths and train discerning character readers, could play a disciplinary role in an unstable commercial world. But an earlier invocation of this biographical hope suggests the
way the genre's contribution was never conceptually straightforward. When
Dickens's *All the Year Round* called for a "modern Plutarch" to produce a set
of lives to complement *Self-Help,* one that would focus instead on the criminal "men who have helped themselves," the prescription given is confusing:
"The compilations of this character that have been already attempted, are
too wanting in simplicity, too overloaded with technical details. . . . We want
something more concise, more biographical, and less apologetic—a Newgate
Calendar, in fact, for the use of schools."[35] Character is key: the "more biographical" will be efficacious whereas "technical details" obfuscate. And yet
the notion that "more biographical" equals simpler complicates the picture
of how the efficacy will be achieved. This Newgate Calendar would offer
the essence of the characters of those it portrays, drawn in stark moral lines
that avoid the complications and potential for apology that "details" might
entail. But it would therefore withhold the concrete representation of those
activities that might give practice in analyzing character or that might help
to instruct a less adept reader by modeling the analytical path from signs to
essence.

    Furthermore, features that we would imagine to be critical to biography's disciplinary utility—a skeptical, or at least objective, attitude toward the subject; an exposé orientation, aiming to reveal hidden or unknown truths—were treated with ambivalence in contemporary discussions of biography. The lionizing attitude that makes the character representations of *Fortunes Made in Business* seem untruthful was less obviously misleading in the views of many Victorian theorists of biography. Objecting to the practice of biography-as-exposé, Margaret Oliphant not only questions the propriety of revealing private information but also doubts that such revelation is really more likely to achieve truth. Representing character by opening "old drawers and wardrobes," displaying the subject's "vacant clothes, with any twist that attitude or habit may have lent to them," may mean that one represents merely accidental details, as opposed to the essential, the "characteristic of his soul."[36] The accidental, the everyday, the "little web of petty susceptibilities"—the stuff of a realist approach to character, right down to an echo of Eliot's metaphor of the web—is not where character truths can be found; instead it is what the reader must "disentangle" character from.[37] In fact, Mrs. Oliphant goes so far as to argue that it is the biographer's "plain duty . . . to refrain" should he find that "an exhibition of personal idiosyncrasies" would "lessen or destroy [the] good name" of his subject—not, she clarifies, revelations of "hypocrisy or concealed vice, which it might be to the benefit of public morals to expose," but the inconsistencies and peculiarities that define the realist notion of individualized character.[38]

In constructing her defense of protective, venerating—even lionizing—biographical practice, Oliphant echoes not only the pattern of hero making of contemporary business biographies but even their tropes:

> That fine St. George, who has given an emblem of spotless valour and conquest over the impure image of fleshly lust and cruelty to two great nations . . . turns out, they say, to have been an army contractor, furnishing the shoddy of his time to the commissariat; and a great deal the better we all are for that exquisite discovery. . . . How many more could we add to the list? till at the end nobody would be left towards whom we could look with any sentiment more reverent than that which we feel for our greengrocer. That this is not the true sentiment of humanity, nor in accord with any law of natural right and wrong, must be evident to the most cursory observer.[39]

Although Oliphant's essay doesn't treat business biography directly, her figures of debunked heroes are commercial—emblems of the everyday, corruptible relations of market society. There is a truth beyond the world of greengrocers and army commissariats, Oliphant suggests, and the role of the biographer is to reveal it, even if doing so requires covering over what green-grocers and army commissariats—and bankers, creditors, employers, and many novelists and readers—might have had in mind when they conceived of the truth of character. Romanticizing one's subjects—seeking the "generous and noble spirit" undeterred by the "little web of petty susceptibilities"—might be the only chance to find this transcendent truth.[40]

Margaret Oliphant, like Thomas Carlyle before her, positioned hero worshipping as a means of seeking higher truth as well as a challenge to the reduction of character under capitalism.[41] In reversing her example by rendering greengrocers (or woolcombers or steel manufacturers or bankers) as St. George, business biographies adopted a model promising a different and greater truth than might be achieved from close reading of the private, everyday life—but a model that had frequently excluded or opposed businessmen of all varieties and the values they espoused. In other words, business biographies took an available concept of the heroic as a transcendent kind of character truth and attempted to wrest the terrain of heroism back from capitalism's critics. The result not only challenged these detractors but also helped change the terms in which capitalism's various practitioners could conceive of the uses and meanings of character.

In a somewhat later essay, Leslie Stephen addressed the place of fact and narration in life writing, expressing concern that contemporary biographers were overly wedded to the scientific, observable detail, too apt to create "a blue-book in which all the evidence bearing upon the subject can be piled like a huge prehistoric cairn over the remains of the deceased, with no more apparent order and constructive purpose than the laws of gravitation enforce spontaneously." Stephen's alternative was biography as a carefully wrought "work of art" aiming to reveal "a character"—"something, with a beginning, middle, and end, which can cheat us for the time into the belief that we are really in presence of a living contemporary."[42] Though the clichéd romances of *Fortunes Made in Business* seem a far cry from Stephen's ideal of biography as "a work of art" marked by formal care and the depiction of "a" character that is both living presence and textual construct, in one crucial sense the two forms are similar: for Stephen, as for those anonymous biographers of commercial Aladdins, the life is most fully expressed in and as story. If the biographers take this further, to a point where the stories' status as truth seems to have little to do with their relation to the real, Stephen's brand of biographical realism nonetheless implicitly recognizes that the lifelike presence it constructs is based on a "cheat," a "belief" achieved through narrative art. And this link, which Stephen's late-Victorian statement renders explicit—the shared emphasis on truth achieved through story—helps smooth the path from Samuel Budgett to the "galaxy of industrial knights" in *Fortunes Made in Business.*

I close my discussion of the shifts in modes of character with Samuel Smiles, perhaps the most prolific and widely read of the business biographers, whose work suggests the fruitful tension that biographical character narratives generated. For the most part, Smiles's theories of character tend toward the realist. In *Self-Help,* for instance, his suggestion that "human life is made up of comparative trifles" and that "it is the repetition of little acts which constitute . . . the sum of human character" implies that the biographical method must dwell in the description of incidentals.[43] As he executes his biographies, Smiles blends quotidian scenes with career highlights from his subjects' childhoods through their working lives, only occasionally indulging in the overblown rhetoric of romance.[44] By and large, his texts focus on the "little acts" and "trifles" intended to create a sense of living individuality: the assortment of music boxes that played nonstop while the inventor and ironworker Henry Maudslay sat at his workbench, or the "large unconsumed surplus" of snuff that would collect in the folds of his waistcoat as he sat intent at his labors, puffing out in a cloud when he stooped to reach for a tool; or the railway engineer George Stephenson's outward scolding and inward pride when he witnesses his son Robert recreating Benjamin Franklin's kite experiment and administering electric shocks to a pony.[45]

The characterological reality effect produced through the accumulation of "trifles" is considerable. But in Smiles's tales the tension between an orientation to an individualized "real" and the presence of convention and textual form is very close to the surface. As biography after biography followed a trajectory of struggle and triumph, through sheer volume his texts consolidated a generic romance narrative.[46] Thus, by 1879 a reviewer ambivalent about the relative merits of the two modes in biography could praise Smiles for managing both simultaneously. On the one hand, the review holds that biography's advantage over history lies in its ability to communicate the "little personal traits which reflect the distinctive lights of a marked individuality" and criticizes biographies for producing "historical romance where the actual has been ingeniously merged in the ideal."[47] On the other, the reviewer's distinction between real character and romance (and his sense of the superiority of the former) becomes blurred, as those "little personal traits" slide from being markers of character to being "admirable matter for the reality of romance." "Thus," the reviewer continues, "in singling out those self-reliant individuals who have raised themselves to distinction by self-help, Dr. Smiles has hit on a most happy vein. Who can fail to follow with the closest interest the achievements of those adventurous engineering knight-errants, who vanquished by the vigorous efforts of their brains the material obstacles which had been baffling our progress?"[48] "The reality of romance": this reviewer's conflation of the two modes in discussing Smiles, the transformation of his "self-reliant individuals" into generic "knight-errants," suggests the way the biographies provide a model in which even the gestures of realism could be easily assimilated into the formula of romance.

The Transformation of Business Character

Beyond these literary developments, however, lies a larger transformation in the forms of character within the commercial world, one that business biographies both reflect and help to foster as they vacillate between the mimetic density of realism and the narrative formulas of romance. Over the last third of the century, as the economic and financial system grew more complex, the promise of character knowledge as a corrective force within the market is retained, but more attenuated, compact forms of representation are allowed to stand for character, and many registers of the word's meaning are put in play. From early in the Victorian period the term *character* had been applied to institutions or instruments referring to their degree of reliability; in describing the "character" of a bank or a bill of exchange, for example, one suggested whether it was backed by strong economic foundations and stable and trustworthy men. *Character,* in such cases, could imply quantitative reckonings, but it also invoked a moral register and a human content that was supplemental to the numbers, but essential to evaluation. Thus, during the 1830s debates over joint-stock banking, for instance, a bank manager called to witness before the 1836 Secret Committee on Joint Stock Banks objected to a proposal to require the publication of balance sheets on the grounds that they were an inadequate representation of a bank's financial situation because they could display only the "amount" and not the "character" of the bills it had accepted.[49]

This was not an inevitable stance for the bank manager to take. Classical political economy had developed the notion that a number, such as a price or a discount rate, could encapsulate a great deal of information about matters such as risk, which included discriminations of personal character. This was a persistent feature in genres of business writing such as company information books, which incorporated (and represented) character judgments in part through the interest rate that they would offer a particular associate. The relationship of numbers to different kinds of information therefore cannot be treated as a simple matter of exclusion, in which numerical representation cuts out whole areas of signification, since numbers were often charged with different kinds of meanings. But the bank manager's position resists such representations and asserts that the crucial aspect of character lies beyond the reach of the numerical form, requiring other kinds of description and interpretation. And the rhetorical difference is not to be underestimated. As Gordon Bigelow has argued, the emphasis on numbers in the political economy of William Stanley Jevons, for instance, was an effort to purge "prolixity" from economic discourse, transforming a messy mix of "moral, social, or characterological questions" into a lean, measurement-driven science of quantities.[50] If numbers don't evacuate those questions entirely, in every instance, they certainly change how the questions might be perceived as the numbers conceptualize the content they represent.

Some of these rhetorical and conceptual differences can be felt in investment manuals from the middle and later part of the century—texts that were both descriptive and prescriptive, presenting instruction to novice investors. Two features stand out in the treatment of character in Francis Playford's 1855 *Practical Hints for Investing Money*. First, when the term comes up as Playford offers reassurance to potential investors, it evokes a content that is decidedly personal and socially established. Playford writes of the character of actors in the Stock Exchange, especially brokers; the "standing and character" that brokers "must necessarily have," in his description, is a matter of diffuse social determination, cared for and cultivated among "friends and employers." Second, it requires writing: in most cases, the broker's character must be buttressed by "a testimonial signed by six respectable householders, recommending [him] as a fit and proper person to exercise his calling."[51] No doubt such testimonials were neither biographical tracts nor novelistic character portrayals, but rather exercises, perhaps pro forma, communicating little detail about the would-be broker's habits, beliefs, and morals. Nonetheless, the written testimonial points to social existence as the place where character is exhibited, and the stipulation that it be confirmed by six signatures suggests that the representation of character is imagined to require some expanse.

In Samuel Beeton's 1870 investment manual the use of *character* is more variable. Beeton holds onto multiple meanings even as he talks numbers: "the difference in the price of railway stocks is regulated by the character of the company and its future prospects, in the same way that the price of foreign stocks is regulated by the character of the Government of the different countries."[52] The first use of the term as a component of a stock price may carry an association with personal character—but it may also merely imply the state of the company: its financial situation, its historical performance, and so forth. But the second appearance of *character*—within the same sentence—as a component of price grows more complex. The "character of the Government" turns out to refer to a moral aspect of character ("honesty"), which can be determined by looking to a number, price: "The character of the country for honesty may be checked by the price its Government loans command in the market."[53] Price becomes a shorthand for probity, overshadowing (or encompassing) other ways of describing the "character" of a country—whether through the personal, with accounts of its political and economic actors and their reputations and trustworthiness, or through the institutional, with descriptions of its laws and enforcement mechanisms, and so forth.

In drawing a connection between the changing terms of character in business biographies and the instability of the meaning of character in investment manuals, especially the rendering of character, defined in moral or personal terms, as price, I am not suggesting an equivalence between romance codes and quantitative representation; the rhetorical differences between the two modes are wide indeed. But there is a crucial similarity: both forms seem to have left behind the thick descriptions of the realist mode, exhibiting a willingness to accept more compact signs—prices or literary conventions— as representative of character. The contrast between the continuous, laborious process of reading and interpreting signs in appearance, language, and behavior and the possibility of imagining a country's "honesty" to be discernible in the price of government loans suggests an important shift in how the term might be employed within the business community. This shift was not total; the realist approach to character remained prominent in commercial discourse, as well as in the contemporary journalism, novels, and biographical writings that touched on business topics. But both the business romances and the numerically minded investment manuals can be seen to advance a similar project of redefinition, accustoming readers to accept *as character* representations that until recently would have been deemed inadequate or beside the point.

Paradoxes of Character: Charisma, Celebrity, and the Impersonal Personal

Up to now I have tended to define this new mode of business character in negative terms, as an emptying out or slimming down. In this section I focus on the productive effects that this new mode shared in and helped generate. Two paradoxes condition these effects. The first is, as I have noted, that business biographies proliferate, personalizing the economic scene at a time when British commercial culture appeared increasingly *im*personal and complex to many contemporary observers, because of legal and structural changes within enterprises and the national financial system. The second paradox is that over time this personalization comes to be more intensified even as it becomes more empty. Though business biographies offered increasingly formulaic, conventional, and de-individualized models of character by rendering their subjects as heroes of romance, they simultaneously worked to surround their businessmen with a heightened aura of charisma that personalized their success to an extreme degree, emphasizing their uniqueness and casting their accomplishments as the results of inherent special gifts and qualities. As business character morphed into business charisma—at once deeply particularized and utterly generic—this paradoxical form offered a response to the anxiety over commercial impersonality, providing new ways to imagine and interpret oneself and others as impersonally personal characters in the changing economic world.

From the start, biographies of businessmen cast themselves as educational tools through which to achieve two aims: learning to interpret the characters encountered in the business world in order to discern the honest from the fraudulent, the inept or lazy from those most likely to succeed; and learning the skills and qualities that were most worthy of emulation. The latter aim, however, looks more ambiguous in texts such as *Fortunes Made in Business*. How, for instance, is the reader to emulate "the magic of mechanical power and inventive genius applied to the cheapening of some article of every-day consumption," when "magic" and "genius" are unique and unbidden powers?[54] The texts frequently portray what is crucial about their subjects' work as a matter of unrepresentable and therefore compelling glamour. Talk of "secret toil" and "intricate and delicate operations" stands in for the mundane details of the process of invention in the story of S. C. Lister; the scene of Sir Henry Bessemer's days and nights of study and labor is a "fast-locked chamber, holding within its unseen and mysterious monster."[55] Even if the necessity of guarding proprietary trade secrets lies behind this uncommunicativeness (as Bessemer's biography suggests), the workaday explanation pales beside the dramatic rhetoric. The result of these tropes is to turn the businessman from a representative and imitable example to a larger-than-life figure whose achievement stems from unique, innate qualities that can be admired, but hardly learned or even fully comprehended.

Max Weber's concept of charisma captures the effect generated by this personalization of business success, though with important differences. Charisma, in its purest form, was the quality that stood against modern apparatuses such as institutions, routines, and rational rules and calculations: the loyalty of officeholders to "impersonal and functional purposes" and the "dehumanized" bureaucracy, "welcomed by capitalism," whose "specific nature" and "special virtue" (according to its proponents) was that it "succeeds in eliminating from official business love, hatred, and all purely personal, irrational, and emotional elements."[56] Charisma, in contrast, is all personal: those who have it are "holders of specific gifts of the body and spirit"; the charismatic leader's claim to power lies in an internal personal conviction that he is "innerly 'called'"—a conviction that then inspires recognition and "devotion . . . oriented to his person and to its qualities."[57]

Biographies such as Arthur's or Smiles's certainly convey a sense that their subjects are special, and they personalize that specialness with their focus on the individual. But *Fortunes Made in Business* ups the ante, giving free rein to a variety of rhetorics of charisma. The revalorization of magic is perhaps the most extreme and telling example. The magician is one of Weber's ur-figures of charisma, holding within himself mysterious, possibly supernatural powers to transform the ordinary course of things.[58] In earlier Victorian writings on business the suggestion of charismatic power expressed through the language of magic as often as not implied something suspicious, even criminal, as in David Morier Evans's portrait of the dishonest railway promoter George Hudson, whose "name seemed to possess a talismanic value," increasing share prices whenever it was mentioned.[59] But the suspicious take on magic is absent from *Fortunes Made in Business*. Scientific inquiry is exuberantly described as if it were alchemical investigation (Bessemer spending nights in his "fast-locked chamber"). "Mechanical power" is "magic," and machines are "formidable monsters" tamed. The growth of English industry is an enchantment of the landscape: if "local pessimists" in Queensbury, where the Foster family built mills, factories, and machine shops, had been able to look into the future, "they would have seen such a dispersion of cloud and shadow from their vision as would have almost made them believers in the truth of the old-world legends of magic and sorcery."[60] Charismatic power is no longer a force that clouds the truth, a tool of shady operators; instead it is honored as a driving force behind British development and is celebrated in life stories.

Thus, the charismatic businessman represented a new model of economic man, motivated by a mysterious, self-contained strength of personality that subordinates the biographies' accounts of hard work, thrift, and prudent investment to its glamorous aura. This difference from modern economic rationality was key to Weber's conception of pure charisma, which held that the "decisive" element defining charisma was that it "rejects all rational economic conduct," indeed, that it "is the very force that disregards economy."[61] But the particular charismatic rhetoric developed in business biographies proved to be a flexible player in the economic field. The charismatic businessman transcended economic laws and forces. Strength of will seems to motivate and enable his actions, swamping the processes of calculation. The charismatic model established a powerful practical fantasy that countered more mechanistic models of economic subjectivity and addressed concerns that economic life was dominated by systems, institutions, and forces unaligned with discernible personal and social agents.

The charisma modeled by the biographies of *Fortunes Made in Business*, in particular, was also suited to its moment in being self-consciously a product of—and dependent on—stories. In this, it both shares features with and differs from Weber's model of charisma, according to which "men do not obey" the holder of personal charismatic authority because of rules or traditions, but rather "because they believe in him." Generating and maintaining this belief is the problem of charisma, the reason why it is "by its very nature . . . specifically unstable."[62] Though charisma claims to derive its power not from the people's voicing their belief but from the inspired, internal force that demands and deserves this recognition, it is a model that requires making appeals, and in anything other than a situation of direct witnessing, these appeals will require stories: accounts of the prophet's or magician's miracles, of the businessman's uncanny ability to turn all his ventures to profit.

At the same time, however, though Weber recognizes that the belief grounding charisma is unstable, he holds it to be sincere, whereas it is much more difficult to discern the status of the belief generated by the self-consciously conventional narratives of *Fortunes Made in Business*. How should one take an attribution of charisma—of deeply personal, unique gifts and qualities—that is achieved through cliché? What happens to charisma when all the tales told to construct it start to sound the same? And when they make little effort to disguise their status as stories—indeed, when they highlight the stories they reference? *Fortunes Made in Business* constructs a form of charisma characterized by a curious mix of elevated individuality and clichéd repetition, in which the only belief necessary is in the fact of stories themselves. Rather than being opposed to the modern principle of routine, this mode of charisma emerges through it, with stories as the vehicle for routinization.[63]

Because its power was generated through narrative, routinized charisma offered a particularly supple mode through which to reimagine personal business and the transactions of character in a dynamic association of stories, belief, and economic relations—an association commonly traced through the concept of credit. There are many similarities: "credit" has named the process—at once unconscious, logical, and cognitive—that readers enact in their encounters with fiction, in which categories such as belief, truth, and probability or plausibility are weighed and articulated on what Catherine

Gallagher has called a "suppositional ontological plane," where the reader's acceptance is "only solicited conditionally, on the revived Aristotelian terms not of 'belief' but of suspended 'disbelief.' "[64] But where crediting, in this model, involves a suspension of disbelief so that the fictional world of a text may be fully (if provisionally) entered, the play with conditionality that routinized charisma enacts in business biographies never quite demands the same degree of immersion. We are not asked to credit a narrative world in which Bessemer "really" fights imps in the patent office. Instead, as the biographies highlight fictionality in what is, after all, a genre tracing the lives and characters of actual businessmen, the discontinuity disturbs the text's referential coherence and shifts the terms on which belief and suspended disbelief are solicited.

If the biographical impulse had been to supply character fact, truth, or essence to manage the risks of the market, the new mode flagrantly played with this ideal, offering gestures toward revelation and promises of disclosures that are never quite satisfied. When the authors of *Fortunes Made in Business* promise intimate knowledge and instead compare their subjects to familiar heroes of literature and legend, the reader might experience disappointment at receiving what feels like grist for the mill of charisma, rendering all the businessmen the same. But on the other hand, by being so up-front with its codes and its conventions, it makes conscious the action of suspending disbelief: the text itself acknowledges that it is offering a story where it promises to give the truth and invites readers to recognize this and go ahead and participate in the biography's construction of business charisma anyway. It offers, in other words, a way of simultaneously, self-consciously, assenting to and disavowing the claim that the businessmen have special personal qualities, knowing all along that one is accepting a generic construction—that there might be something more to be told. (And the proliferating volumes of business biography always have more stories to offer, even if they are the same as what came before.) If there might be something other than the story one encounters—some deep character truth that a detail signals or that remains unrevealed—the charismatic mode denies that this is the key to interpretive power. When *Fortunes Made in Business* asserts of Mr. Dawson of the Low Moor Company that "there is a tradition that his children were so badly off for clothes that they used to run about the lanes in tattered garments and barefooted, but that is a statement that probably requires to be taken *cum grano salis,* seeing that such stories exist with regard to most self-made personages," it makes its apparatus clear and almost begs the reader to apply the grain of salt to any other narrative contained within its pages.[65] But because self-consciousness admits knowingness, it does not undermine the text's efforts to construct charisma; rather, it enables a version of charisma that permits and even depends on such knowingness. The dynamic by which such a biography produced both the illusion of personal knowledge and a readiness to live with the understanding that the knowledge is illusory made it a useful mode for business—accustoming readers to accept, not that the stories offered were adequate or complete representations of character, but that the fact of the stories contained a power that was truth enough in the reader's own world of money and credit, a power in which one could, provisionally, believe.[66]

For the authors of *Fortunes Made in Business* the self-consciousness extends to a passage of representational self-reflection with a strikingly theoretical turn. In fact, the questions it engages mirror those posed by literary theorists: How do we describe the nature of our "belief" in fiction? How do we evaluate the probable and the plausible in fiction—and with reference to what? How do different modes of writing—romance, biography—construct and claim to capture truths about the world? Remarkably, the text locates a principle of power precisely in the uncertain terrain these questions mark. Ruminating on its deployment of fiction, *Fortunes Made in Business* suggests that no divide exists between the textual forms of romance and the real world, because romance is a principle of life in contemporary Britain embodied in "the breath of the men and boys, and even of the women." Citing Arthurian legends, fairy tales, the *Arabian Nights, Pilgrim's Progress,* and the plays of Shakespeare (the "echo" and "embodiment" of the "trumpets of romance"), the text argues that

all these creations of imagination live in the popular mind in company with what is their great exemplar, Robinson Crusoe. It is idle to say Crusoe is not an historical personage, and is only a fiction, and not even a legend. . . .

We may, if we like, entertain a doubt whether Crusoe was really born in Yorkshire in the year cited; but we go on practically giving faith to all the main story. It was not that Defoe was so cunning a writer, but that we are ever ready to believe him. We may not be over-curious either about the Giant Blunderbore, or as to what order or genus of dragon St. George killed, and whether the brute was graminivorous or carnivorous; but whatever the world may discuss, we give about as good credence to these tales as we do to many articles of our faith.

All this is no digression, but a way of getting home to facts, which we may not so readily understand if we look at them dryly, as delineated by what is called common sense, and what is often common nonsense, when offered as a representation to the body of mankind.[67]

Though the subjects celebrated in the pages of *Fortunes Made in Business* may achieve greatness through their mastery of "common sense," their embodiment of the kind of scientific spirit that *would* be interested in pinning down the genus and diet of St. George's dragon, those approaches are not the only route to truth. There is no need to imagine a "historical" Crusoe, whose date and place of birth might be verified; the story of Crusoe is a fiction, but not "*only* a fiction" (my emphasis). And as fictions can deliver a deeper truth than a historical or scientific account of the real, far from fearing the fictionalization of lives and the replacement of realist character truths by romance conventions and charismatic exorbitance, readers should embrace the process. To recognize fictions—to "entertain a doubt whether Crusoe was really born in Yorkshire"—and to still "go on practically giving faith to all the main story" makes the reader a worthy participant in building the romance of contemporary British business.

"Melmotte" versus Melmotte: Names, Character, and the Charismatic Mode

The year before Laurence Oliphant's pseudo-autobiography of Albert Grant and his company appeared, Anthony Trollope published *The Way We Live Now,* a novel whose villain, the larger-than-life swindling financier Augustus Melmotte, is also thought to have been based on Grant. Following Melmotte's suicide, his daughter, Marie, is left to mull over her family history and her prospects. Because she lacks the usual connections that might be expected to provide insights, she turns to the biographies published "as a matter of course . . . within a fortnight" of her father's death in order to catch and capitalize upon the public's tide of interest. But rather than helping, these biographies merely multiply the stories that contribute to Melmotte's already vast and confounding legend, giving "various accounts . . . as to his birth, parentage, and early history"—disagreeing, in fact, over so fundamental a matter as Melmotte's "true name."[68]

Historically minded readers have shared with Melmotte's fictional public the curiosity and the ultimate uncertainty over this "true name." Grant is merely one possible model, joined by numerous real-life and literary precursors, most famously George Hudson, the so-called Railway King; John Sadleir, the embezzling M.P./bank director; and *Little Dorrit*'s Merdle, whom Dickens based on these same recent historical figures. (John Sutherland has proposed no fewer than eight possible originals for Melmotte and many more possible antecedents for his South Central Pacific and Mexican Railway scheme.)[69] Built out of repetitions of repetitions, Melmotte is utterly familiar even as he is described in terms of absolute distinction—both the story of the moment and a story that everyone seems already to know.

Melmotte, then, represents an almost exaggeratedly apt version of the nonreferentiality—or pseudo-referentiality—that Poovey suggests characterizes the breakup of the fact-fiction continuum, as literary writing becomes oriented toward a self-enclosed aesthetic formalism rather than assuming an informational role. Here is historical reference run amok—a plethora of possible factual cases that the novel "seems to, but does not, help readers understand."[70] I would suggest, in contrast, that the problem of Melmotte's nonreferentiality (or surplus referentiality) is exactly the point of connection between the novel and its contemporary "credit economy." Melmotte's blurring of factual and fictional reference (Grant, Hudson, Sadleir, Merdle . . .), his existence as a creature of stories both before and after death, cast him as a fictional case that highlights the new mode of business charisma: both full and empty, personal and impersonal, exorbitant and routine, generating power through stories that simultaneously solicit belief and disavow it. The "gestural" quality of this representation—in which an extratextual reality is pointed toward but not really elaborated—finds a parallel dynamic in the changing representation of character in commercial practice, where "character" becomes, more and more often, a gesture toward a *kind* of meaning by a sign that doesn't elaborate that meaning.[71] That we don't know the "true name" of Melmotte, in other words, may not be the point that emphasizes the split between fact and fiction; instead it may suggest the new ways this continuum remained richly productive for writers, literary and otherwise, and for business.

I close this chapter with a reading of the different forms through which Melmotte is meaningful as an instance of business charisma, from the generic stories in which his charismatic power is generated to the routinized way this power is understood. In particular, I analyze the form that represents one of the most compact signs of the personal, the name, juxtaposing "Melmotte" with other instances of names from the Victorian investment world, in particular those that appeared in company annual reports and investment prospectuses. And finally I analyze Trollope's exploration of character as a response to charisma, as he shifts from representing "Melmotte" to representing Melmotte, the developed, psychological realist character.

Even before his death prompts the flood of biographies, their familiar narrative forms structure the representation of Melmotte. As he stands at the apex of his achievement on the brink of his entry into Parliament, Melmotte casts himself in their terms, echoing the rags-to-riches story of self-making as he marvels that "he, the boy out of the gutter, should entertain at his own house, in London, a Chinese Emperor and English and German Royalty" (2:113). But his overreaching consists in misunderstanding the authorship of that story. Pondering his legacy, Melmotte claims creative power over his tale, invoking Horace's claim to immortality through poetry as he silently chants " 'Non omnis moriar,' in some language of his own" (2:113). In fact, stories like his are not singular but generic, and the public is the author of record.

Spectacular business narratives were already clichéd by the 1870s, received by a knowing and cynical public well seasoned with journalistic and biographical accounts. "The world worshipped Mr. Melmotte," the narrator notes, yet stories told about him do not for a minute inspire the sincere belief of anyone in the novel (1:331). But they are no less powerful for being a matter of routine, generating economic credit even as they are met with habitual skepticism. As Roger Carbury, perhaps the closest thing to a moral center in this biting novel, puts it, "Men say openly that he is an adventurer and a swindler. No one pretends to think that he is a gentleman. There is a consciousness among all who speak of him that he amasses his money not by honest trade, but by unknown tricks" (1:138).[72] This marks a difference from the genres that the novel echoes: rather than delivering a straightforward exposé, it takes the assumption of clichéd familiarity a step further so that there is nothing to expose. Like the speculators and chatterers in his society, we may not know all the details of Melmotte's history and business practices, but we always know the truth of Melmotte: "In the City Mr. Melmotte's name was worth any money,—though his character was perhaps worth but little" (1:33–34).

Thus, when Trollope represents the emergence of rumors of Melmotte's criminality, they are so familiar as to almost not need saying: "In the third edition of the 'Evening Pulpit' came out a mysterious paragraph which nobody could understand but they who had known all about it before" (2:76). As the subsequent tumble of the value of his name indicates, a great many people seem to understand the paragraph—that is, seem to have "known all about it before." Even those who attend his dinner for the emperor of China are by and large ready to believe Roger's evaluation of Melmotte: "A failure! Of course he's a failure, whether rich or poor;—a miserable imposition, a hollow vulgar fraud from beginning to end" (2:44). In fact, the narrator asserts, "the greater part of the people assembled did believe that their host had committed some great fraud. . . . It was so probable that such a man should have done something horrible!" (2:103). "Of course," "it was so probable": as the embodiment of stories that everyone already knows, Melmotte is a type—a stereotype even—a fact recognized by the *Times* in its review, which noted that "men of the Melmotte type, who shoot every now and then with meteor-like suddenness across the London sky, are only too familiar to us all."[73] Whether it represents him as likely to succeed or to fail on a grand scale, any story about Melmotte—or "the Melmotte type"—can be met with an "of course."

Trollope's construction of "Melmotte" registers not only a shift in the public—whether in their sophistication about commercial narratives or in their level of commercial morality—but also a change in the way those narratives and terms such as *character* are operating in commercial discourse. To say that Melmotte's power emerges through stories, accruing to his name even as his character is (correctly) valued at little, is not exactly to say that character has lost economic significance. More accurately, in many of the texts of investment practice in particular, character stands out very clearly as what it has in many ways always been: a horizon of meaning, a *promise* of possibilities—for individual responsibility, for moral evaluation, for knowledge—that can only be gestured toward. The rhetoric of investment documents helped to institutionalize this gestural form of the personal and to construct the routine that gave business charisma so much of its practical power.

The name is one device of particular importance. Names crowd the materials of Victorian investment with an insistence that testifies to the continued value of offering gestures toward the personal. Investment prospectuses, for instance, varied in form, but their openings are relatively standard: a listing of the company's capital and share offerings followed by the names of directors, accompanied by their occupations or other marks of distinction (fig. 1). Annual and semiannual reports offered by companies to their investors followed a similar pattern, listing the names of current directors, solicitors, accountants, and so forth. These lists met legal requirements for disclosure. But their rhetorical, suggestive effects go further. They conjure the *idea* of personal responsibility, as much as they assure the fact. And after the trumpeting of investment numbers (in which the potential capital often dominates the paid-up, visually as well as in the accounting), names offer a reassuring gesture of solidity: real people, after all.

In designating individuals, names point to the possibility of character knowledge. But this remains a fairly empty gesture, since in themselves the names and the documents didn't provide access to character. Instead, the names of these eminent men were signs that the company had at its helm—well, eminence, if nothing else, or wealth, or personal or political connection, or possibly expertise. The descriptions attached to the names could signify,

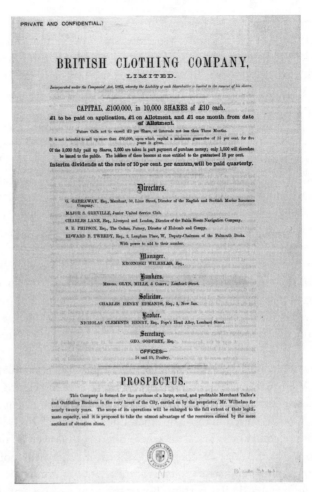

FIGURE 1. Prospectus of the British Clothing Company, Limited. (London, 1865). (Guildhall Library, City of London)

or claim to signify, through a wide range of qualifications and activities and with differing degrees of precision: to take just one example, among the five directors listed in an 1865 prospectus for the British Clothing Company, Limited, are "a merchant," a "Director of the Bahia Steam Navigation Company," and a member of the "Junior United Service Club" (see fig. 1).[74] Thus, what the names and descriptions on prospectuses and reports indicated was as often as not a broad sense of the "quality" of person who believed in the undertaking, more than a specific sense of individual character or indications of relevant expertise. As such they were intended to reassure potential investors that in pledging their faith (and their money), they would be, in more senses than one, in good company.

It is possible, of course, that the names listed on a prospectus or report did convey information to a certain audience. Particularly within the milieu of the City, or within a particular industry, names—and the people they belonged to—might have been familiar enough that no further description or narrative of history or qualifications seemed necessary. Some of the faith the names inspired, furthermore, might have accrued not through immediate personal acquaintance, but rather through knowledge of and trust in the friend or associate who passed along the prospectus in a gesture shaped as intimately interpersonal by the document's "private and confidential" stamp (fig. 1).[75] But this kind of personal knowledge, and even second-order personal knowledge, was certainly not always in play. And as the connections become further removed, the community of trust that provides the foundation for taking the names as meaningful becomes more diffuse, and the offer of names becomes increasingly formal and gestural.

To illustrate the relative emptiness of these invocations of the personal, I offer an example from both investment genres. First is the name of John Sadleir, which winds into and precipitously out of the reports of the London and County Bank for eight years at midcentury. In the year-end report from December 30, 1848, the directors declare that they have "the satisfaction to announce that John Sadleir, Esq., M.P., has been elected Chairman, a gentleman whose general habits of business and intimate knowledge of the system of district banking eminently qualify him for that position."[76] More narrative detail than this—what these habits and knowledge were, how he attained them—is not given, as if either the assertion alone is meant to suffice or the new chairman is well known enough that no stockholder would require more. Over the course of the next few years, one piece of character evidence is given, as the reports praise the benevolence of the chairman in establishing a sort of pension or disability fund, the Sadleir Provident Fund. In the half-yearly report of June 1856, however, no direct mention is made of Sadleir's suicide in February of that year, following the discovery of his embezzlement of £200,000 from the Tipperary Bank; his story has now been reduced to "the peculiar circumstances which have transpired since the last Meeting," which have prompted the directors to seek extra auditing. Furthermore, the narrative states, "since the last Meeting five of your former Directors have ceased to be Members of the Board."[77] The names of these directors are never specified directly—they have simply vanished from the list, replaced by others—nor is the story of their transgression spelled out. In the next half-yearly report, the provident fund is mentioned, but it is no longer named for Sadleir.[78] The stories behind the names are left to biographers, journalists, and, in Sadleir's case, novelists such as Trollope and Dickens.

The next example of the degree to which names played a role that was literally formal may be illustrated by a provisional prospectus for the Bank of West Africa, Limited, dated 1879 (fig. 2). In this document, blank spaces are reserved, to be filled with the names of directors, solicitors, and so forth.

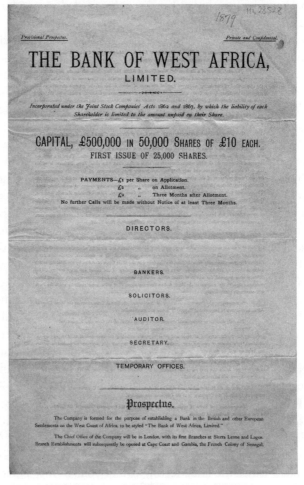

FIGURE 2. Provisional Prospectus of the Bank of West Africa, Limited (1879). (London Metropolitan Archives, London; Reproduced with permission from Standard Chartered Bank. © Copyright 2013 Standard Chartered Bank. All rights reserved.)

The names are thus themselves incidental to the course of the company's development—a matter of filling in the blanks. One name might not, per- haps, do *quite* as well as another, but the blank may be filled in any number of ways—if not by Notable Man X, then by Respectable Man Y. Viewing the prospectus in its earlier, provisional stage highlights the dynamic: the director, who is shaped by the rhetoric of the final prospectus into a figure who grounds the company, instead occupies a contingent position similar to the potential investor, only one step further along—someone who has been made to believe in the company or at least to credit its possibility for profit. The names on the prospectus conjure a community of believers that a poten- tial investor might choose to join, and in asserting the existence of this com- munity they make it easier to take the step of declaring belief by investing. One commentator, critical of this sleight of hand, went so far as to suggest a new classification, "ornamental directors," whose "ornamental names," "not to be bought for an old song," were a crucial part of the "fine art" of "the drafting of prospectuses." By constructing a category that is decorative, artifi- cial, and commodified, in which the name may be split from and irrelevant to the ethical care and personal identity it purported to guarantee, the writer's satiric tone calls for that guarantee to be reestablished. But in the prospectus such purity would be impossible: the names were always, crucially, a "draw."[79]

When Trollope's Hamilton J. Fisker, the sharp company promoter from San Francisco, makes the gathering of names his first task upon arriving in England, he astutely gauges the importance of the personal. Fisker attaches the name of a young Englishman, Paul Montague, to the "brilliantly printed programmes" for the proposed company, without Paul's knowledge or ap- proval (1:78). He prevails upon Paul to gain an introduction to Melmotte, the businessman of the moment (whom Paul doesn't know well at all), writ- ing out a letter that Paul recopies and signs. When the introduction is suc- cessful, Fisker puts the same prospectus before Melmotte and announces, "I want to have your name there": "And he placed his finger down on a spot on which it was indicated that there was, or was to be, a chairman of an English Board of Directors, but with a space for the name, hitherto blank" (1:83).

In the inclusion of Paul's name without his knowledge and the false pretenses of his fill-in-the-blank signature on the letter of introduction, Trol- lope captures both the necessity and the meaninglessness of names as signs of the personal. Furthermore, as I have suggested, the facts that Melmotte's name might be thought to communicate are at best unclear or at worst indic- ative of a very bad character. And yet the addition of Melmotte's name has the desired effect. In terms of generating profits it is as good as a real prod- uct: as the narrator notes, making a comparison to another source of quick

riches, "Mr. Fisker had 'struck 'ile'" when he obtained Melmotte as director
(1:205). By the end of the chapter in which Fisker pays his visit, the railway is
spectacularly launched: "it was felt that Mr. Melmotte was himself so great
a tower of strength that the fortune of the Company,—as a company,—was
made" (1:84).

Because the effect of Melmotte's name originates in the routinized charismatic mode—grounded in stories that everyone has heard before, that no
one sincerely believes, but that claim support in a generalized, impersonal
"it was felt"—its unsoundness is palpable. But any name on a prospectus,
functioning as a gesture toward the personal that may or may not communicate content, produces its effects by invoking and enabling a shared social
performance of belief without any necessary ground. The charismatic mode
and the ordinary operations of character, dissimilar in many respects, in
fact have much in common. Though charisma magnifies its difference into
enchantment, magic, or worship, its counterpart is likewise dependent on
cognitive processes associated with fictions: the suspension of disbelief that
sets the limits of credit; and the construction, through a proper name, of a
designated entity that may or may not have expansively defined properties.[80]
Routinized charisma merely exaggerates and institutionalizes the element exceeding the rational, calculable, and knowable that is present in any appeal
to the personal.

It is tempting to read the explicit reference to business biographies in *The
Way We Live Now* as an assertion of the novelist's superior claim to purchase
on the territory of business character, countering the enchantments and mys-
tifications of the charismatic mode with an omniscient realist penetration of
the "inner life" that biographies promise but don't deliver—and thus offering
firmer grounds for adjudicating credit.[81] And as the stories about Melmotte's
probable fraudulence multiply, Trollope attempts to address the power of the
Melmotte *type*—the charismatic creature of stories—by turning him into a
particularized, psychological *character.* At the dinner party for the Emperor
of China, as Melmotte faces down the rumors that threaten his success, a
lengthy internal monologue renders him transparent:

> Perhaps never in his life had he studied his own character and his
> own conduct more accurately. . . . No;—he could not run away. He
> soon made himself sure of that. . . . Looking back at the hour or two
> that had just passed he was aware that he had allowed himself not
> only to be frightened in the dinner-room,—but also to seem to be
> frightened. . . . But he would not falter again. Nothing should cow
> him,—no touch from a policeman, no warrant from a magistrate, no

defalcation of friends, no scorn in the City, no solitude in the West
End. He would go down among the electors to-morrow and would
stand his ground, as though all with him were right. (2:105)

Up to this point in the novel the reader has no *absolutely* firm grounds for
judging whether Melmotte is a fraud or a legitimate success. But as we enter
Melmotte's mind with the immediacy provided by free indirect discourse, it
becomes increasingly clear that he is attempting to manage some sort of commercial scam. And as the novel progresses up to the moment of his suicide,
we keep the same closeness: we follow him through the streets, we watch his
violent attempts to persuade his daughter to sign property over to him, we
watch him enter Parliament to make ill-considered speeches, we watch him
drink too much, all the while privy to his reflections on the game he has kept
up and his desperate efforts to keep it going further.

However, some curious features intrude on the representation of Melmotte's subjectivity through the period before his demise. First, the moment
where we get closest to being granted evidence of his criminality is represented with an excessiveness that is striking and ultimately mysterious. On
the day of the election, as rumors run wild, Melmotte returns to his private
office in the house he has rented, bolts the door, burns several papers from
his desk, and disposes of their ashes. And that's not all: one final document
gets the special treatment of being put "bit by bit into his mouth," where it
is chewed "into a pulp till he swallow[s] it" (2:119). Although this feels like
a moment in which the reader is granted full access—to the private office,
behind the bolted door—the scene finally withholds as much as it reveals,
never telling us what these documents actually contain. It seems likely that
they relate to Melmotte's forgeries—but then, which ones? Those of Dolly
Longestaffe's name, which allow him to mortgage Pickering Park? Those related to the shady-seeming purchase of properties in the East End? Perhaps—
but then nearly two hundred pages later Melmotte reflects, "As to the dead
man's letter, and as to Dolly Longstaffe's letter, he did not think that any
sufficient evidence could be found," a superfluous contemplation if he had
already destroyed the evidence (2:298). His forgery of Marie's name and that
of his clerk, Croll, come after the scene, so it can't be those. And what about
the over-the-top detail of the one document that is too hot to be burned but
must be torn, chewed, and eaten? The novel announces that there is something singular about this paper but never tells us what it is.

The privileged glimpse into privacy is, of course, the particular terrain
of the novel, and especially omniscient narration—the essence of the fantasy of fullness that fiction can appear to offer.[82] Just what it actually reveals,

however, is decidedly uncertain. In fact, the passage seems to highlight not that apparent fullness, nor the novel's special purchase on character truths that can combat corruption in the marketplace, but rather its limitations, the "incompleteness" of its fictional entities.[83] Melmotte turns from his disposal of evidence to his breakfast, accompanied by the pile of newspapers in which stories of his turpitude are told, reading them "without a quiver in his face or the slightest change in his colour" (2:119). In the space of one scene, then, Melmotte is constructed as a likely criminal by one set of papers representing public opinion, while his literal incorporation of another paper attests to the criminality of his character. But finally the promise of revelation that the scene holds forth is strangely empty: we know not much more and not much less about Melmotte at the end of this last on-paper representation, in the pages of a novel, than what the voices of public opinion always have "known," without it making any great difference. There is something *beyond* character, in other words—call it facts, or evidence, or perhaps a gesture to another, unrepresentable real—which it is necessary to know and which the novelist doesn't deliver. That character, which the novelist *is* supremely well placed to reveal, remains effectively coterminous with the judgments of the marketplace—which move independently of any moral interest or even any financial reality—and this nullifies its power to combat the challenge of the charismatic mode within the economic sphere.[84]

The charismatic mode constructed new ways for character representations to be experienced and transacted by producers, readers, and consumers: as narratives that skated along the fact-fiction continuum and that could be acknowledged to be fictions without necessarily losing their force; as evidence of the "reality of romance" whose power should be embraced. Blurring truth and fiction, sidestepping moral and rational calculation, business charisma made capitalist enchantment a matter of routine. But even as it undercut character's (elusive) promise of individuality and plenitude to guarantee truth and moral responsibility, charisma intensified the personal and kept it at the forefront of the economic scene. Melmotte was "blow'd up vid bigness," in the words of his clerk, Croll (2:449). The circularity of the image (he gets bigger because he is big) highlights the insubstantiality of charismatic power. But it does not negate the power itself: in the routinized charismatic mode, helped along by narratives and their willing, knowing readers, personal business finds new opportunities for making it big and, perhaps, blowing it up.

PART II

LOCATING CHARACTER IN COMMERCIAL REPRESENTATION

3

Reading Ruin

FAILURE AND THE FORMS
OF CHARACTER, 1849–1865

THE OPENING TIRADE OF THE TROUBLED SPEAKER IN ALFRED, LORD
Tennyson's 1855 poem *Maud* attacks the notion that his was an era of stability and prosperity.[1] "Civil war" is a more apt description of the national
state of affairs, he fumes, though the sword has been replaced by commercial competition (27). The immediate impulse for this bitterness is personal:
"a vast speculation had fail'd," and the speaker's father, ruined in the event,
has died under indeterminate circumstances (9). A torrent of questions follows as the father's ruin seems to shatter the possibility of knowledge, from
matters of fact ("Did he fling himself down? who knows?") to matters of
judgment ("Villainy somewhere! whose?") (9, 17). The speaker seems particularly tormented by the challenge ruin poses to his knowledge of character—
his father's and even his own. *Was* the father maddened by despair? Is the
speaker, "raging alone," preparing to inherit the paternal fate of madness or
death (53)? In fact, is he so unstable a character that he is likely to "passively
take the print" of his age, feeling neither "hope nor trust," ready to cheat
others as his family was cheated? "Why not?" the speaker wonders. "Who
knows?" (29, 30, 30, 32).

Tennyson's sense that ruin in his "recklessly speculative age" was an occasion that prompted questions and required interpretation was shared by
journalists and businesspeople alike.[2] In 1860 the *Economist* suggested that
"the revelations of the Court of Bankruptcy cannot be expected to be the
pleasantest which we can conceive." "It contains the *debit* side to the greatness of our commerce. We see elsewhere the traces of the energies it awakens
and the blessings it confers. We read there a record,—a very imperfect and
incomplete record, no doubt,—of the vices which it fosters and the risks by
which it is attended."[3] As the passage moves from the glories of commerce
to its gloomy and even sinister underside, the verbs shift. The "blessings" of
commerce are self-evident, available for all to "see." To understand its prob-

lems requires a more laborious, mediated process of reading, requiring exposition and interpretation.

Efforts to furnish opportunities to read ruin were in no short supply in the mid-Victorian period. In the space of roughly a decade *Maud* finds company with *Dombey and Son* and *Little Dorrit* (1855–57), William Makepeace Thackeray's *The Newcomes* (1855), Elizabeth Gaskell's *North and South* (1854–55), and George Eliot's *The Mill on the Floss* (1860), to give just a few canonical examples. As literary writers turned their gaze and their abundance of words to the representation of ruin, outside the literary sphere a debate occurred over the place of reading and the form of representation in addressing failure. Between 1849, when a new bankruptcy law was introduced that established a system of certificates classifying bankrupts according to culpability of character, and 1861, when this system was abolished, the debate was particularly intense.

To note the way that ruin was conceived as a representational and interpretive problem at midcentury is to broaden a critical focus that has often centered on the discourse surrounding the debtor and his or her ethical status and character.[4] This focus, as useful as it is, leaves the impression that those who contracted obligations and failed to pay them were the primary object of concern as Victorians grappled with the necessity of credit. However, the mid-Victorian emphasis on the problem of *reading* character in the transactional relationship of lending and borrowing places a heavy burden on the creditor: each real-life tale of ill-fated speculations, collapsed banks, or overextended traders potentially stood as a rebuke to the character-reading capacities of the participants. In fact, many Victorian commentators blamed creditors as much as debtors for the state of things: *creditors* had lost their discrimination, their sense of individual responsibility, seeking protection in the law when their own efforts were manifestly lacking.

This emphasis on the reading powers of individual creditors privileged the embedded, interpersonal relationships characteristic of personal business. The contrary impulse—looking to law, seeking systematic and standardized responses that might address flaws of character reading—tended toward abstraction and rationalization. In this chapter, I analyze these competing dynamics in midcentury debates over bankruptcy reform, which generated pressure to create a rationalized market out of an uneven array of interpersonal relationships of debt and credit. *Could* character be abstractable, systematized? Was this even desirable, or was character's implication in socially embedded modes of knowledge—and its resistance to abstracting modes—part of the value it brought to commerce?

Two textual representations of character and debt form the center of my analysis. The first is the midcentury classification system that assigned certificates according to the culpability of the bankrupt's character. The second is Eliot's novel *The Mill on the Floss,* a story of the financial ruin of a miller, Mr. Tulliver, and the sexual ruin of his daughter, Maggie. I argue that the debates surrounding the character certificates' intervention in market relations and Eliot's novelistic explorations of abstract and embedded or sympathetic modes of knowledge emerged out of a larger, shared cultural concern. In particular, I suggest that Eliot's construction of a simultaneously interested and disinterested, authoritative and sympathetic narrative voice represented a fantasy that an approach to character representation could be found that would overcome the discontinuities generated in the experience of failure and the limitations of both overly interested and overly abstracted character judgments. At the same time, her translation of the struggle to narrate the truth of characters-in-debt through familial and sexualized representations of personal connection highlights the way that the personal continued to pose a practical challenge to the establishment of market rationality, one that finely tuned approaches to character reading and representation could not, finally, overcome. Eliot's novel's narration—and the mode of realism that it epitomized and fostered—marks both a high point in the confidence in literary writing to moralize the marketplace through its attention to character and a moment of divergence, shifting the ground on which presumptions about character and representation in everyday commercial life rested.

The Experience of Ruin

At the beginning of the third book of *The Mill on the Floss,* "The Downfall," Eliot's blustery, obstinate miller Mr. Tulliver perceives a great deal of flexibility in his state following the loss of his lawsuit to his nemesis, the lawyer Wakem. Riding home from a meeting with his lawyer, he contemplates the steps that have led to his predicament. Beyond the lawsuit costs, three factors stand out: a mortgage on the mill, held by a Mr. Furley; an agreement to act as surety for a friend, the auctioneer Mr. Riley, who dies and leaves him with a £250 debt; and a rash agreement to give a bill of sale on his household goods to an unnamed creditor who loans him £500 when, in a fit of pique, he insists on paying back his wife's sister, the formidable Mrs. Glegg. Tulliver clings willfully to the possibility that he will be able to work out an arrangement with these creditors so that he will not be "obliged to turn out of his old place, and look like a ruined man."[5] In Tulliver's first inkling of its approach, ruin is a matter of appearances, something that may be staved off by skillful management of creditors—playing on their friendly feelings and their self-interest—so that the debt is prolonged, shifted around, but not incorporated in a defining, visible sign. Though his thoughts evince subtle changes—for instance, deeming "right and natural" a sudden willingness to turn for assistance to another sister-in-law, after earlier insisting that he would not be beholden (173)—Tulliver's character seems as yet relatively unaltered: impetuous, self-regarding, generous, and deluded.

The situation changes catastrophically when he learns that the unnamed creditor, feeling anxious about the debt, has made over the bill of sale to none other than Wakem, a blow that leaves Tulliver prostrate, not to return to full consciousness and health for some months. During this period his household is auctioned off, the mill and farm equipment are sold to Wakem, and the possibility of averting true financial ruin is denied as the proceeds from all transactions are found not to cover the debts. Now the signs of character transformation are many and dramatic. Mrs. Tulliver "seemed aged ten years" by the sale (209). The maturation of Tulliver's son Tom is similarly accelerated, as he is forced to step into his father's place to provide for his mother and his sister Maggie and to work to pay off the creditors and clear the family's name. Maggie's character perhaps maintains the most consistency, remaining prey to what her brother and her friend Philip Wakem would call enthusiasms; but her enthusiasms become more solemn and tend toward renunciation rather than expansiveness. And in perhaps the strongest image of transformation Mr. Tulliver is translated into a new, lower class, as Tom enters the house and sees "a coarse, dingy man," the bailiff, "sitting in his father's chair, smoking, with a jug and glass beside him" (178)—a figural translation that becomes actualized as Mr. Tulliver enters Wakem's service as a wage worker managing the mill.[6] To lose the identity of property owner is to lose himself, his sense of agency in the world. "I'm nought but a bankrupt," he tells his wife. "It's no use standing up for anything now" (231).

But significantly, Tulliver's sense of this transformation is given a psychological, rather than a purely economic origin. Wakem's takeover of the bill of sale, which prevents all the miller's schemes for face-saving arrangements and puts him under the thumb of his bitterest enemy, is in purely economic terms no different from the scheme of going to work for Furley, the original mortgage holder. By making the final cause of Tulliver's downfall as much psychological as financial, Eliot insists on ruin as a fundamentally transformative experience. And in doing so she aligns herself with a position moralizing debt and failure that was a key component of Victorian middle-class ideology. An 1851 *Economist* article celebrating the moral progress of the Victorian era, for instance, singles out for praise that "*debt*, which used to be regarded as an indispensable characteristic of a man of fashion, is now almost everywhere scouted as disreputable," substituting a middle-class notion of respectability for the aristocratic, fashionable reputation that easily incorporated debt.[7] Eliot recognized the deep hold this notion had taken on her in a letter thanking her publisher, John Blackwood, for an extra payment recognizing the success of *Adam Bede,* written as she was working on *The Mill on the Floss:* "I certainly care a great deal for the money, as I suppose all anxious minds do that love independence and have been brought up to think debt and begging the two deepest dishonours short of crime."[8]

However, *The Mill on the Floss* also registers an awareness that the solemn view of debt may no longer have had a complete hold on her imagined readership. In an ironic paragraph added in revision, Eliot makes the "narrow notions about debt" held by the "old-fashioned Tullivers" a matter of the novel's historical setting that "may perhaps excite a smile on the faces of many readers in these days of wide commercial views and wide philosophy, according to which everything rights itself without any trouble of ours" (244). Eliot's representation of what Nancy Henry has astutely characterized as a "laissez-faire" rationalization for misconduct or dishonesty joined a long line of complaints that debt and failure had become routine, losing their power to shame and dragging down the state of commercial morality.[9] Indeed, by the middle decades of the nineteenth century many observers were complaining that the bankruptcy and insolvency laws had become overly soft. Meetings of merchants and tradesmen in London in 1847 adopted the resolution that these laws were "a disgrace to our age and country.... Under their shelter, deceit, reckless trading, extravagance, dishonesty, and every species of fraud may be practiced with impunity; the Debtor is demoralized and the Creditor unprotected."[10] As the bankruptcy commissioner R. G. C. Fane complained in an 1848 pamphlet, "modern changes" in the law "have entirely *reversed* its spirit. It *was* a system of excessive severity; it is a system of excessive leniency. Formerly the Debtor was at the mercy of the Creditor, now the Creditor is at the mercy of the Debtor."[11] Ten years later the *Economist* still found reason to complain, decrying recent reforms' "sentimental and inordinate sympathy with debtors,—unfortunate debtors—just as if there were no such thing as unfortunate creditors," and the *Times* asserted that there was "no question at the present moment so important to the commercial world as that of amendment of the bankruptcy law."[12]

What were the contemporary circumstances that would make midcentury businessmen agitated and the Tullivers appear obsolete? The answer does not seem to be an overwhelming increase in the number and cost of failures, though these are difficult to pinpoint exactly.[13] Official bankruptcy was expensive and time consuming, and many creditors came to private arrangements with debtors (such as insolvency, trust deeds, and compositions), the losses from which are harder to estimate. (Such a private arrangement seems to be what the Tullivers negotiate, though the family expresses confusion over whether or not Mr. Tulliver has been made a bankrupt.) Changes in commercial law, most notably the 1855 introduction of limited liability, may have played a role in conjuring a specter of a flood of unpaid debts. The gradual phasing-out of imprisonment for debt, too, seemed to many an indication that debt was coming to be regarded more casually, as something less than the life-altering experience of which prison seemed an apt symbol and instantiation.

But significant as these changes may have been, I suggest that much of the concern over the problem of ruin at midcentury may have derived from its highlighting intransigent tensions over the balance between personalized and abstracting market tendencies. In the first place, in a capitalist economy dependent on credit for its smooth workings, debt could not be a clear-cut marker of individual moral worth. The man who employed credit, having only "a little capital, or no capital at all but his character and the confidence of others," might be more likely to develop that character further, acting with energy and vigilance in his commercial pursuits.[14] His capital-rich counterpart, in contrast, might be a safer bet, but that very safety might be less of a stimulus toward self-development. Indeed, as Boyd Hilton has argued, the evangelical economic model saw credit and debt as occasions for moral trial and character development, with bankruptcy and failure representing a healthy check on excesses. By midcentury that model was breaking down, partly as a result of longer experience with cycles of failures that seemed to have no clear moral origin.[15] Because the relation between credit and capital was cyclical—with credit a step on the way to gaining capital, which then became a step toward gaining credit—the business practices of credit and debt did not seem to be fundamentally accountable to an outside moral authority or to a predetermined narrative pattern in which an action had predictable and justified consequences.[16] What mattered was simply at what point the cycle was stopped: if it was at a moment of success, the practices were right; if not, wrong. Thus, the *Economist* made this pronouncement: "As every one, merchants as well as bankers, trades on credit, to do so is not wrong: the wrong is to do so in a way not to succeed. It is not wrong to give an acceptance: it is extremely wrong not to pay it."[17] Morality could seem to be determined by outcomes rather than by anything intrinsic to individual actions.

Even as the fuzzy line between credit and capital, debt and solvency, rendered it difficult to judge on any basis other than outcomes, it was recognized that outcomes themselves were often not fully under an economic actor's control. The combination of these factors meant that the history of

the law of debtor and creditor in England was marked by a tendency toward leniency on practical grounds that stood in perennial tension with the
impulse to strictness on moral ones. From the sixteenth century forward,
bankruptcy law recognized that new economic forms entailed a necessary
element of risk: "traders" could fail through no fault of their own because of
their dependence on suppliers, unreliable transport, and so forth, or through
the failure of others.[18] Even as bankruptcy addressed this recognition by
offering the possibility for discharging debts, provisions for the possibility
of moral assessment were maintained to avoid encouraging irresponsibility.
The granting of the "certificate of conformity," the discharge certificate that
enabled the bankrupt to resume trading, was one occasion in which the conduct of the bankrupt could be examined and judged.

Not only did credit and debt trouble easy judgments of moral character, but they also highlighted the difficulties in balancing the claims of the
individualized, often highly personal relations between creditor and debtor
with the need to rationalize the credit market. Mr. Tulliver's debts—to
friends and family, as well as more distant acquaintances and even unknown
creditors—and his efforts to arrive at private arrangements vividly suggest
that unevenness. The Victorian bankruptcy-reform debates are dominated
by questions of whether and how to rationalize this uneven market and how
this will affect the assessment of character. Two components to the debate
stand out: first, the effort to overcome distinctions between creditors and
to render their treatment uniform; and second, the question of who should
have authority to judge a debtor's affairs and his character—officials of the
courts or creditors who had a personal interest in the debtor's affairs.

When the 1831 Bankruptcy Act established a new court of bankruptcy
and instituted a system in which the bankrupt's estate was administered by a
court-appointed assignee—a permanent, appointed official—rather than an
assignee chosen by creditors, reaction among businessmen was mixed. Particularly controversial was the proposal to shift control away from creditors.[19]
After all, an aggrieved writer wrote to the *Times,* "Who . . . is so much interested in the expeditious and economical winding up of a bankrupt's estate as
his creditor, who knows his affairs and has the best opportunity of judging of
every circumstance connected with them?"[20]

Significantly, the letter writer bases his claim for the creditor's right to an
active role in the debtor's affairs not merely on the creditor's economic interest but also on his superior knowledge and judgment. Fane's 1848 pamphlet
made a similar assumption, complaining that the system's "evils" emerged
when the bankrupt's release "came to depend, not upon what the creditor
really believed, or rather knew, as to the cheat that had been put upon him,

but upon what he could prove to the satisfaction of a Court of Justice."[21] In both of these examples, the creditor is represented as the ultimate standard of knowledge about the case; in the second, especially, this is rendered almost mystical, as the internal standard of the creditor's belief is equated with knowledge and cast as superior to the standards of legal proof. To insist on the preeminence of creditor knowledge was to insist that the relationship of credit and debt was moral and interpersonal. And as the *Times* letter makes clear, the creditor's self-interest in the relationship, far from seeming to impinge on his capacity for judgment, was instead claimed to produce accuracy and insight.

However, the value claimed for the interpersonal did not mean that private arrangements between creditor and debtor, called compositions, were embraced. Because they avoided publicity many felt compositions acted as "cloaks of all sorts of fraud," enabling friendly or intimate creditors to make more favorable arrangements than others.[22] Furthermore, compositions created an imbalance in knowledge. As Fane noted in testimony before a House of Lords Select Committee in 1849, because "the failure must be known to the debtor's friends and connexions," it was a matter of justice to "the general public (any one of whom may thereafter be asked to give him credit)" that they should have access to the same information.[23] Publicity was not merely a way to *protect* an extant "general public"; it was a way to help *create* a general public out of a system of particular relationships.

The tension between particular and general relationships in the credit market, both of which made epistemological and moral claims that found support in Victorian thought, bedeviled other aspects of the response to ruin. Publicity worked not only on the individual creditor but also on the family of the bankrupt, whose fear of exposure was invoked as a way to minimize losses from bad debts. When a parliamentary committee expressed concern about the intent to use disgrace as a tactic, by acting "upon the fears" of a bankrupt's "relations and friends," William Hawes, the chairman of a London merchants' committee, replied that "in most cases those relatives and friends have to pay, and more severely at last than they would have done if the career of the debtor had been sooner checked"—dismissing concerns about emotional costs as irrelevant, except as a means to minimize financial ones.[24] And an 1854 commission report claimed that the affective toll—"the pain" that a bankrupt "knows his wife and family will endure" through the imposition of the assignee—was an even more effective deterrent to failure than publicity.[25]

The threat that a family would be sold up, their household examined with appraising rather than loving eyes and their distress advertised in pub-

licly posted notices, was thus an active component of strategies for minimizing losses. Novelists' attention to this aspect of the experience of ruin speaks
to its importance. The disciplinary effect of publicity of the sale at Dorlcote
Mill is shown affecting Mr. Tulliver's family, not the miller himself, who lies
ill and oblivious to intrusions and exposure. But his son Tom is sent hurry-
ing out of town at the sight of a flyer advertising the sale, posted "as if on
purpose to stare at him" (206). Mrs. Tulliver cries as she imagines bargain
hunters examining the engraved initials on her prized Dodson teapot and
suffers as cherished possessions are "identified as hers in the hateful publicity
of the Golden Lion" (209). Though the narrator gently mocks Mrs. Tulliver's identification with her things at this crisis moment, the intimately personal shame that both she and Tom experience is treated as an occasion for
sympathy. In calling for a sympathetic response to the suffering of the family that is affected, inadvertently, by the failure of one member, Eliot turned
a conventional concern for the pain of creditors and shareholders harmed
by the debtor's failure to a reminder that there were others who bore no responsibility who were also hurt—this time by the settling of accounts. "Even
justice makes its victims," she notes, and the devices that rectify debts—
"allocaturs, filing of bills in Chancery, decrees of sale"—are "legal chain-shot
or bomb-shells that can never hit a solitary mark, but must fall with widespread shattering" (215).

But the presumption of familial privacy and innocence that elicited sympathy for the debtor and his family also represented another threat to rationalization, as the mix of affective and economic bonds rendered the family
suspect. Families were perceived as vehicles to hide money and property that
might be used to pay debts or as shelter for evasive debtors. Over the years,
therefore, bankruptcy reform stressed the need to regulate the conduct of
the family of the debtor. The 1849 act, for instance, diminished the special
status of the wife by declaring the court might summon and examine her
about her husband's estate.[26] Provisions were made to prevent the settlement
of property on children or other persons except upon marriage.[27] Outraged
cries to close the loophole charged that marriages were being conveniently
arranged.[28] Emotional connection and family histories meant nothing in
the disposition of property; one case, for instance, held that a bankrupt who
concealed property, "although of small intrinsic value and prized by him for
the sake of family recollections and associations," could not have the suspension of the certificate of discharge lifted.[29]

The pursuit of transparent, rational standards for the relationship of
creditor and debtor has a familiar, even unsurprising, logic. But as the law's
treatment of family demonstrates, in effect this rationalization meant a loss

of privilege for relationships that were ideologically and practically prized in the Victorian period, such as family and friendship. This was met with some concern on practical as well as moral and emotional grounds. Friends and family, after all, did not merely moralize and provide solace; they were also potential sources of financial assistance. The interference of a rationalizing law in such relationships threatened to undermine their social *and* economic value. Thus the *Economist,* for instance, lamented the law's provision "to deprive the bankrupt" of any property that might "descend, be devised or bequeathed, or come to him otherwise than by his own personal earning," after the certificate of discharge was granted. Such a provision, the writer feared, could wind up creating a dangerously uprooted, isolated market agent: destroying a bankrupt trader's "hope of aid from friends," it would place him in a state of "statutable outlawry . . . far more likely to injure the commercial continuity, by rendering the bankrupt a desperate person, than to benefit his creditors."[30] In smoothing out the market so that all kinds of property were valued the same, and all parties rendered alike so as to prevent "preferences" being given to any "particular creditors," the rationalizing bankruptcy laws altered the social moorings of the credit market, building its foundations on procedural equality rather than individual connections.[31]

One of the more famous innovations of Victorian responses to ruin, the three-tier character-classification system for discharge certificates that I will explore in the next section, was an attempt to mediate the sticky problems posed by the uneven credit market. Adopted in 1849, the certificates, with their simplified classifications determined by court arbiters, seemed to represent the triumph of a rationalizing, objective perspective on the moral and characterological challenges of ruin. But the vigorous debates that followed until the system was abandoned in 1861 suggest how the certificates failed to resolve the tension between the values of objectivity, disinterest, and reason and the compelling claims of interest, particular relationships, and embedded knowledge. For George Eliot, whose work was often preoccupied by the exploration of these modes of knowledge about characters and society, the debates offered a ready staging ground for these issues to emerge with the Tullivers' ruin in *The Mill on the Floss.*

Classifying Characters, Recovering the Real

Speaking before a Select Committee of the House of Lords in May 1849, William Hawes, the chair of a London committee to reform bankruptcy laws, made a recommendation in favor of classifying the discharge certificates granted to bankrupts according to a system designating distinctions of character. "The certificates of conformity should be in three classes," he argued, "one indicating extreme fraud, and the others merely indicating cases of insolvency. We think, if the class to which each certificate belonged was added to the publication in the Gazette, it would afford, without any further inquiry, most useful information, and be of great service to the commercial world." Three times the committee members pondered whether the new certificate would entail other consequences. Hawes replied that the character classification would be enough in itself: "It would be a great boon to an honest man on getting a first class certificate; it would be a recommendation in future life, and something to aim at, that he had passed unscathed through adversity." The committee then wondered about the form of the certificate, asking Hawes to "take the trouble of drawing the three forms of certificate; one rather praising, another neutral, and the third a little condemnatory." But this was not quite what Hawes's group had in mind. Instead of the even minimally discursive certificates imagined by the Select Committee questioner, Hawes responded that "the suggestion which has been already made in that respect was, that they should be merely 1st, 2d and 3d, without any descriptive words."[32] Ultimately the 1849 Bankrupt Law Consolidation Act adopted a form of certificate that included more than just numbers, but the categories themselves bore most of the burden of conveying character. The judge would declare a finding that the bankrupt's "conduct [had] been satisfactory" and would grant a first- or second-class certificate (not distinguishing further between the two categories), or that the bankrupt's "conduct [had] not been satisfactory," which meant a third-class certificate.[33]

The London committee and the many bankers, merchants, and tradesmen who supported it favored classifying certificates in order to give the public determination of character an active role in the credit market. For the innocent bankrupts—the merely unfortunate trader whose first-class certificate could be taken to stand as a testament and the careless or improvident trader who received the second-class certificate—as well as for their malicious third-class counterpart, the fraudulent trader, the statement the certificate made about their characters was to stand as second chance or punishment in itself. For potential creditors, the certificates could determine the terms on which credit would be extended to the former bankrupt, if at all, and thus represented a way to minimize risk by factoring character into lending decisions.

But in eschewing "descriptive words," the London committee advocates a strangely abstract model of the variable, character, that they constructed as crucial. The exchange in the committee hearings demonstrates a vacillation between abstraction and precision, between the rationalizing impulse that the simplified three-tier model represents and the privileging of the kind of embedded personal knowledge that character implied. This dynamic would characterize much of the debate over the laws of bankruptcy and insolvency over the next decade. Though the classification of character certificates was first proposed by a warehouseman and was greeted with enthusiasm by business interests, it quickly became controversial. The classification system's appeal—its simplicity and its application by disinterested officials, promising an objective standard of judgment that all future creditors would be able to grasp and use—proved illusory in practice. Far from providing an example of accurate, objective character assessments, the variation in classification by judges left in place all the questions about how character should be determined. And the certificates themselves, with their minimalist rhetoric, failed to answer doubts about the way the bankruptcy process produced narratives of character. As these dissatisfactions persisted through the 1850s, such consensus as there had been on the role of character in addressing failure began to break down, with two divergent responses emerging. In the first place, commentators moved away from the ideal of disinterested, rationalized, abstract judgment that the classification system had represented, championing instead once again the power of creditors' self-interest as the key to promoting accurate and useful character assessment. At the same time, however, others argued for shifting the focus of the bankruptcy process away from character as an element of *business* calculation, claiming the judgment of character should be left to the courts as a matter with legal and social ramifications, but not intrinsic to the main commercial concern: recovering as much of a debt as possible.

It did not take long after the adoption of the scheme of character classification for qualms to emerge. The month after the Bankruptcy Act established the system, an *Economist* review of a book on the act took special notice of the author's concerns that certificate classifications would prove unwieldy, quoting in particular a section in which he worries that "the particular opinions and tendencies of mind of each commissioner will render it a very uncertain and sliding scale whereby to test mercantile character."[34] These concerns proved prescient: far from producing an objective standard of character judgment, the bankruptcy courts over the next few years put on a display of the continued power of "particular opinions." There was, in the view of one commissioner, "no moral, legal, or commercial standard on which to base a decision as to the classes of certificate"; thus one commissioner awarded first-class certificates in 60 percent of his cases, while another's rate was just 13 percent.[35] As it was applied, the classification schema could not sustain its aura of objective truth, and by the time it was abandoned in 1861 the easy-to-understand, shorthand descriptions of the three-tier system had come to seem merely imprecise. The approach that replaced it told a more concrete and individualized (if still brief) story by noting any untoward circumstances attendant on a bankrupt's discharge, for instance recording the length of time a certificate had been suspended and the reasons for the suspension or whether any imprisonment had been ordered. One legal commentator suggested that these new principles would "afford to the commercial world far more reliable information, as to the previous character of the discharged bankrupt who may again seek their confidence, than was attainable under a system of classification so extremely vague in its definitions, and construed with such widely divergent interpretations."[36]

Disappointment with the classification scheme's pretensions to objectivity was not the only reason it met with distrust during the decade it was in operation. By assigning character assessment and the administration of estates to bankruptcy officials, the 1849 law struck some commentators as contributing to a dangerous evasion of creditor responsibility. The *Economist,* in particular, treated skeptically the very possibility that legal reform was the key to safeguarding creditors and the credit market, arguing that "the only effectual guard is individual vigilance, prompted by self-interest." Traders must be made to understand that the best defense against losses was to be found not in law, which might "lull that vigilance to sleep," but in "their own care, vigilance, and intimate knowledge of the character of those they trust."[37] The law's new attempts to be muscular on behalf of creditors could have precisely the effect of atrophying the crucial faculties of prudence and reading character. With this argument the *Economist* lines up with earlier champions of the superior judgment of embedded, interested creditors. Character judgments were crucial, these held, but they were most useful when produced by individuals in the thick of commercial activities and exchanges, rather than after the fact of ruin by disinterested officials applying an abstract system.

The article's emphasis on the timing of character judgments highlights one reason that the certificates produced such dissatisfaction. In the peculiar temporality of credit, where the morality of taking on debt could not be judged until it had reached its conclusion, the certificate was a testimonial to contingency and discontinuity, even as it proffered a confident statement that a character could be fixed and evaluated. Failure was a crisis, a moment that produced a break in the narrative of a working life. The certificate was permission to start afresh; at the same time it also promised a bridge between the two stages of life: the character one had before the crisis was the character that would carry over into the period of second chances. However, this involved a leap of faith: the ruined person, after all, had shown himself to be (or to seem) creditworthy at one moment, but to have failed to bear out that trust. The certificate's offer of a fixed evaluation thus came to appear as "whitewashing," covering over a meaningful change with the sleight of hand that the bankrupt was reborn but yet maintained a continuous character.[38] The certificates, then, highlighted a problem with relying on character at all as a way to contend with business risks: character was enacted, rather than possessed—part of a story that had not yet achieved closure—and a textual judgment rendered at one moment might prove flawed down the road.

Over the course of the decade, frustration with the bankruptcy system persisted. Late in the 1850s the *Economist* denounced the institutional efficacy of the Court of Bankruptcy. But its complaints are themselves beset with ambiguities. The court is, on the one hand, too "rigid": "too uniform and inelastic in its practical operation," containing "no principle of dealing with different cases according to their intrinsic merits," especially "where the character and transactions of the insolvent are in the estimation of creditors above all suspicion." In fact, the article complains that creditors "have little or no influence." On the other hand, within the same paragraph the system is described as too subject to chance and sentiment, such that "where just dissatisfaction and suspicion of fraud exist," whether or not a serious investigation is made is determined by "whether the petition be in the hands of a friendly or a hostile creditor."[39] The article suggests both that rationalization had not been achieved, if accident and creditor feelings still played a role, and that the effort to make the system responsive to shades of moral responsibility had likewise floundered: creditors felt cut off and, despite the gradients available, felt that the certificate was an overly blunt instrument.

Perhaps spurred by the new wave of failures in the commercial crisis of 1857 and by the new company laws and limited liability, which changed the terrain in which credit and investment markets operated, dissatisfaction once again came to a head in the late 1850s. And joining the longstanding concerns over the way character stories were brought into the bankruptcy system, a new line of debate emerges over exactly what the role of such stories should be or whether they should play a role at all. While many commentators continued to value judging character as a means of disciplining debtors and creditors, some shifted the focus away from individual cases, arguing instead that a more generalized social usefulness should be the measure of success. The *Economist* article just mentioned, for instance, goes on to complain that one problem arising from the avoidance of the bankruptcy system lies in lost opportunities to figure out the narratives—factual and moral—of failure. "There is . . . no clear discrimination as to the merits or demerits of each case—no sufficient investigation as to the true origin and causes of the insolvency," the author notes.

The honourable and prudent trader who may have fallen a victim to
a mere temporary and unlooked-for misfortune—who has been in-
duced to suspend payment at the first moment he suspected himself
unable to meet his obligations in full, out of a regard only to the interests of his creditors—who has declined at the risk of involving others
to use the means at his disposal and to trade upon a name and credit
which he enjoyed, to bolster himself up and to attempt to regain a lost
position at the hazard of making it worse,—is confounded and mixed
up in one common catalogue of misfortunes with those who have
for years been in a state of hopeless insolvency—who have exhausted
every means of raising money—who have made every sacrifice of
their creditors' property that was necessary to sustain appearances for
the moment and to postpone the evil day as long as possible—who
have trafficked in accommodation and fictitious paper, fraudulent in
its character—and who are forced to suspend only when some sudden derangement of the money market renders all second-rate and
suspicious paper unnegotiable.

Employing and reaffirming the power of stories, the exemplary mininarra-
tives in this passage, with their dash-heavy punctuation, create a breathlessly
emphatic sense of their status as plots. To fail to discriminate between these
different plots would be, the author notes, "extremely detrimental to the true
interests of trade."[40]
    But more is at stake than a simple failure of justice or a risk that business-
men will be duped by shady traders whose careers have not been checked.
Instead, the failure to tell the stories entails a "great loss to the community,"
a loss of knowledge that matters not because it denies the "just appreciation
of . . . character" on an individual level, but because it fails to illuminate "the
causes which lead to what may be termed national disasters; and . . . the best
means for preventing them in future." To enable this social knowledge, the
author proposes a new model for investigating and narrating cases of ruin: a
"competent tribunal, armed with sufficient authority to reach the facts and
history of the case," should prepare and publish an "authentic report . . . for
the benefit of the creditors, who should then by a legal process have a right to
decide as to the mode in which the estate should be wound up." All the facts
of the case would thus become known through an "authoritative medium,
acting for the creditors and not employed by the debtor." This level of exposure
would leave the public comfortable to judge whether the conduct of a debtor
had been acceptable enough to make composition an appropriate measure or
whether he had been reckless or fraudulent so that "nothing but the Court of

Bankruptcy would do justice to its exposure."[41] Though the makeup of the "tribunal" or "authoritative medium" is not specified, the legalistic resonance of the first term and the mediation of distance and closeness implied by the second suggest that the aim is to balance the claims of creditor interest and the desire for an objective perspective.

Other writers took dissatisfaction with the system's use of stories a step further to argue that whatever their merit, it should not be the responsibility of business to find out the stories behind ruin. Instead they claimed business should focus simply on the efficient recovery of assets, leaving the rest to the law and the state. Two years after publishing the previous article, the *Economist* set forth "a business-like view of the court of bankruptcy." A bankrupt's creditors, the author notes, have as their object "a prompt, equitable division of the bankrupt's assets." But the bankruptcy court has been "occupied with different considerations": finding out "why the bankrupt has failed, whether he ought to have failed or not, whether he is blameable or not, in what degree he is blameable, whether he ought to have a certificate or not, what sort of certificate he ought to have." The focus on moral narratives, character determination, and so forth is misplaced, the writer suggests: "All these questions are matters of public policy, or are interesting solely to the bankrupt himself. None of them are material to the creditors."[42] The article's title overstates the degree to which business abjured its interest in the stories and the moral character of bankrupts. But the view assigning character questions to the courts and the state and property questions to creditors did gain traction within the business community by the early 1860s. For instance, in 1864 the Associated Chambers of Commerce argued for the "fundamental principle" that "questions affecting the person or the character of the bankrupt, or abstract questions of law, belong exclusively to the court, but the duty of realizing and distributing the estate belongs exclusively to the creditors."[43]

In slightly more than a decade, then, business interests went from proposing a measure that insisted on evaluating and documenting character as part of the process of dealing with failure, and from insisting on the superior capacities of interested creditors to put together the story of a failure and to make moral judgments, to an explicit disavowal of creditor interest in playing a role in the moral "winding-up." This is not to say that business lost all concern for finding out the moral status of its agents: in reminders to maintain a vigilant faculty of judgment; in the new certificate's replacement of classification with a straightforward précis of the events deemed morally significant in a case of ruin; and even in the insistence that *some* entity—the courts, the state, or an "authoritative medium"—find out the stories behind failures for the benefit of the nation, a continued concern with character and storytelling is in evidence. Still, although the shift is incomplete, the new willingness to suspend participation in determining moral justice in favor of concentrating on material efficiency is striking. As business took a step away from character, however, other institutions and actors addressed the gap. The legal system, acting with a sense of civic responsibility to a wider market, continued to insist on its own capacity to uncover and render judgments of the moral histories of failure. As the *Law Magazine* put it in 1869, "the state had a duty to interfere and demand an explanation of a debtor as to why he could not pay his debts—it was a question of 'right and wrong' and not just of dividends."[44] Journalists delighted in recounting stories of failures, great and small. And novels, with their often complex formal and epistemological concerns about questions of interest, objectivity, and narrative perspective, took up the issue of ruin and its implications for character. Insofar as business ceded terrain on character, it could do so in part because its concerns were being worried over and addressed—though not always resolved, and not always in ways that business interests would have approved—on other grounds.

The Authoritative Medium

As George Eliot began *The Mill on the Floss,* debt and money were on her mind in a new way: because, for the first time, she could imagine getting them off her mind. In her earlier years she had witnessed the bankruptcy of her sister Chrissy's husband and the efforts of her brother Isaac to help take care of the family following the husband's death. In 1854 she saw John Chapman, the editor of the *Westminster Review,* face bankruptcy and finally work out an arrangement with his creditors with the assistance of family and friends. And for years during the 1850s she lived with George Henry Lewes in small quarters as they both worked to pay off debts that had quite often been contracted by Lewes's wife. With these experiences, Eliot had enough experience with debt and its effects on the debtor's connections to make her reference to the dishonor of debt while thanking Blackwood for an extra payment more than pro forma. *The Mill on the Floss* occasioned complicated contractual discussions intended to capitalize on the success of *Adam Bede;* helped by Lewes, Eliot was able to negotiate terms for the new novel that made her wealthy.[45]

But beyond any personal reasons for the interest in debt, the broader cultural, economic, and political preoccupation with bankruptcy during the 1850s represented a field that offered a ready staging ground for the explorations of abstract and embedded or sympathetic modes of knowledge that had absorbed Eliot in her aesthetic reflections and fictional practice. The questions raised in bankruptcy-reform debates—could impartial standards of character be defined? could a disinterested judge determine a fair and truthful account of a failure? did sympathetic gestures to debtors risk demoralizing them and commercial society more generally? were financially interested creditors likely or unlikely to arrive at fair judgments of debtors? what did failure mean for the continuity of a person's character?—all these were in some sense instantiations of epistemological dilemmas and arguments that preoccupied Eliot throughout her career.

To say that the issues surrounding bankruptcy made up a central ground for Eliot's exploration of abstraction and particularity or embeddedness is to highlight a key, and sometimes overlooked, component in the Victorian debate over these perspectives. A number of accounts of Victorian literature and culture have examined the dynamic tension between what has been called, variously, detachment or objectivity as a means of pursuing knowledge and more embedded, subjective, or situated forms of knowledge. Sensitive to the ways objectivity was itself still being established as a value in the scientific practice of the period, critics have often framed the contrast as one between abstract theoretical thinking that found expression in a scientific objectivity premised on the suppression or overcoming of the self and an epistemology that centered on a defined, situated, and self-conscious observer.[46] Such accounts have suggested that Victorian authors are frequently engaged in efforts to mediate between the two positions. For instance, George Levine's *Dying to Know* uses the radical disembodiment and self-suppression in accounts of scientists and scientific inquiry as an emblem of objectivity. Amanda Anderson, in *The Powers of Distance*, highlights Eliot's contrast in "The Natural History of German Life" of two knowledge-seeking modes: abstract, generalizing sciences such as political economy that formulate rules for predicting and explaining human behavior and a more embedded model of participant observation. For Eliot, Anderson notes, the development of the faculty of sympathy is what abstraction threatens and participant observation promotes. And as she describes other authors who have attempted to mediate between these ways of knowing, sympathy remains a key term in the "interested" side of the equation. This emphasis on sympathy as a characteristic or corollary of "nondetached" epistemologies emerges from many Victorian writers themselves, and it tends, for this good reason, to come to mind when bipolar models of ways of seeking knowledge—disinterested, abstract, and scientific versus embedded and particular—are invoked in accounts of Victorian culture today.[47]

However, the bankruptcy debates of midcentury suggest that a different element might be cast into the mix. The position of the creditor who has a special purchase on the truth *because of*, not in spite of, his interest and implication in the bankruptcy can't be easily accommodated to the notion that interest and embeddedness lead ineluctably to sympathy. Indeed, the economic interest that the creditor embodies is one kind of interest that we assume *both* the detached, objective and the embedded, sympathetic perspectives were to disavow as a stumbling block and a moral impediment to truth. The idea that economic interest could make the successful pursuit of truth *more* likely has thus tended to receive less attention than it might deserve in analyses of the Victorian struggle to evaluate the claims of detachment and interest, especially since it was one of the particular innovations of nineteenth-century thought.[48] The bankruptcy debates are an occasion to reconsider that struggle in order to see in a concrete situation how a perspective that had powerful adherents and a powerful intellectual history in political economic thought comes to be (to a degree) written out of the equation by Victorian literary writers and their later analysts.

As Eliot refined her realist aesthetic in *The Mill on the Floss,* working to produce a particular notion of historical character and to improve her readers' sense of character, she thematized and dramatized different positions within the spectrum of disinterest/abstraction—embeddedness/sympathy and argued explicitly against the notion that economic interest is the key to understanding characters and motivations. But the lessons in character and interpretation that her narrative practice poses present an impossible challenge in the transactions and interactions of daily life: as history and psychology are constructed as the keys to character in Eliot's novel, the grounds for determining character are pushed further and further out of the range of ordinary access.

Very early in *The Mill on the Floss* Eliot presents an extended commentary on character evaluation in which questions of economic interest come to the fore. Seeking a tutor for Tom, Mr. Tulliver asks for a recommendation from the auctioneer and appraiser Mr. Riley, a man who makes it his business to come to accurate judgments of value. After a long discussion in which Riley attempts to persuade the dubious Tulliver that a young clergyman, Stelling, is his man—a discussion peppered with references to Stelling's connections, to Riley contacting Stelling's father-in-law in order to advance the placement of Tom, and to Riley's recommendation holding a great deal of weight with Stelling's family—the narrator embarks on a long challenge to the reader's likely interpretation of details like these. Initially the narrator seems to ally herself with the reader, saluting the imagined reader's insight into Riley's character—"as you perceive, he was a man of very obliging manners" (22)—thus conjuring an interpretation so as to submit it to scrutiny.

And what she determines is that the reader, in paying attention to these details, is likely to be misled:

> [Riley] had really given himself the trouble of recommending Mr Stelling to his friend Tulliver without any positive expectation of a solid, definite advantage resulting to himself, notwithstanding the subtle indications to the contrary which might have misled a too sagacious observer. For there is nothing more widely misleading than sagacity if it happens to get on a wrong scent; and sagacity, persuaded that men usually act and speak from distinct motives, with a consciously proposed end in view, is certain to waste its energies on imaginary game. Plotting covetousness, and deliberate contrivance, in order to compass a selfish end, are nowhere abundant but in the world of the dramatist: they demand too intense a mental action for many of our fellow-parishioners to be guilty of them. It is easy enough to spoil the lives of our neighbours without taking so much trouble: we can do it by lazy acquiescence and lazy omission, by trivial falsities for which we hardly know a reason, by small frauds neutralised by small extravagancies, by maladroit flatteries, and clumsily improvised insinuations. We live from hand to mouth, most of us, with a small family of immediate desires—we do little else than snatch a morsel to satisfy the hungry brood, rarely thinking of seed-corn or the next year's crop. (23)

One of the most obvious purposes of this first lengthy narratorial digression on the process of interpreting character is to undercut the understanding of character as grounded in one fundamental motivation, self-interest, with rational patterns of behavior following from it. The "distinct motive" and "consciously proposed end" that the "too sagacious observer" has discerned is explicitly linked to economic rationality as the passage goes on: "Mr Riley was a man of business, and not cold towards his own interest, yet even he was more under the influence of small promptings than of far-sighted designs" (23). Riley's references to Stelling's father-in-law, Timpson, indicate self-interest, the narrator suggests, but not the kind the reader might expect: Riley does not have an agreement with him, but rather a vaguer hope that his recommendation will make Timpson, who has "a good deal of business, which he knew how to put into the right hands," think of him (23–24). Self-interest is a motive, but expressed in an ad hoc, scattershot way, not leading to a clear narrative explanation of behavior.

In a later episode, Eliot deepens the critique of taking economic self-interest as the key to interpretation when she casts it as merely one of a num-

ber of motivations—and not the first—for Wakem to buy the mill. Eliot
begins by describing Wakem's pleasure at the thought of humiliating Tulliver, who had been an annoyance, then describes his inclination to dabble in
"practical rural matters." Only then do we hear that Wakem has determined
that the mill will be a "capital investment." Even this is not allowed to stand
as an uncomplicated, straightforward statement of rational self-interest.
The sentence immediately follows this assertion of what *should* be the only
motivation that needs mentioning (the mill as good investment) with the
qualification "besides, Guest & Co. were going to bid for it" (224). Wakem's
financial motivation, in other words, is itself intimately linked to the more
psychological and social desire to assert his status in town by snatching a
"capital investment" out from under "a ship-owner and mill-owner who was
a little too loud in the town affairs as well as in his table-talk" (224). By making the supposedly primary motivating force of human nature into merely
one part of a complex mixture, Eliot downgrades it. The reader who takes
the view that we all act out of pure self-interest may have too blunt a notion
of what that interest consists of and the behaviors it may produce, seeing
deliberate action where motives may be muted or haphazard.

To say that economic self-interest is not the singular motivating force
directing human behavior, and that it therefore should not be considered
above all else when describing human character, is not the same thing as saying that economic self-interest presents a cognitive or moral impediment
to character judgment. However, undercutting the primacy of self-interest
undermines one of the premises that gave it epistemological force: that self-
interest would cause a rational, clear-sighted evaluation of character and situations. In passages like the early one on Riley and the later one on Wakem,
Eliot insists that even within the sphere of business (where even if you didn't
see self-interest as paramount in all aspects of human behavior it might be
thought to have its fullest scope) behavior is guided by multiple psychological and social factors: emotions, relationships, social competitiveness, and
so forth. And thus self-interest can't be abstracted from those other qualities
that it is supposed to overcome in situations where character judgment is
required. To illustrate the failure of self-interest to lead to good judgment,
the novel notes that Riley, the appraiser, whose job depends on making eval-
uations, in fact is less than adept at this in part perhaps *because* he is led by
self-interest. Riley wants to make the recommendation, in order to look good
to his friend and business associate and to bolster his standing with Timpson;
he thus needs to see Tulliver as able to take advantage of this recommendation, which he claims will be a good one "for any one that's got the necessary
money." He then asserts, with a confidence that proves to be misplaced, "and

that's what you have, Tulliver" (19). The critique of self-interested judgment is underscored when Riley is himself shown to be implicated in Tulliver's bankruptcy: he has asked the miller to be a surety for a loan, missing his precarious financial position, and has died leaving Tulliver responsible. While the novel dramatizes a relationship between acute character insight and business savvy in the scene in which Tom's partner Bob Jakin sells his wares to Aunt Glegg, recognizing her stinginess and turning it to profit, the scene takes place in a comic register that blunts the challenge it might pose.[49] It cannot trump, for instance, the novel's most telling critique of the purported link between business judgment and moral judgment: the representation of Tom, who stands as an emblem of good business thinking through much of the novel but who is shown to drastically undervalue the character of Maggie, with whom the sympathies of the narrator (and through the narrator, the reader) most palpably lie. In attempting to shape the reader's sense of how one should properly come to evaluate character, then, Eliot begins by questioning the role of self-interest and continues to cast doubt on its effectiveness at moments throughout the novel.

If Eliot quickly undercuts the view that characters are led primarily by self-interest, and through it to good judgment, she also uses the early passage describing Riley's recommendation of Stelling to raise the issue of general or abstract and particular perspectives as ways of gaining knowledge, especially of persons. The grounds for Riley's recommendation, it turns out, are much more tenuous than his confident response would lead one to believe. Instead, Eliot takes the reader through various steps in narrative distance. Riley "had no private understanding with the Rev. Walter Stelling; on the contrary he knew very little of that M.A. and his acquirements":

> But he believed Mr Stelling to be an excellent classic, for Gadsby had said so, and Gadsby's first cousin was an Oxford tutor; which was better ground for the belief than even his own immediate observation would have been, for though Mr Riley had received a tincture of the classics at the great Mudport Free School, and had a sense of understanding Latin generally, his comprehension of any particular Latin was not ready. . . . Then, Stelling was an Oxford man, and the Oxford men were always—no, no, it was the Cambridge men who were always good mathematicians. But a man who had had a university education could teach anything he liked; especially a man like Stelling who had made a speech at a Mudport dinner on a political occasion, and had acquitted himself so well that it was generally remarked, this son-in-law of Timpson's was a sharp fellow. (23)

From the initially posited incorrect presumption that Riley knows Stelling so well as to be in league with him, Eliot leads us further and further from the ground of personal knowledge: someone named Gadsby (who never appears within the novel's diagesis to be judged directly by the reader) vouches for Stelling, with the tenuous qualification of having a cousin at Oxford. Then follows an appeal to common knowledge about the characteristics of Oxford men, which is not even completed before it is undercut, leaving the reader doubting the trustworthiness of the assertion about both Oxford and Cambridge. From "what everybody knows" of Oxford, or maybe Cambridge, men—in which the "everybody" is linked to no specific consciousness or consciousnesses—we move to "what everybody says" about Stelling after his political speech. Here, though there is more of a sense that real speakers are behind this than in the previous example, the impersonal passive phrasing "it was generally remarked" leaves the reader with no notion of the agents doing the remarking: their number, their astuteness, their interests are all unclear, as is the question of whether Riley himself witnessed the speech.

By displaying the levels of abstraction through which a supposedly personal judgment and recommendation may be filtered, Eliot leads the reader to question the kinds of character statements that commonly pass as having their origins in personal knowledge. But there is a tension in the passage between Eliot's critique of the reliance on abstracted perspectives and her own ironic narrative perspective. Eliot's irony depends on an intimate penetration of the motivations and consciousness of the character represented, often in free indirect discourse or in an even more direct collapsing of the narrator's voice with the character's thought (Riley's "no, no, it was the Cambridge men," for instance, a slip into the direct representation of his internal voice). But the narrator represents, of course, another kind of abstracted perspective, especially insofar as she has this privileged access to a character's interiority and history. And strikingly, as the passage progresses into a further challenge to the reader's interpretation of Riley's character to this point, with a plea for the reader to hold off on judging him harshly, the narrator's vision becomes wider and her voice more tuned to the general register. Rhetorical questions frame themselves as speaking a truth that would compel general assent: "Why should an auctioneer and appraiser thirty years ago, who had as good as forgotten his free-school Latin, be expected to manifest a delicate scrupulosity which is not always exhibited by gentlemen of the learned professions, even in our present advanced state of morality?" (24). Gnomic statements abound: "It is always chilling in friendly intercourse, to say you have no opinion to give"; "a man with the milk of human kindness in him can scarcely abstain from doing a good-natured action" (24). With the quasi-proverbial invocation of Shakespeare, the language itself borrows from a common stock. And with the reference to the laws of nature in the image of the "inconvenient parasite" whose welfare is cared for, and its quasi-utilitarian justification that Stelling will benefit by the recommendation, the narrator invokes abstract principles of a different sort (24).

To be sure, there is an ironic edge to all of these appeals to the general, as there is in the investigation of the particular circumstances of Riley's thinking. But the mixture of appeals to the general and accounts of the specific in which the narrative voice enters the character's nonetheless has the effect of producing a certain sympathy, especially the sympathetic process, described by Rae Greiner, of "going along with" another mind.[50] It is significant that it is hard to tell whether a rhetorical question like "why then should he not recommend Stelling?" (24) is an example of free indirect discourse reporting Riley's rationalization or a rhetorical question aimed to highlight the reader's assent to a general truth. The ambiguity, which depends on the reader's inclusion in the general perspective, puts the reader in the character's place, enacting a variety of sympathetic exchange. This is somewhat different from the dichotomy that has been drawn, for instance by Anderson, from Eliot's interest in participant-observation as a way to approach the world, which sees a strategy attempting to "mediate between sympathetic immersion and detached analysis and judgment."[51] The narrative strategies that produce sympathy here depend as much on the rhetorical power of abstraction and appeals to the general, and the narrator's ability to give it voice, as on immersion in the character's particular situation. As Greiner suggests, "a full and impersonal comprehension of the human situation is achievable only by way of human situatedness," but it is the "oscillation between proximity and distance" that produces the best ethical response.[52]

The passage thus moves toward a consolidation of the power of the narrative voice as a perspective that can penetrate the particular, analyze and define the general, and mediate between the two to generate a new, sympathetic mode of interpreting character. This demonstration of and argument for narrative authority is not necessarily an unusual posture for a Victorian novel to adopt and certainly not out of keeping for Eliot, whose narrative voice has often been described in terms of its wisdom, its "grown-upness"— or, from a more skeptical standpoint, its moralizing, its intrusiveness, its tendency to turn social questions into matters of psychology or ethics. But viewed against the various uses of and expectations for character that I have traced in this book, it looks somewhat more strange. The discourse around failure in the 1850s, with its emphasis on the need for creditors to apprehend character clearly as a means of avoiding losses through bankruptcy and insol-

vency, placed character at the forefront of legal, political, and economic debate. Eliot's early meditation on character interpretation in the Riley passage,
while maintaining an instructional aspect, does little to bolster the reader's
confidence in his or her own interpretive capacity. In fact, the reader is prepared, in part, to accept the assertion of narrative authority as the chapter
winds up because the early part of the passage has assiduously worked to shift
the balance of interpretive authority away from the reader—even, or perhaps
especially, the diligent one—and toward the narrator.

Eliot begins, as noted, by positing an observant reader: "as you perceive,
he was a man of very obliging manners." But this perceptiveness quickly turns
into a problem; the imagined reader is not "sagacious" but "too sagacious"—
"misled" by his very competence with the details of the text as he concentrates
on the "subtle indications" that Riley has been motivated by self-interest that
the narrator acknowledges dwells in her account of the exchange between
him and Tulliver. The reader's mistake has been not only to assume the pre-
dominance of self-interest but also to assume that the appraiser behaves as
if he is in a narrative—"with a consciously proposed end in view" and with
"plotting covetousness"—one that resembles the vision of a "dramatist." The
reader has, in other words, done a good job of noticing the subtle details
that contribute to a portrayal of character but has nonetheless failed to interpret Riley correctly because he has seen him *as* a character, supplying a
story that grows out of a theory to make sense of the details he observes.
The extended passage that follows detailing Riley's history, his connections,
even his thoughts, suggests that the reader's inadequacies will be inevitable:
by positing a real life that is unlike the structure of stories, that proceeds
through small actions responding to "immediate desires," as opposed to a
future-oriented narrative pattern, and by fleshing out that real life with histories, complex networks, motivations and thoughts, and accidents and contingencies that only a narrator can provide, Eliot builds her narrative authority
on top of readerly failures that are not so much failures *of competence* as they
are competent failures.[53]

A later passage introducing the character of Wakem to the reader highlights once again the narrator's authority. "You have never seen Mr Wakem
before, and are possibly wondering whether he was really as eminent a rascal,
and as crafty, bitter an enemy of honest humanity in general" as Mr. Tulliver
has represented him, Eliot begins, directly offering the reader an opportunity
to examine the way character knowledge is achieved: "It is really impossible
to decide this question by a glance at his person: the lines and lights of the
human countenance are like other symbols—not always easy to read without
a key. On an *a priori* view of Wakem's aquiline nose, which offended Mr Tul-

liver, there was not more rascality than in the shape of his stiff shirt-collar, though this too, along with his nose, might have become fraught with damnatory meaning when once the rascality was ascertained" (219). The passage that follows Mrs. Tulliver's meeting with Wakem shows a movement from generalizations and abstractions that sound suspiciously like the "maxims" that Wakem himself is said to avoid judging by (223)—and that the narrator later will call into question as she condemns the "man of maxims" who derives moral judgments from "general rules" without "patience, discrimination, impartiality," and "fellow-feeling" (435)—to specific thoughts, feelings, and secrets. On the one hand, Wakem's relationship to Tulliver is compared to that of a pike to a roach, in a kind of fable; the description prompts references to "human nature" and to aphoristic statements about the relative pleasures derived from different ways of defeating an enemy (222). On the other, the narrator introduces Wakem's particular complex of psychological motivations—snobbery, business interest, competitiveness—and adds the secret that he has an illegitimate son. This son serves almost no plot purpose: he provides a tangible positive reason why Wakem would want to buy the mill, and a quick reference to his proving a disappointment later on provides a rationale for Wakem to agree to sell the mill back when Philip proposes it. But he does stand as an emblem of the way the private and secret is made central in Eliot's account of character truths.[54] And he underscores the power of the narrator, who is the only source for this secret. In fact, it is hard to imagine a "key" for character interpretation, if a key for reading symbols is something that holds general significance, something that can be taken to other occasions for interpretation. As the passage ends, it returns to its generalizing mode in a playfully proverbial tone, referencing a "remark of a great philosopher" underscoring the importance of understanding psychologies that may be different from our own: "fly-fishers fail in preparing their bait . . . for want of a due acquaintance with the subjectivity of fishes" (224). The narrator advances a general rule that we must know subjectivity to make judgments, but in the example of her text the only possible keys to that subjectivity emerge in an ad hoc way, delivered by a narrator who alone has access to subjectivity's private content.

Audrey Jaffe has described the omniscient narrator as "a fantasy of knowledge, mobility, and authority" that "can come into being only in contrast to limitation, which is constructed in the form of character."[55] In *The Mill on the Floss,* Eliot's omniscience comes into being also in contrast to the limitations with which she hems in her readers, who over and over are positioned as trying and failing to read the character signs they encounter. What was at stake in breaking down the reader's sense of competence and bolstering the narrator's power? Viewed within the bankruptcy debates of the late 1850s, the strong assertion of narratorial authority that this passage establishes early in *The Mill on the Floss* offers a compelling fantasy to a culture that was obsessed with knowing how to read character but dubious about its abilities and undecided about whether objective or embedded perspectives would give the best purchase. In one sense, though their final products are as different as can be, Eliot's narrator shows the same kind of skepticism about the abilities of her reader as did the proponents of the certificate, who longed for a simple, objective shorthand that would bypass messy particularities and individual idiosyncrasies and inadequacies in reading character. Her effort to demonstrate the shortfalls of standards of character judgment that take interest as the key motivation leaves the reader with the need for some new model. Rather than a simple classification, however, Eliot goes to the other extreme, presenting complexity, moral ambiguity, and historical continuity with a confidence and authority that the certificates never managed to achieve. But like the certificate, determined by disinterested judges, Eliot's model delivers character from elsewhere, evading, as Jaffe puts it, "presence" and its "consequences"—consequences that would leave creditors and debtors, readers and characters, seeking the "truth" of character in psychologies and histories to which they can't have access, through signs that will not fail to prove limited.[56]

"I only wish I could write something that would contribute to heighten men's reverence before the secrets of each other's souls, that there might be less assumption of entire knowingness, as a datum from which inferences are to be drawn," Eliot wrote to Charles Bray in the midst of composing *The Mill on the Floss*.[57] It is a striking statement, seeming to undermine a goal (knowledge of character) and a practice (drawing inferences from particulars) that were important features of realism and its demands on readers, as practiced by Eliot and others, and to fly in the face of the widespread desire to imagine a way to access character truths. But in order to create the "reverence," Eliot first has to construct the secrets. By pressing at what Dorrit Cohn has called the essence of fictionality, the "penetrative optic" that gives access to interior consciousness—dramatizing character, invoking inadequate interpretations, and then offering both expansive and penetrating views as correctives—Eliot enables a fantasy of a full representation of character, a perspective and form that can authoritatively bridge apparently discontinuous histories, probe motivation, and offer glimpses of interiority.[58] This model, placing character truth in interior thought and feeling, historical details, and other details that will only be able to be delivered by an omniscient narrator, leaves the reader—or the observer of actual persons—at a distinct disadvantage.

By aligning Eliot's reader and an everyday observer of character, I do not mean to suggest that actual observers would confuse real people for novelistic characters nor that they would ordinarily *expect* to achieve in their own lives the access that is fiction's special illusion. But Eliot's model of character does represent an imaginative horizon shared across different interpretive situations (though more or less out of reach), the common ground evidenced by the creation of a center of authority in the novel's narrator that echoes the cultural and commercial wish for just such authority brought to the fore by episodes of failure and debates over policies to deal with it. The *Economist* writer who in 1858 longed for an "authoritative medium" to mediate between the interests of creditors and an objective perspective on debt might have found an example in Eliot. In her uncanny ability to channel the thoughts, feelings, and memories of her characters and to place them within a wider historical and cultural field, Eliot's narrator seems to fulfill the medium's role. But the question of the narrator's interest is more complicated than a direct parallel would suggest. The *Economist* writer clearly began with the presumption that the creditor's interests were paramount—the medium would be *"acting for the creditors and not employed by the debtor"*—even as a certain objective distance was suggested to be desirable. The narrator of *The Mill on the Floss,* in contrast, seems able to probe and even enter the interests of *many* characters through gestures of sympathetic imagination. This critical difference suggests the way that though Eliot's posture of authority speaks to the same fantasy that was expressed in the bankruptcy debate, it simultaneously charts a path that challenges the commercial model of interest and the state/legalistic model of disinterest that formed its two poles.

I have been emphasizing Eliot's narrator's abilities to span the general and the particular, to speak with an authority as if from on high, separate from the fray experienced by her characters. However, at a couple of moments Eliot's narrator embeds herself within the novel, adding a peculiar, intermittent aspect of flesh-and-blood presence. The novel famously begins with a dreamy scene of memory, set up as if it were an interlude in a conversation between reader and narrator. The narrator's bodily presence is suggested by making her subject to weaknesses of the flesh; she has "dozed off" in the midst of telling us of the Tullivers, waking to find her arms "really benumbed" at being pressed against the arms of her chair (8). She is constructed as a real presence within the dream memory, too, as she takes the reader in present tense past the river, which seems "like a living companion," and watches the little girl who becomes Maggie as the story proper opens (7). A somewhat different insistence on the physical proximity of the narrator to the story occurs later in the novel, when the narrator steps back from the plot to give the reader a historical perspective on St. Ogg's in order to contextualize the characters. In this moment when her more expansive, abstracted perspective comes to the fore, she simultaneously steps forward to replace distanced textual knowledge with a perspective constructed as more immediate, guiding her "refined readers" into the town to give them a more direct vantage onto commercial scenes and agricultural products that they would so far know only "through the medium of the best classic pastorals" (103). A change from the manuscript version of the novel personalizes the textual sources that are invoked as she presents the history of St. Ogg's: the impersonal "there are several manuscript sources" became in revision "I possess several manuscript versions" (104n5), a double-edged image suggesting that histories are multiple and textual, but also that they have an aura of immediacy as the products of embodied writers (manuscripts as opposed to printed books) and that the narrator has a personal connection (through possession) to this immediate access to history.

Such suggestions of the physical presence of the narrator remain merely gestural in the novel; the narrator never really is placed in a defined, narrated relation to the characters. An oddly deliberate gesture like this requires explanation. By suggesting that the narrator is a "real" person, one with tangible connections to the town and its inhabitants, Eliot creates a posture that, as Harry Shaw has noted, asks her reader to consider the narrator as subject to the "constraints of history" in the same way as her characters and her readers, in order to bolster the narrator's ethical authority.[59] Certainly the gesture of making her narrator a more tangible presence, only to transcend the limitations of particular consciousness, creates a stronger image of the ideal moral practice of sympathy that Eliot lays out for her reader. But whether this gesture suffices to render Eliot's narrator subject to the "constraints of history" is much less clear, for in a crucial respect—especially noteworthy in a novel that centers on economic as well as sexual and social ties and obligations, in which characters are represented as bound to one another by a dense network of financial, emotional, and familial responsibilities and exchanges—Eliot's narrator is without the particular interests that these relationships involve.

However, as *The Mill on the Floss* progresses, Eliot refigures the question of interest by transforming the language of debt and spreading it across the social field. Indeed, as the economic debt of the Tulliver family is worked off, losing its force as a motor of the plot, it is replaced by new invocations of debt that come to characterize social, emotional, and familial bonds.[60] As the narrator plays different instances of the language of debt against each other, the ties that it invokes are multiplied and the balance of interest is shifted.

On the one hand, a pattern representing human and social connection in terms of debt gains prominence and authority as the novel progresses. Early in the novel, for instance, Maggie's childhood vow to kiss Philip is depicted as a "void" promise, going unfulfilled because the gender and sexual norms of adulthood interfere with its realization (166). This emotional debt, indeed, might be seen to provide a motivating force for the working out of the financial plot, rather than the other way around, as Poovey has recently argued, as this debt structuring Maggie and Philip's relationship comes to be imagined (by her cousin Lucy Deane, as well as by Philip and Maggie herself, to an extent) as a way to resolve the Tullivers' ruin by returning them to their original property. Indeed, Maggie is the central figure in this pattern; perhaps the strongest representation of human connection as debt occurs as Maggie fends off her attraction to Lucy's intended, Stephen Guest, and makes her decision to return to St. Ogg's after their journey down the river, invoking the language of claims, debts, and obligations to make her case: "we owed ourselves to others, and must conquer every inclination which could make us false to that debt" (416). Stephen responds by picking up on the language of debt, asking "who can have so great a claim" on Maggie as he does, and then twists it to invoke the slate-cleaning of bankruptcy, suggesting, "We must accept our own actions and start afresh from them. . . . In a few hours you will be legally mine, and those who had claims on us will submit—they will see that there was a force which declared against their claims" (418, 419). The well-known passage imagining the reaction of the "world's wife" to Maggie's actions, which declares disapprovingly (in the voice of the world's wife) that she had been "so much indebted to her friends," nonetheless represents Stephen's analysis as correct: the world's wife *would*, ultimately, be willing to clear the score and allow a more or less fresh start to the couple if they were to return married (428, 429). Maggie's choice to remain indebted—her steadfast sense of obligation to her home, her past, her family, and her friends in the face of such willingness to "start afresh"—is part of what produces her as a moral center for the novel; the debts Maggie imagines are those things that embed her in her history and in her family and community. By refusing the fresh start and insisting on human relationships as debts, Eliot places the keys to character knowledge in individual emotional and psychological ties, formed over time in personal histories.[61]

In this, as in all of Eliot's extraordinarily complex novels, there always seems to be an "on the other hand." Another strand in *The Mill on the Floss* is critical of using debt to model representations of emotional and social relationships. The "world's wife," after all, is not represented as a particularly acute moral arbiter, and the use of debt to characterize Maggie's relation to

her family is therefore perhaps suspect. At an earlier moment Philip bris-
tles at his father's suggestion that in maintaining a connection to Maggie he
hasn't made him the proper "return" for his indulgences and care, rejecting
his father's use of the language of debt: "You have been an indulgent father
to me; but I have always felt that it was because you had an affectionate wish
to give me as much happiness as my unfortunate lot would admit of—not
that it was a debt you expected me to pay by sacrificing all my chances of happiness to satisfy feelings of yours, which I can never share" (371). For Philip,
for Tom, who takes on the burden of his father's emotional debts (his hatred
of Wakem) as well as financial ones, and even for Maggie, for whom readers
have chafed as she follows her feeling of obligation to the past, sensing in
particular that fulfilling the debt to Philip with marriage would be an unsat-
isfying conclusion to her story, human-connection-as-debt can look like a
model that tramples individual choice and independence.

The tension between the moral force that the model of debt holds in the
novel and the competing view that debt is a stifling and ungenerous way to
imagine human relationships can be to some extent reconciled by recognizing the differences in the kinds of debt invoked in both circumstances. What
allows debt to generate a sense of moral authority is for it to be embraced by
the debtor, as when Maggie voluntarily chooses her home obligations, recognizing the importance of the ties to the past, to her community, to her family.
When a creditor's position and interest in the debt are invoked or implied,
the relationship becomes suspect, as when the world's wife or Mr. Wakem
implies some interest in payback. The former position, embraced as it is by
Maggie, seems to be where the novel leads. And the language of debt recurs
elsewhere in Eliot's oeuvre as a way to figure the claims of the social: "every
bond of your life is a debt," says Savonarola in *Romola*.[62] However, if we all
become debtors through our immersion in a social world, then we must also
all be creditors to each other. What Eliot attempts to do, then, is to imagine
a new kind of interest for creditors—interest without the "self-" attached.
As players in relationships of debt, she suggests, we become "interested," and
through this interest, this recognition of embeddedness, we may gain access
to the deepest moral truths of character, emerging from the emotional, familial, and community histories that debt represents. But to preserve the moral
clarity and authority that the recognition of mutual indebtedness can provide, we must never conceive of ourselves as having a *particular* interest, one
that redounds to ourselves as a creditor seeking repayment. The narrator of
The Mill on the Floss represents this model of interest without self-interest:
disembodied and departicularized enough that even choosing the gendered

pronoun with which to refer to it has proven difficult, yet not absolutely so and still part of the social fabric; connected, but without a self that can make claims.[63]

A scene that challenges multiple contemporary resonances of debt and bankruptcy helps to illustrate Eliot's attempts to rethink notions of claims and interests and the role narrative was imagined to play in this reevaluation. As Mr. Tulliver lies unconscious, the family gathers to sort out his affairs, and the matter of his loan to his sister's husband, Mr. Moss, comes up. Mrs. Moss reveals that a note promising to pay the £300 loan exists, and the family confronts the issue of whether or not to destroy it. Such an act was considered tantamount to the destruction or theft of the creditor's property in bankruptcy law. The 1849 Bankrupt Law Consolidation Act, for instance, makes it a felony, punishable by transportation or imprisonment, for a bankrupt not to "discover all his Real and Personal Estate, and how, and to whom, upon what Consideration, and when he disposed of, assigned, or transferred any of such Estate (and all Books, Papers, and Writings relating thereunto, except such Part as shall have been really and bonâ fide before sold or disposed of in the way of his Trade, or laid out in the ordinary Expense of his Family)." It was a misdemeanor to "destroy, alter, mutilate or falsify any of his Books, Papers, Writings, or Securities."[64]

Tom's role in this debate departs from the rigidity with which he treats most questions of conduct throughout the novel.[65] A case in point: Tom believes his father to be bankrupt, though this is revealed to be merely the product of his "untechnical mind," which sees no distinction between asking creditors "to take less than their due" and bankruptcy (216). But despite his belief that his father is bankrupt, Tom isn't led to take advantage of bankruptcy's provisions to wipe away debts; instead, directed by a stricter code of responsibility than the law technically required, he labors to repay his father's creditors. In contrast, in the scene debating what to do about Moss's debt, Tom favors destroying the note, insisting that his father never meant to ask for the money, preferring to treat it as a gift to his needy sister. In fact, the scene shows Tom as steadfast in upholding an antirationalized code of property ethics as he is in upholding a strict code that debts should be repaid—both models that bankruptcy challenged, with its assertion of a uniform standard of properties and debts that looked past their social embeddedness and its affirmation that debts could be wiped clean. Affirming the priority of a generational principle about the relation of fathers and sons and of the sibling relationship over the rationalized relationship of debtor and creditor, Tom says, "I ought to obey my father's wish about his property" (194). In upholding these principles of social connection over economic reasoning, Tom grounds connection in a debt that has no self-interested creditor.

This challenge to the rationalizing tendencies of bankruptcy law prompts cries of approval from Maggie and her aunt and seems intended to evoke the same in the reader. But the approval is not imagined to be automatic; the reader is led through various arguments intended to support this affront to current principle.[66] As Eliot delivers the debate, Tom's uncles Pullet and Glegg express the prevailing view that destroying the note would be an alienation of property that could draw the attention of "the constable" (193). Mr. Glegg, indeed, explicitly raises the issue of the creditors' perspective on the action: "I've been a creditor myself, and seen no end o' cheating" (194). Significantly, though, this comes at the very moment where he accedes to the plan to destroy the note, overriding the creditors' self-interested perspective on the morality of the action: "we shouldn't be doing any wrong by the creditors, supposing your father *was* bankrupt. . . . If he meant to give your aunt the money before he ever got into this sad work o' lawing, it's the same as if he'd made away with the note himself; for he'd made up his mind to be that much poorer" (194). For Mr. Glegg and Tom, the key to justifying their action is to consider Mr. Tulliver's decisions in a temporal perspective—to get the narrative straight. As Tom concisely puts it, if Mr. Tulliver "had made up his mind to give [Mrs. Moss] the money before he was in debt, he had a right to do it" (194). The debate over the note is one of the rare occasions in which Tom steps in and narrates a story, a memory of the conversation he had with his father in which his wishes were made clear; he blushes and hesitates as he tells it, but it is the power of creating a narrative in which motivations, intentions, and interests are traced through time and understood from a perspective that acknowledges debt as a mode of deep connection that permits their claim for the justice of sympathetic action. The act of narration is the act that can make the notion of interest without self-interest real—and that can trump the claims of self-interest to get at the truth as it considers the historical, emotional, and social ties that construct a character and his or her actions of moral consequence.

As *The Mill on the Floss* took up the challenges that ruin presented to a commercial culture preoccupied with the role of character, it undermined this role even as it elaborated a mode of writing character that seemed to fulfill the fantasy of complete knowledge. Eliot's mode of realism, with its emphasis on psychology and history as the sites of character truths, promised to fill in the details and to bridge the historical gaps highlighted by business failures and the forms of character evaluation, such as the classification of certificates, that were proposed to deal with them. However, that historical and psychological emphasis, and the assumption of narrative authority in positing and delivering these hard-to-access aspects of human experience, paradoxically meant less room for readers to take the lessons of their novel reading into account in everyday commercial practice. In addition, Eliot's reevaluation of interest, constructing a posture that enacted a movement between embeddedness and abstraction, challenged the role of self-interest in producing accurate moral judgments. As Eliot's mode of writing character grew in prestige and influence, therefore, it tended to crowd out the specific epistemological claims of interested, commercial character judgments.

The bankruptcy debates, and the response of business to the problems ruin posed, form a kind of flashpoint in the career of business character, in which fault lines between changing literary discourses of character and the needs of business emerge. To a degree, then, the story that this chapter has told seems to track the pattern of separation between the literary and the economic that Poovey has argued typifies nineteenth-century writing, as self-referential formalism becomes the norm in literary fiction. To the extent that Eliot and other novelists succeeded in constructing psychological depth and historical complexity as the truth of character, it became more likely for the split between character knowledge and efficiency to be instituted in the business community's responses to ruin. By the early 1860s recovering the "real" in the aftermath of ruin could have different meanings depending on whether one's instrument was the novel or the double-entry account ledger.

However, fault lines are not schisms: if there is separation, there is also a continued pressure, a mutually constructive friction, as literary and business character move alongside each other. Character does not vanish from business calculations, concerns, or practices, as the next chapter will make clear— and novelistic and realist modes of reading and representing character do not become entirely irrelevant to participants in commercial activities. Nor do commercial modes of interpreting character lose all force in reading. For instance, the persistence of businesslike language describing the effectiveness of the Dodsons in *The Mill on the Floss* in E. S. Dallas's review of Eliot's next novel, *Silas Marner*, demonstrates that Eliot's assumptions of authority and her arguments for a sublimity of character against approaches that treated people as collections of data to be interpreted were not wholly successful: "Mean as the Dodson family are, yet, having the elements of their character before us, we see that they are calculable elements, and we can forecast their legitimate results."[67]

Perhaps most important, however, the mid-Victorian responses to ruin may prompt us to reconsider the status of form and formalism in arguments about the Victorian writing of business. In their own way, bankruptcy reformers engaged in formal experimentation, trying out different modes of narrative and nonnarrative representation to achieve an authoritative version of character. We should not underestimate the distinctions between the products of their efforts to create a self-contained, complete character form and the psychologically and historically rich forms that novelists worked to elaborate. But neither should we overlook what they may have in common. In the bankruptcy debates, self-contained formal completeness represents less a point of rupture between fiction and business writing than a shared fantasy. Formalism is one in a set of possible representational responses to the challenges of commercial practice, rather than an endpoint or fork in the road. As such, the will-to-form signals the urgency of maintaining a perspective that keeps business and literary writing on common historical ground.

4

The Heir Apparent

GENDER AND THE TRANSMISSION OF TALENT
IN MARGARET OLIPHANT'S *HESTER*

ONE OF THE MOST ENDURING MYTHS OF THE VICTORIAN BUSINESS
life story is captured in the concept of self-help. Despite business biographies' recognition of the influence of family origins and assistance, and despite the very real roles that context, relationships, and institutions played in molding an actual life in business, in the Victorian cultural imagination the self-made businessman enjoyed pride of place. With his creation of the commercial fabulist Josiah Bounderby, the Coketown manufacturer in *Hard Times,* Dickens trained a parodic focus on this quality of self-making and the stories that enabled it to be taken for granted. It is Bounderby's remarkable, invented, autobiographical *narrative* that is a masterpiece of self-making—not his life. And it is the assistance and love of family that Bounderby most explicitly denies in order to enact this self-making. Cast aside by his heartless mother, left to a drunken grandmother (or so his story goes), womb and bosom are replaced by the gutter; rather than the sustenance of family lifting him up, his rise becomes an individual triumph over the muck that might have sucked him down. "Don't you deceive yourself by supposing for a moment that I am a man of family," Bounderby informs the well-born dilettante James Harthouse upon his arrival in Coketown, and though the immediate context for the term implies political and social connection, Bounderby's self-narration makes clear that in not being "a man of family" he is independent also of ordinary domestic origins.[1]

More specifically, however, Bounderby's self-authoring seems determined to root out not just family but mothers. Mother and grandmother are elaborately and imaginatively rewritten, while the father who died when Bounderby was young barely figures as a narrative presence in the industrialist's tales. In countering this self-construction, Dickens's narrative of the industrialist's character pays similar attention to the maternal. Many of the novel's most powerful emotional effects, in fact, are achieved by highlighting the pathetic figure of the living mother, Mrs. Pegler, shunted aside with a pension and required not to contact her son, who nonetheless ventures to town now and then to "take a proud peep" at him.[2]

This strong maternal focus is not strictly necessary to *Hard Times*'s challenge to the notion that business success is grounded in the pure assertion of personal character and individual will. As the biographies I discuss in chapter 2 suggest, both fathers and mothers (and their kin) might be sources of capital, and both contribute to the formation of character through education and example. The reasons why Dickens and Bounderby would nonetheless place special emphasis on *female* family members are, in many ways, overdetermined. As vehicles of social critique, mothers are symbolically resonant of the ethic of care absent in the Coketown world. A mother who works—as Mrs. Pegler does, keeping "a little village shop" in order to give her son educational advantages and pay for his apprenticeship—carries particular ideological baggage, saddling Bounderby with a realistic marker of lower-class origins that he combats with his fantastic account of triumph over poverty and disconnection.[3]

Reading Bounderby's stories through the historical lens of contemporary concerns with business character, I add another observation about the focus on mothers: it calls biology into the text. By highlighting Bounderby's *maternal* line, Dickens emphasizes the familial tie—the mother-child relationship—that most directly asserts a biological bond. In fact, through a debate that gained steam as Victorian science grew more and more interested in the processes of heredity and evolutionary change and their relationship to character and ability, mothers represented not merely a relationship that could undermine the notion of self-making but also a crucial biological contribution to the raw materials of the self with which one started. The common belief that scientists confronted placed mothers at the center of the mystery of the origins of genius: "men of talent," as one writer put it, "are always indebted for what gives them distinction to their mothers, either in the way of an inheritance of natural ability, or through the means of unusually good nurture and education."[4] Bounderby's narrative denies nurture and education—the help that he received from his mother. And as he disavows his mother's business talents—her ability to keep that "little village shop," to "pinch" and "put by"—he denies her potential contribution to his natural ability as well.[5]

What is present as a trace in Dickens's text—the possibility of a biologically based, inherited "talent" for business—emerges more directly in business biographies and journalistic accounts, in which biological tropes such as heredity and instinct become increasingly frequent. Debates over scientific understandings of the relation between mind and body, and of the heritability of mental and moral qualities, generated new ways of conceiving of character, breaking it down into parts, imagining its measurability, and placing it (or its components) within evolutionary narratives. As it was invoked in business contexts, the concept of heredity intensified the personal, offering explanations for success and decline that were lodged in the body. Here was a new promise: highlighting physical origins would address the perennial problem of character's openness and indeterminacy as a historical, performative, and narrative form, always subject to change. In the hereditary, materialist conception of character, elements of talent or aptitude came to share equal prominence with ethical and temperamental tendencies. Conceiving of these elements of character in terms of inborn traits could make the personal live up to expectations for efficacy in the marketplace, as new, apparently empirical grounds for truth, backed by the prestige of science, would supplement or supplant the knowledge gained in everyday character transactions through reading and interpretation.

And yet that promise of a new, determinative empiricism was elusive. Though the language of heredity personalized, it also dispersed character qualities throughout familial lineages, rendering them intergenerational properties whose transmission was not always predictable or constant. They might decline, mysteriously vanish, appear in unlikely or inappropriate places. Atavistic reversions could present unpleasant surprises. In a pre-Mendelian intellectual context, there was no firm consensus about how exactly the transmission occurred nor about just what was being passed on. Could talents *particular to business* be defined and transmitted? Or only more general personal qualities—aptitudes, intelligence, moral or characterological inclinations—that would be commercially beneficial but less specifically demonstrative? Could hereditary business talent really be isolated from other familial contributions, or did nurture (education, example) or social connection and influence confound its effect? More to the point, were properties of hereditary talents being confused with other forms of property: was an apparent familial instinct or genius for business really just an effect of earlier familial success—not talent breeding talent, but family capital breeding family capital? With so much uncertainty in professional scientific discourse, perhaps it is no wonder that many popular appropriations of scientific language invoke biological concepts as a new aspect of enchantment—a new language for designating what remained ultimately mysterious.

Other scientific or pseudoscientific notions that linked character and mind to physical sources—phrenology, for example—made appearances in commercial discourse. But heredity became particularly significant. First, as

I have suggested, it shaped discussions of self-help, suggesting physical limitations to the transformative possibilities theoretically available through
the conjuncture of character and capitalism. In addition, heredity was an especially salient conceptual framework to bring to the context of the family
firm, an organizational form that retained an enormous significance across
the economy, from small, local businesses to the highest reaches of finance.
(The Rothschilds, icons of international finance, were a favorite example of
business instinct running in the family.)[6] The question of intergenerational
succession—how a firm would survive and thrive when leadership was family
bound, as it passed from older to younger members—made the issue of the
transmission of talent a source of concern.

Heredity presented yet another conceptual challenge in a commercial
context that was normatively masculine since, as my reading of Bounderby's
story suggests, the language of heredity drew women into the picture. As
Gillian Beer has noted, "the new emphasis on genetic descent as the primary
means of storying the past" made it "necessary to recognize the generative
power of the mother," offering women a point of entry into narratives (and
institutional forms: Dombey *and Son*) from which they had been marginal-
ized.[7] In an 1866 address to the British Association for the Advancement of
Science, W. R. Grove took note of the way that "the long-continued conventional habit of tracing pedigrees through the male ancestor" had made it easy
to forget "that each individual has a mother as well as a father, and there is no
reason to suppose that he has in him less of the blood of the one than of the
other."[8] Add the gendered laws and norms of property, inheritance, and labor
to the "conventional habit" of thought about intergenerational relationships,
and the unsettling, anomalous effect that heredity might have in bringing
women into the active story of the family firm becomes apparent. It was easy
to conceive of women as vehicles infusing property into a firm through marriage. But the implications for understanding business character as well as
women's economic subjectivity were less clear when women were imagined
as vehicles for transmitting talents and character traits that they were not, in
principle, supposed to express fully themselves.

In this final chapter I examine how biological concepts shaped visions of
commercial character, offering new puzzles along with promised reassurance,
new languages to contain uncertainty even as they introduced sources of
risk. The scientific, physicalized model of character represented a powerful
alternative to the models represented in literary writing. Margaret Oliphant's
1883 novel *Hester*, centered on an intergenerational drama that is both familial and commercial, offers a case through which to explore the representational challenges that literary writers experienced as they engaged the new

science and the expectations for character in the culture of personal business. Published the same year as Francis Galton's *Inquiries into Human Faculty and Its Development*, which first introduced the term *eugenics*, the novel's representation of generational tensions within a family bank is preoccupied with the formation and expression of character within the competing imperatives of self-making and familial determination. However, *Hester* stages these concerns through a plot that highlights glitches, indirections, and, most significantly, gender reversals as it traces the transmission of "business genius" through the family. Reading *Hester* alongside contemporary discussions of the heredity of business talent, I argue that the novel's unconventional mapping of talent, heredity, and gender challenged its readers to reevaluate not only the categories through which they conceived business character but also the narratives that shaped them. In the case *Hester* develops against the privileging of heredity lies an assertion of the novel's continued authority to represent commercial character and the value of its instruction in interpretation for readers navigating the character transactions that an everyday life in business entailed.

"Bon chien chasse de race": The Heritability of Business Talent

In an epigraph from Charles Lamb's ballad "Hester," Oliphant's novel opens by foregrounding the role of nature in character formation:

> I know not by what name beside
> I shall it call: if 'twas not pride
> It was a joy to that allied
>   She did inherit
>
> . . . .
> She was trained in Nature's school.
>   Nature had blest her.
> A waking eye, a prying mind,
> A heart that stirs, is hard to bind:
> A hawk's keen sight ye cannot blind.
> Ye could not Hester.[9]

The "springy," uncommon girl of the epigraph, namesake of the novel's eponymous youthful heroine, is formed by inheritances and "Nature"—even her training, her nurture, is "Nature's." Her characteristic spunkiness is an animal quality, innate and irrepressible as a hawk's sharp eyesight. The opening pages continue the theme, constructing a family history of sorts through which the reader is invited to consider the operations of inheritance and nature on the Vernons, proprietors of a bank "second only to the Bank of England in its stability and strength" and progenitors of Hester and the older female cousin, Catherine Vernon, on whom the novel focuses most attention.

This initial family history maps the commercial drama of Vernon's bank onto variations in quantities and qualities of the Vernons' "genius for money" (5). The term *genius* has a complex history, but across its range of significations it frequently implies a quality that is inborn or intrinsic, something that might be developed but not instilled through instruction. By introducing genius through this family history and detailing with relative precision its variation through four generations, Oliphant draws the concept into a frame that is very much of the moment, echoing *Hereditary Genius,* Galton's influential study purporting to find statistical evidence for the biological and transmissible nature of talents. Beginning in familial terms with John Vernon, "the grandfather of the present head of the firm," the narrator posits that he possessed a "special gift," comparable to the "genius which produces a fine picture or a fine poem" (5). Not precisely equivalent to intelligence or industriousness—"wiser men" and "men as steady to their work" did not experience the same success—the inborn "genius" appears as mysterious as magic or fortune: though he doesn't quite know how, John's "investments always answered," he escapes panics and a run on the bank that "ought" to have ruined anyone, and it appears to "the popular imagination" that "under his influence the very cellars of the banking-house . . . filled with gold" (5). His son Edward's "genius" was of a different sort, being the "genius for keeping what he had got" (5). The next generation brings difficulties, sons who died young and "went wrong" (6), leaving a still younger generation—Catherine and her cousin John—in whose era the bank undergoes yet another crisis. When he takes over as head of the firm, the younger John's leadership failures and his extravagance threaten the bank with another run, which is only averted through his cousin Catherine's talents—and a large quantity of her "mother's money." These talents are claimed as a paternal inheritance, as Catherine responds to praise for her "head for business" with the declaration, "I hope I am not old Edward Vernon's granddaughter for nothing" (20). (The infusion of maternally derived property, in contrast, receives no triumphal notice.) And in the aftermath of the bank's rescue, as Catherine takes over its leadership, her successes prove that she had "more than her grandfather's steady power of holding on": she "was, indeed, the heir of her great-grandfather's genius for business" (22).

Oliphant's insistent use of the language of inheritance in this opening, incorporating the transmission of property but even more emphatically illustrating a hereditary transmission of talent, is part of a larger pattern in contemporary representations of business. For instance, an 1882 *Blackwood's* article, "Romance in Business," addressing the remarkable multigenerational success of the Rothschilds, gives enthusiastic credit to their "hereditary instincts" and "natural business aptitudes." Though the article casts these in conventional, racialized terms as features of the Rothschilds' "Jewish blood," it also particularizes them as aspects of a blood*line:* "*Bon chien chasse de race;* and it is remarkable how the heirs of the family have taken after their founder."[10] The French expression, roughly equivalent to the English strain of proverbs implying resemblances between parents and children ("like father like son"), heightens the biological resonance by invoking the language of dog breeding ("*race*"). The article recognizes the role played by the transmission of property (carefully reserved to the Rothschild family through intermarriage, it notes) and knowledge, but the real distinctiveness—what merits the adjective "remarkable"—is the hereditary resemblance. Other accounts of rather less illustrious families saw similar signs of heredity at work. The collection *Fortunes Made in Business* includes the ninety-year history of the Low Moor Ironworks, which also finds good business in the blood, deeming it "somewhat remarkable that the business instincts and great natural abilities of the founders of these works should have been inherited so fully by their descendants." For the Peases of Darlington, another of the collection's multigenerational sagas, "great commercial ability and integrity, combined with a strong gift of foresight and an indomitable enterprise, have been hereditary."[11]

Business instincts, aptitudes, abilities, integrity, genius, talent: treating these as traits that can be passed down like blue eyes or curly hair, these passages render the secret of success a matter of the body. This corporeal focus was not altogether new. Business writers shared in the Victorian fascination with the possibility of reading character through physiognomy and phrenology, recommending readers avail themselves of "mental science," learning to "analyze character" through "its external signs as written on the head and on the face." Young men deciding on a profession could thus read physical manifestations as clues to their aptitudes, while merchants hiring clerks were directed to seek visible markers of applicants' characters.[12] In scientific writing, everyday commercial practice was a common site through which to imagine and raise questions about the relationship between the mind and the physical body or about the proper analysis and measurement of mental processes and character.[13] The conjuncture of scientific, biological, and commercial languages of character pushed the focus inward, as brain, nerves, and "blood" became privileged loci of mental, moral, and characterological investigation. And as business character took conceptual root in the body, it simultaneously was pushed backward (and forward) in time by scientific interest in the relationship of mental traits to evolutionary processes and descent.

In an 1877 lecture before the Midland Institute, Birmingham, the physicist and popular science educator John Tyndall evoked the puzzle of how sense impressions were translated into actions through nerves, emotions, intellect, and muscles with an illustration of "a merchant" sitting "complacently in his easy chair":

> A servant enters the room with a telegram bearing the words, "Antwerp, &c. . . . Jonas and Co. have failed." "Tell James to harness the horses!" The servant flies. Up starts the merchant wide-awake, makes a dozen paces through the room, descends to the counting-house, dictates letters and forwards despatches. He jumps into his carriage, the horses snort, and their driver is immediately at the Bank, on the Bourse, and among his commercial friends. Before an hour has elapsed he is again at home, where he throws himself once more into his easy chair with a deep-drawn sigh. . . . This complex mass of action, emotional, intellectual, and mechanical, is evoked by the impact upon the retina of the infinitesimal waves of light coming from pencil marks on a bit of paper. We have . . . terror, hope, sensation, calculation, possible ruin, and victory compressed into a moment. What caused the merchant to spring out of his chair? The contraction of his muscles. What made his muscles contract? An impulse of the nerves, which lifted the proper latch, and liberated the muscular power. Whence this impulse? From the centre of the nervous system. But how did it originate there? This is the critical question.

The pleasures of narrative—the quick pace of sentences and events, the atmospheric detail of the snorting horses—and the familiar trope of market excitement constitute Tyndall's merchant as a recognizable figure, one whose particular character traits (decisiveness, for instance) allow him to play an active role *as* a character in his commercial drama. But as the scientist reflects on and reshapes the story, the merchant is transformed into an almost mechanical system—latches lifted, powers released—that captures the entire narrative possibility of his situation ("terror, hope, sensation, calculation, possible ruin, and victory") in one ultimately mysterious nervous "impulse."[14]

The shift that occurs within Tyndall's anecdote is broadly representative of the way psychological and evolutionary science came to represent character, as holistic accounts fractured into smaller component pieces—often, in theory, localizable, with physical origins, and measurable. Galton's efforts to measure character, perhaps the most famous (or notorious) instance of this tendency, treat the representation of character as a statistical project aiming at "the simplest and most precise measure" in which "carefully recorded acts, representative of the usual conduct," are listed, "separately verified, valued and revalued, and the whole accurately summed."[15] Though narrative representations often shared these preoccupations with typicality and detail as means to derive character, Galton's interest in measurement and heredity presses for precision, slicing character into often hyperparticularized traits. Arguing that the "capacities" of man should be measured as a career service, to determine what work he is fit for, Galton suggests, for instance, measuring the capacity of energy, or "the length of time during which a person is wont to work at full stretch, day by day, without harm to himself, in obedience to an instinctive craving for work." This characteristic is familiar from any number of biographical accounts of extraordinarily industrious businessmen; however, Galton's approach translates the characterological term *industriousness* into *energy*, a term with a physical connotation and with the body as its primary locus. "True tests" of the characteristic of energy, therefore, would be "physiological and of considerable delicacy." They would focus on a concrete bodily phenomenon, measuring "the excess of waste over repair consequent upon any given effort." The measurement of this physicalized character is conceived in economic terms: measuring capacities is equivalent to measuring one's "stock-in-trade," and measurements of the depletion of energy would indicate a "loss of capital which, if persevered in, must infallibly lead to vital bankruptcy."[16]

Galton's transformation of "industriousness" into the measurable physical capacity "energy" nonetheless describes a trait applicable to a wide range of commercial interests and pursuits. Like genius, ability, intelligence, and "high moral characters," other qualities whose heritability Galton emphasizes, energy/industriousness fits within a model that construes business character as a general ethical-temperamental tendency.[17] But the categories in Galton's investigations frequently swing between qualities such as these and more narrowly conceived capacities that focus much more precisely on specific skills and talents. Thus *Hereditary Genius* claims that judges inherit "judicial ability." The "statesman's type of ability" is broken down into particular components; these include features such as "high intellectual gifts," whose characterization as "hereditary" might not occasion much surprise, and others, such as "tact in dealing with men" and "power of expression in debate," which might.[18] Although businessmen are not well represented in his sample of eminent men, qualities particular to business are isolated.

Galton describes one family, for instance, possessing, as a hereditary trait, a "curious saving, mercantile spirit."[19]

Such highly particularized instances muddy the distinctions between talents passed on as a natural inheritance and talents learned and developed through familial and social examples and practice. Strange as some of these examples might seem, however, they were not out of line with contemporary scientific discussions of heredity, in which the question of whether characteristics developed through the lived experience of individuals could become heritable remained very much a matter of debate. Informed by Darwin's work on instinct and the still-influential theories of Lamarckian inheritance, the current scientific thinking was relatively hospitable to the notion that habits or actions—such as one would undertake in the practice of law, statecraft, or business—as well as the mental and moral tendencies that these actions would develop, might be transformed into heritable qualities.[20] Galton himself was skeptical about the degree to which the transformation of action into biological, heritable matter occurred. In fact, he invokes occupational examples to cast doubt on the possibility ("I am assured that the sons of fishermen, whose ancestors have pursued the same calling time out of mind, are just as sea-sick as the sons of landsmen when they first go to sea").[21] But many prominent scientists believed firmly that actions, habits, and conscious thought and choices could be imprinted on the nervous system or modify brain structures and could thus be transformed into heritable traits. The evolutionary psychologist Henry Maudsley, for instance, contended that a person's "persistent disuse of moral feeling, and a persistent exercise throughout his life, of those selfish, mean, and anti-social tendencies which are a negation of the highest moral relations of mankind," might "succeed in manufacturing insanity in his progeny" as an atrophied moral capacity is passed on in an unusable state.[22] In fact, despite Galton's skepticism, the persistence of notions of the heritability of acquired characteristics helped to create an intellectual space within which the more finely tuned inherited traits and capacities in his theory made sense. Whatever the mechanism—whether there was some kind of original, physical substance that was expressed in a "mercantile spirit" or whether acting with a "mercantile spirit" made that spirit flesh—the discourse of heredity gave the material body a key role in personal business.

Popular representations eagerly picked up the theme, conceiving of everything from handwriting to expression as heritable. One writer cites his acquaintance with cousins who shared "the same quick, hurried manner, and a trick of commencing their sentences with an exclamation," peculiarities that the writer suggests must come from a "remote ancestor" as the parents did not exhibit them.[23] From a more skeptical angle, a parodic response to Galton's notion of inherited faculties testifies to the way they implied a new way of breaking down character. The "desire 'to found a family,'" "contemptible" to ordinary ways of thinking, should be redescribed in Galton's terms as "a magnificent ambition. . . . no longer a vulgar wish to perpetuate the name of Robinson, but to bequeath to a grateful country in perpetuity the wit, the humour, the administrative talents, or the power of multiplying four figures by four figures in one's head, which is now the attribute of Master Jack Robinson only, and may be lost forever by a mésalliance with a dull heiress!"[24] The mundanity of multiplication, as well as the particularity of the talent it denotes, renders the notion of inheriting such specific mental traits ridiculous. Galton's studies were criticized for describing as hereditary effects that might just as well have originated in familial influence or connections; as this same skeptical writer notes, one family's twenty-six lawyers "possessed a most extraordinary hereditary genius—*for getting on at the bar.*"[25] But the argument, here and elsewhere, focuses on whether there is a particular, inherited "judicial ability" that can be separated out from other explanations of success. The fact of the criticism suggests that the notion of inherited, narrowly focused, often occupationally defined mental qualities had enough conceptual traction to make it matter for debate.

This broad willingness to countenance the heritability of all sorts of behaviors, talents, and dispositions conditioned the ground on which assertions of inherited business capacities might be offered and received. It was possible to imagine specific, focused business talents, separate from other more general or specific qualities that might be associated with everyday commercial activities (Thomas Edison, for instance, was said to be a "true scientist," with "no room in his brain for business talent").[26] And it was possible to imagine inheriting those particular traits. But even as accounts of business heredity implied specificity—*business* abilities, *business* instincts, *business* aptitudes, integrity, genius, talent—the abundance of nouns marshaled in their descriptions leaves the content suggestively vague. Hereditary business qualities could be moral (integrity) or intellectual (talent or aptitude); they could be subject to control and development (abilities) or beyond the reach of reason and will (instincts). In defining success as the product of inborn traits, the language of hereditary character formation promised more precision than it finally offered.

As a result, the scientific language of business character shares much with its contemporary, and apparent rhetorical opposite, business charisma. Innate, unbidden, the hereditary business trait is deeply personalized and often strikingly elusive. When it registers as instinct, in particular, the intrinsic quality of mind that accounts for business success bypasses—or, as Kathleen Frederickson has argued of the evolutionary model that informed contemporary writers such as Walter Bagehot, exists in "back-formation" toward—all the norms of conscious rational calculation and self-development that were elsewhere placed at the heart of capitalist endeavor.[27] A reader encountering in a biography a description of "the true inventor's instincts" that lay at the base of S. C. Lister's triumphs in the field of silk waste, or of Josiah Mason's "rare gift . . . of seeing, as if by instinct, what was possible and what was outside reasonable range" in the business of pen making, was not given a model of business ability that could be mimicked or learned.[28] Instead, instinct joined the panoply of forces that made market relations less than predictable, rational, and calculable.[29]

In fact, very often commercial instincts and gifts cannot even be understood by those who possess them. In *Hester,* the illustrious ancestor in the bank, John Vernon, was unable to explain how his "special gift" worked; the "popular imagination" mythologizes his success into cellars filled with gold. The quasi-magical appearance of this profit is not confined to fiction; rather, fictional tropes extend into nonfiction accounts of the business world, casting the language of heredity into the terms of legend. "Bankers and merchants from the City who turned everything they touched to gold, in virtue of an hereditary birthright," were at the heart of the speculative frenzy of the mid-1860s, for instance, the *Saturday Review* claimed in 1871.[30] The ambiguity in the description—was the bankers' power attributable to biologically hereditary traits or to a familial "birthright" of connections and commercial influence?—suggests the way that scientific language generated mysteries as much as explaining them, forging an imaginative space that leaves behind the promise to determine the real, material forces driving business life and instead creates Midas-bankers out of the everyday actions of City men.[31]

With concreteness always out of reach, hereditary business character opens up an unexpected horizon of enchantment. But where charismatic enchantment builds its power despite—or because of—the way it exceeds the norms of realist explanation, the alliance of languages of enchantment and science diminishes the authority science offers in the encounter with personal business. Take, for instance, the question of succession within a firm, a moment of instability requiring assessments of personal character and aptitude to which models of heredity might seem especially relevant. In one post-Victorian history of the commercial system, Ellis T. Powell's *The Evolution of the Money Market, 1385–1915* (1916), "physiological" terms derived explicitly from Darwin and Herbert Spencer structure a Gothic effect: the "deathless corporate organism" is "capable of accumulating and transmitting experience" over time "by means of a corporate identity," suggesting that a legal fiction—the corporate personality—has come to take on independent life, becoming an uncannily embodied conduit passing on experience as if genetically through its disembodied form.[32] Gail Houston's astute account of the genre implications of the eruption of the Gothic in this uncanny rendering of anxiety over corporate power and identity can be usefully extended by considering the scientific metaphor in the context of the everyday relationships of the corporation.[33] Powell takes the Bank of England as his example; however, it is not necessarily the most representative choice in a context in which familial control frequently persisted even within a corporate form. The hereditary model highlights those individual members that make up the firm, specifically the relationship between the corporate form and *their* personalities—their mental qualities and capacities—and their living, dying, and reproducing bodies. Only apparently deathless, the corporation operated on a different timescale from the human; however, its persistence depended on those minds and bodies that brought it to life. In this context, in other words, the hereditary transmission of business knowledge and power was not just a question spurred by Gothic fantasy but a real—even realist—problem as well. And in such realist terms, the move to supernatural explanation becomes less a fantasy of exorbitant corporate power and more a signal of explanatory weakness and the limitations of knowledge. When crisis hits Vernon's Bank, in the opening of *Hester,* the memory of John Vernon's inexplicable, quasi-magical "special gift" demonstrates that weakness: it offers no tangible model of knowledge and practice for the firm's current leaders to follow, and the reappearance of the gift via biological transmission through the family's bodies is uncertain.

Succession and transmission—in fact, intergenerational relationships in general—are tangible points of vulnerability in commercial accounts. The entries in the information book of the merchant firm Antony Gibbs and Sons, for instance, hit notes of anxiety around these moments. The "senior" in one family firm "finds the money for the junior who is rather a harum-scarum sanguine young man"; his paternal indulgence toward a successor might taint business practice. Succession upends whatever character knowledge has been gathered and marks a moment of suspension as the qualities of particular firm members are absorbed, shed, or transformed. Fathers grow intemperate, and their sons do "not inspire us with much confidence." Heads of firms die whose "thorough respectability + prudence" are taken to guarantee confidence, only to be replaced—sometimes not even by sons, but by clerks who carry on the firm's name and business but whose personal qualities are unknown.[34]

While the late Victorian science of heredity claimed, on the one hand, that sons might be more likely to succeed than clerks, on the other its genealogical projects and statistical assumptions undermined the offer of character legibility that it held out. Galton's studies of twins trumpet the priority of nature over nurture in forming human character; however, they argue partly from examples of twins who seemed to have been "perfectly dissimilar in character, habits, and likeness" from birth and who maintained their dissimilarity despite receiving (according to Galton and their families) identical upbringings and influences.[35] Families did not *always* reproduce identical— or even similar—"natural" characters. Galton's family histories argue for the statistical likelihood that ability clusters within a family, but in doing so they must note the family members who don't achieve the lofty heights of "genius." The principle of reversion to the mean suggested that extraordinary ability was by no means necessarily followed by equally extraordinary progeny. (A *Times* notice about a lecture by Galton emphasizes this issue; located on the same page as the stock market tables, its point about the difficulty of prediction might just as easily carry over into the newspaper's other columns.)[36] As firms and their associates encountered the issue of succession, heredity's probabilistic claims cut both ways, leaving its contribution to character assessment in doubt with property on the line.

Finally, heredity's association with evolutionary models presented a similar conundrum. The late Victorian economy, facing agricultural depression, continued commercial panics and shocks, and increased competition from other countries, was poised tenuously atop an imagined evolutionary scale that threatened to tip backward. The priority placed on tradition and familial and social continuity suggested that British business might be degenerating, as the principle of hereditary *property*—and the desire to preserve family property and family businesses for new generations—clashed with the unpredictability of the heredity of *talent*. (Galton himself suggested that the "free power of bequeathing wealth" was one of the markers of civilization that helped "spoil a race," interfering with natural selection "by preserving the wealthy, and by encouraging marriage on grounds quite independent of personal qualities.")[37] As a result, the natural course of commercial adaptation was at risk. An 1881 letter to the editor of *Bankers' Magazine,* for instance, fretted that too many banks were "aristocratic and exclusive," concerned to work "in a groove, and with what we may call their exclusive traditions," rather than "adapting themselves to the changing times."[38] The trope of blood, furthermore, anchored the issue of the reproduction of the individual commercial organism—and the broader population of firms—in a biological, evolutionary paradigm. For instance, one leading economist diagnosed the 1879 failure of the City of Glasgow Bank as the result of its hidebound leadership and prescribed "the constant infusion of fresh blood" into boards of directors to prevent stagnation and work toward transparency and openness, countering the coagulating factor that personal loyalties could generate within a longstanding board.[39] Carrying property and talent through the firm and through generations, but not always in tandem and not always predictably, "blood" was an ambivalent marker, signaling the possibility of dissolution as much as incorporation.

When the Baron Lionel de Rothschild, head of the Rothschild enterprise in Britain and the "last surviving, though the eldest, son" of the firm's founder, Nathan Meyer Rothschild, died in 1879, the occasion presented an opportunity for the *Bankers' Magazine* to reflect on the difficulty that family relations represented to knowledge of commercial character—and that personal qualities might represent to the relations of family business. "The business abilities of a man of great wealth are sometimes mixed up with the influence of that wealth itself by those who judge him merely by reputation or from casual intercourse," the writer suggests. "They think that because a man is wealthy and born to a great hereditary business position he cannot fail of success." The writer strongly disputes this evaluation, calling it "very erroneous," and goes on to use the case of Lionel to demonstrate the distinction between mere hereditary position and active business talent. With "powerful judgment and keen insight into affairs" and an "accurate knowledge of his business," the deceased was "at the head in business qualities of that great branch of commerce which he so long controlled."[40] "Business qualities"—elements of character and talent—and hereditary position matched up, in his case. But they are separate entities. That such a discussion emerges around a figure like Lionel de Rothschild, who emblematized, in many respects, the hereditary transmission of business ability (*"bon chien chasse de race"*), suggests the way hereditary wealth and position may interfere with a clear evaluation of personal qualities. If his skill could be overlooked or doubted, so could another man's inherited property and position mask his personal incapacities. The congruence of particular, personalized business talents—"business qualities"—and an inherited commercial position in this case by no means settled the question of how talent and inheritance could be untangled in family firms and their leadership.

"So many Vernons": Gender, Generation, and Character in the Family Firm

Margaret Oliphant's sons were not heirs to a family business. With an artist father who died early (of tuberculosis) and a mother whose literary talents and extraordinary energy were constantly marshaled to support both her own spending habits and those of a widening circle of dependents (including alcoholic brothers), any inheritance they had was likely to consist of personal qualities rather than tangible property. And this inheritance seemed to be in question throughout their too-short lives. Both Cecco and Tiddy, having received through their mother's efforts excellent educational opportunities, were unable to settle into careers. Prone to dissipation and illness that echoed the generation above, they were a steady source of anxiety. Oliphant's own family life, shaped by illnesses and addictions that were widely considered to run in families, made the issue of biological inheritance especially salient, but it also posed questions. Her husband's tuberculosis and her brothers' alcoholism suggested that heredity could be to blame for her children's weakness. These hereditary traits appeared to affect and flow through men. But what role did she play?

If we imagine Oliphant's family as a kind of map of heredity, her own place within it as a site of transmission is unclear. If, as she held, "a son's maternal inheritance was to be judged in moral terms," then it would be difficult to define her positive contribution to her sons' failings.[41] The sons lacked self-reliance and industriousness, qualities that were morally loaded, but this could not be easily attributed to her hereditary contributions (or to her example, for that matter), as she displayed those capacities in spades. They lacked business judgment and aptitude. On this the evidence (such as it was) was ambiguous. Despite her literary talent, her prolific output, and her exertions, Oliphant does not define the energy that she clearly possessed as a *business* skill. Rather, she imagines the "head for business" (as she was to name it in *Hester*) as a particular kind of talent, defining it as such by its absence in her own makeup as she fantasizes about the difference it might have made to have someone interceding for her in her negotiations. Professing that she shared her husband's lack of interest in and knowledge of business affairs, she claims that her success had been achieved despite her deficiencies in this talent, her inability to "fight for a higher price" and negotiate good terms.[42] But because this is a deficiency that she shares with her husband, it can't clearly be designated as *her* contribution. This leaves Oliphant on the heredity map, but without a clear role in transmission. She hasn't apparently passed on her positive, definable qualities; nor is she the obvious source of her sons' deficiencies. She might be a conduit for the addictions that pass from her lineage (indicated by her brothers), but because these are unexpressed in her own character and her female body, it isn't clear. Or she might be simply a bystander, in nature and nurture, to the paternal inheritance that predominated in her offspring.

Many critics have suggested the parallels between the novelist and her creation Catherine, the older woman in *Hester* whose talents and labor make her benefactor to a host of more or (mostly) less worthy relatives.[43] Though the unmarried Catherine and Margaret Oliphant stand in different genetic relation to their dependents, the ambiguous role played by both women in the drama of generational succession represents a less noticed aspect of these parallels. Catherine's representation, in fact, literalizes the ambiguity when she enters the Vernon family tree as a virtual blank in the crisis that forms the immediate prehistory to her leadership of the family bank and to the novel's main action. As Mr. Rule, the bank's clerk, ponders what to do about the threatened failure precipitated by Catherine's cousin John, he runs through the Vernon generations to the present calamity, coming up short when he remembers her presence and her pedigree:

> Vernon's! To think that Ruin should be possible, that so dark a shadow could hover over that sacred place. What would old Mr Vernon have said, he who received it from his father and handed it down always flourishing, always prosperous to—not to his son. If his son had lived, the eldest one, not he who had gone wrong, but the eldest, who was John too, called after his grandfather, he who was the father of—It was at this point that Mr Rule came to a dead stop. . . .
>   The father of——Yes, indeed, indeed, and that was true! (16)

The dash that signals the first disruption in the proper sequence of inheritance, as the elder son's death prevents his accession, morphs into a new disruption, standing in twice for Catherine's name. The function of these latter dashes is peculiar. Both substitute for missing periods, stopping thoughts but simultaneously linking to the upper case of a new sentence. But even as they move forward, the nominal substitution that the dashes represent (especially as the final one doubles, mimicking the conventional placeholder for a name) makes them more than merely connective: they represent a content, a person, whose function in the familial/business sequence is ill defined. In this dual role, they resemble the unspecified nodes in the family trees generated by investigators of heredity. The Xs and Os in Galton's *Hereditary Genius,* for instance (fig. 3), represent unnamed marriage partners, parents, siblings, and even generations, whose names are either unknown or apparently unconnected to the main story of hereditary talent charted by the tree but whose bodies—as sources of content and as connective conduits—might contribute to its meaning and its interpretation.

As Oliphant's history suggests, women's role in the charting of heredity was unsettled, the tension between conduit and content represented by any

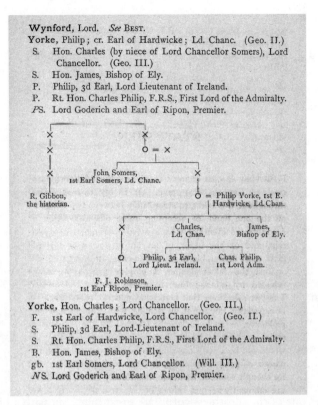

Wynford, Lord. *See* BEST.
Yorke, Philip; cr. Earl of Hardwicke; Ld. Chanc. (Geo. II.)
  S. Hon. Charles (by niece of Lord Chancellor Somers), Lord
      Chancellor. (Geo. III.)
  S. Hon. James, Bishop of Ely.
  P. Philip, 3d Earl, Lord Lieutenant of Ireland.
  P. Rt. Hon. Charles Philip, F.R.S., First Lord of the Admiralty.
  *P*S. Lord Goderich and Earl of Ripon, Premier.

John Somers,
1st Earl Somers, Ld. Chanc.

R. Gibbon,
the historian.

O = Philip Yorke, 1st E.
Hardwicke, Ld. Chan.

Charles,   James,
Ld. Chan.   Bishop of Ely.

Philip, 3d Earl,   Chas. Philip,
Lord Lieut. Ireland.   1st Lord Adm.

F. J. Robinson,
1st Earl Ripon, Premier.

Yorke, Hon. Charles; Lord Chancellor. (Geo. III.)
  F. 1st Earl of Hardwicke, Lord Chancellor. (Geo. II.)
  S. Philip, 3d Earl, Lord-Lieutenant of Ireland.
  S. Rt. Hon. Charles Philip, F.R.S., First Lord of the Admiralty.
  B. Hon. James, Bishop of Ely.
  gb. 1st Earl Somers, Lord Chancellor. (Will. III.)
  *N*S. Lord Goderich and Earl of Ripon, Premier.

FIGURE 3. Family tree of the Yorke family. From Francis Galton, *Hereditary Genius: An Inquiry into Its Laws and Consequences* (1869). (Special Collections, University of Virginia Library, Charlottesville, Va.)

member of a family tree, regardless of gender, posing special questions for females, whose qualities, talents, and potential were often unrecorded or unexpressed. Galton himself was interested in evaluating the question of women's relative contribution to hereditary genius, although he recognized that the task would be complicated because the sources from which he drew his data were unlikely to feature women ("eminent mothers do not find a place in mere biographical lists").[44] Galton's hypotheses and his eugenic prescriptions underscored the crucial presence of women in the dynamic of heritability. His "Utopia—or . . . Laputa, if you will," of scientific mating features competitive examinations for women as well as men, in order to reduce the dilution of talent through marriage to heiresses whose only qualifications were their property.[45] But at the same time his conclusions diminished the role of women imagined in the folk "misapprehension" that talent was transmitted by the mother, deeming women no more likely than men to serve as vehicles for inherited ability.[46] Reviews emphasized this point: *Fraser's*, for instance, suggested that Galton "proves that . . . the ratio of transmission through the male to transmission through the female line is in the large majority of cases as seventy to thirty, or more than two to one."[47] Even Galton's method of genealogical notation rhetorically deemphasized women by typographically and conceptually representing them as inflections of the masculine relationship. Father, brother, and son are "always printed in capitals" as "F. and B. and S.," while "their correlatives for mother, sister, and daughter are always expressed in small italicised type as *f.*, *b.*, and *s.*"[48] (Thus Emily Brontë, for instance, is listed as Charlotte's *b.*, her female brother, so to speak.) Selected out of the original data pool by their relative exclusion from activities of genius and frequently diminished in Galton's analysis and rhetoric, women were left with their "Laputa" role, as participants in scientifically regulated mating in which talent, ability, and physical superiority become, by virtue of Galton's multivalent echo of Swift, sexual commodities in a market governed by reason.

Catherine's entry as dashes in the Vernon family tree typifies the position of women in one sense: she is a surprise, an afterthought to the main, masculine story, especially as it has centered on the varying quantum of hereditary business talent. By spotlighting this anomalous figure, Oliphant places that hereditary notion in focus. In the opening family history Vernon's bank resembles one of the "deathless corporate organisms," but with a biological mechanism for transmitting its essence specified: the Vernon talent for accumulating property is a feature—though not always a consistent one—of Vernon blood, rather than Vernon teaching or experience. Catherine's unusualness seems to confirm this: her skill is not easily ascribed to nurture because as a woman she didn't receive the same business education, even informally, that a boy might have enjoyed. Her early dealings with the bank lie in performing the girlish offices of monitoring her grandfather's consumption of biscuits and wine and inspiring chivalric worship in the clerks; upon her cousin's accession she retreats altogether despite having the right to be consulted as partner. Catherine's business talent blossoms, when called upon, from a latent state that can only be attributed to innate inheritance, apparently eliminating the contaminating effects of education that perplexed efforts to isolate hereditary genius.[49]

However, even as she seems to confirm the relevance of heredity, the other aspect of Catherine's anomalous status within the family tree reopens the question. As a single, childless woman, Catherine embodies familial talent without enacting a biological reproductive role: she represents hereditary content but is not a conduit. Contemplating her retirement after forging a successful career at the bank, Catherine therefore faces the question of succession. With "so many Vernons" to choose from, the problem seems "not difficult" (25). But because the succession is a matter of choice, not a relatively automatic filial sequence, the problems of character interpretation within a familial commercial context are multiplied and foregrounded. As the novel follows the consequences of Catherine's decision, it expands the material of interpretation, weighing different models of character that emphasize the assemblage of inherited traits, the imperatives of self-making, and the psychological and affective demands of family.

Catherine's position as the main action of the novel opens blends masculine and feminine: in her life "the work of a successful man of business" is "increased, yet softened by all the countless nothings that make business for a woman" (24). With streets, buildings, philanthropic institutions, even churches in the town of Redborough named after her, she has attained the local eminence that represents the crowning achievement of so many masculine business careers.[50] As an "old maid," on the other hand, she deviates from the conventional pattern of feminine achievement and reward (24). However, hers is not the typical condition of an unmarried older woman; she may be a "dry tree," but in her unfruitfulness she resembles "Queen Elizabeth" rather than Austen's Miss Bates (24). In fact, with "plenty of money" and a "handsome, cheerful house," Catherine has created an alternative structure of adoptive, affiliative family (24). As an "amateur grandmother in numbers of young households" she experiences quasi-familial affections without the anxieties or limitations of a mother; the "children of the barren" are "in her case . . . more than those of any wife" (24, 25). In fact, Catherine—an unmarried only child—enjoys the names of mother, grandmother, and aunt in these flexible, self-chosen relationships.

In choosing her successor from among the array of Vernons, however, Catherine gives priority to bloodline, favoring three—Edward, her favorite, and the sibling team of Harry and Ellen—who were "descendants of the brothers and sisters of the great John Vernon" and who were "the nearest to her in blood" (25, 26). Though cousins, they call her Aunt Catherine, claiming an intergenerational, proximate, and, as Eileen Cleere has suggested, economically resonant bond and resenting those "many" who call Catherine "Aunt" in what they deem a "fictitious relationship" (26).[51] The ironic handling of their resentment introduces a skeptical note into the novel's treatment of the foundational status claimed for blood relationships, which here are no more and no less fictitious than other modes of affiliation.

In fact, *Hester* frequently matches assertions of flexible and affiliative kinship possibilities with competing claims grounded in blood. With the same unconcern for precision as Edward, Harry, and Ellen (the nephews and nieces who are really cousins), Captain Morgan, a maternal relative of Catherine, jettisons even the principle of consanguinity when he describes Hester as his "great-grandchild in the spirit," slotting neatly into the generational space left by the death of a beloved daughter (87). His actual grandchild, Emma Ashton, who comes to visit in order to find a husband, shrewdly overlooks the fact that she is not blood kin to the cousins of Catherine, adopting the name of cousin and brazenly presuming on the fictional relationship to gain entrance to Redborough society. As one character after another makes kinship a matter of choice, metaphorical likeness, or calculation, sliding between kinship terms and even from one family tree to another, the hereditary model of character set up in the opening account of the Vernon family history begins to unravel.

Insofar as characters maintain their investment in blood as a determinant of kinship and character, the novel suggests that this investment is driven by property rather than emerging from an inherent meaningfulness. Property concerns *make* blood significant; by extension, blood cannot be considered an a priori indicator of a particular familial talent for making good use of property, because the relationship between the two is so intertwined. *Hester* makes this point most directly through its representation of the sneering, seething relatives whom Catherine maintains in the apartments of the Vernonry, a familial charity project for her dependent kin. Unpleasantly insistent on determining degrees of Vernonness as they forthrightly conflate blood and property rights, these relatives resent the unequal distribution of Vernon property to those nearer and farther from the main patrilineal line, even as they accept the principle of blood-linked distribution in rejecting the use of Vernon money for the support of non-Vernons, especially Catherine's maternal relations, Captain and Mrs. Morgan. In this, of course, they conveniently overlook that it was the infusion of Catherine's maternal inheritance that saved the bank; "Vernon" money is, like "Vernon" blood, a mixture. The Miss Vernon-Ridgways join their co-inhabitants of the Vernonry in this resentment of the Morgans, even as, "convinced that the blood of the Ridgways had much enriched the liquid that meandered through the veins of the Vernons," they stew in anger that their own familial contribution has been overlooked (52). As the parasitical inhabitants of the Vernonry translate money into blood and back again, heedless of contradictions that Oliphant's ironic narrative tone makes apparent, the precise distinction of bloodlines appears as an effect of property rather than a source of talent accounting for it.

Though Catherine is amused by the self-centered peevishness of the Vernonry, she draws lines around degrees of "Vernonness" just as carefully. In fact, in spite of the initial assertion of Catherine's openness to affiliative relationships, she is susceptible to the same tendency to fetishize blood. For instance, Edward's apparently affectionate residence with Catherine leads her to transform him imaginatively from cousin to nephew, and from nephew to an encompassing filial relationship in which he is "son and daughter to the lonely woman" (123). His commercial skill becomes, in her view, a concrete manifestation of the rightness and the reality of that designation. Whereas Harry will "never set the Thames on fire" (126), the notion that Edward shares Catherine's familial talent seems to signal the alignment of the imaginative, the affiliative, and the actual, with blood—expressed through talent—confirming indirectly that she has found her true son and heir.

In the bitter unraveling of the certainty that Catherine believes she has found in Edward, Oliphant's novel turns on its head the relevance of family to business implied by the notion of inherited genius. Edward's particular familial trait—his hereditary talent—is, in the end, far less important than his overall character, conceived not as a collection of biologically based traits, but rather in moral and psychological terms as a product of the tension between the demands of family inheritance (hereditary and financial) and the desire for independent self-development. By making her story of a family firm center on a business head who is both female and an adoptive mother, Oliphant emphasizes the danger to business that family can pose. Rather than acting principally as a fount of transmitted, innate talent—and thus a signal of personal fitness for business—or as an institution in which the moral character necessary to safeguard the economy is nurtured, family in *Hester* represents a potential disruption of character development and character interpretation.

Edward's surreptitious speculations with bank property—the bank's clients' savings and Vernon family investments—represent a rebellion against familial trusts and responsibilities as he seeks to establish his independence and to liberate himself from a family role that he experiences as stultifying. Edward's chafing was not uncommon in family firms, in which friction between the possibility of individualistic self-making and the imperative to preserve family property and identity was built into the form. In the letters between partners in Antony Gibbs and Sons, for instance, a flurry of missives to Vicary Gibbs, a brother managing the company's interests in Australia, from his father in England urge him to practice restraint, to avoid embarking on risks that the firm isn't willing to take. Vicary's side of the correspondence isn't included in the collection, but the letters that are preserved characterize his response as one of irritation, centered on complaints that his father was inconsistent in both praising his success and asking him to rein in his expansionary endeavors. His brothers Alban and Herbert join in defense of their father's wishes, the latter finally exploding, in a letter marked "Private," that Vicary's individualistic impulses were posing a threat to the firm: "Consistency in instructions would have made *you* go on swelling until *we* burst."[52]

Replacing the more typical masculine cast of family firm dramas such as this one with a matriarchal business head, Oliphant maps the psychological strain of character development through gender. While the Gibbs men argue openly about appropriate degrees of independent, masculine tumescence, Edward is feminized and delibidinized by his role as Catherine's favorite. Both her chosen and apparent "son and daughter" and at times a kind of substitute, asexual husband, Edward stays in with Catherine or walks with her in the garden rather than joining regularly and openly in Ellen's dances and other mating rituals of the Redborough youth. Edward's initial step toward criminal misuse of the bank's funds and deposits is cast as an expression of resistance to these psychological constraints when he responds to the news that his more plodding cousin and partner, Harry, is pursuing a romantic inclination toward Hester with his first mentions to Catherine of the "prospectuses" and "investments" that are his individuating and energizing secret (128). The physiological metaphor through which Edward imagines speculation—"It would be like pouring in new blood to stagnant veins; it would be new life coming in" (249)—is as much a fantasy of male parthenogenesis as of transfusion. Placing his own mark into the blood of the firm through speculation, and framing it as an individualist rebellion against an "old woman's insane objection to anything daring" (247), Edward asserts a self-generated masculine potency that lifts him above the role of mere hereditary vehicle, a cog in a familial machine.

As he shares his secret in pulse-racing exchanges during his own surreptitious flirtation with Hester, the sexual and psychological charge of Edward's dangerous speculations, enacted to resist an *adoptive* maternal/uxorial force, undercuts the sense that the moral flaw in his character might be simply innate, taking hold when financial opportunities present temptation. Instead, whatever Edward's inborn tendencies, the overlapping emotional and financial demands of family and firm, and the nurture that they represent, take narrative priority. Figured through a maternal substitute who helps shape his character with affection and support, pressure and demands, but not a direct hereditary transmission, Edward's criminal actions are finally represented as motivated by a psychology formed in familial *experience,* not blood inheritance. When he feverishly blames Hester and heredity for his own actions, suggesting that he has "taken the disease" that "must run in the blood" from her father John through Hester as a sexual vector, the strain in his reasoning undermines the notion of hereditary character further (404). No matter what role might be played by nature and nurture, the final responsibility for making character rests, Oliphant's novel insists, in a person's active choices.

In its treatment of the place of character in business, then, *Hester* undercuts the contemporary interest in locating particularized, hereditary business qualities; though Edward has inherited the family trait, its meaningfulness is, finally, utterly suspect, circumscribed by a nonphysiological model of moral character and psychology. Rather than providing a hereditary key to Edward's commercial performance, family adds layers of affective experience that make his character less rather than more predictable and that present a hindrance to character reading. Again, the unconventional gendering of Vernon's bank helps to emphasize the point. A female businessperson such as Catherine figures the blend of family and business more directly than might a father. The affective ties that prevent Catherine from assessing Edward accurately—the sentiment that renders her normally "keen perceptions . . . of no more use to her than the foolishness of any mother" (245)—are framed as maternal. The ironic conversation in which they discuss speculation seems to point to a skepticism about feminine emotion in business, as Edward asserts that it would be "silly" to think of "a woman's incapacity for business" in Catherine's presence, prompting her misguided, motherly interpretation of his smile as "full of affectionate filial admiration and trust" (245). But as the chapter goes on, the salience of this feminine blockage to character reading comes to seem primarily metaphorical and metonymical, merely one aspect of a range of psychological issues and familial relationships that complicate understanding. Masculine intragenerational competition and sexual rivalry—a complex of familial relationships—help to energize Edward and to define him, producing his character as a discomposed "wonder" to himself and even to observers who don't share Catherine's—or Harry's or Hester's— affective predispositions (248). It isn't, in other words, simply that emotional ties, captured by the example of maternal love, interfere with character assessment within a family firm. Instead, that confusion of affect and judgment is just one part of the novel's insistence that family, defined experientially rather than merely through consanguinity, presents a complexity that easily trumps heredity's promise to isolate inherited traits as the keys to reading business character.

Making the Old Stock New

Mr. Rule, the loyal, long-serving clerk in Vernon's bank, has his doubts about Edward, though his attempts to communicate them to his besotted principal are limited to pregnant silences in response to her enthusiasm. Of the novel's other candidate for heir apparent to Catherine—the young Hester—his judgments are simultaneously certain and puzzled. "She is not like his daughter," he confidently asserts, referring to Hester's irresponsible father, John. But nor does she resemble her mother, known to all by the wifely appellation Mrs. John: the lively and original Hester is not "that poor lady's," Rule suggests. What Hester is, instead, is a hereditary surprise, a reappearance of "the pure old Vernon stock" in a female body, with no apparent direct means of transmission (84). In this assessment Rule echoes the judgment of the narrator, who initially introduces Hester as an inheritor of the family trait: she is "apparently of the old stock, with a head for business, and a decision of character quite unusual in a child" (29). In fact, the character Hester most resembles is Catherine, her bitter rival, as several of the novel's characters are quick to point out, from Mr. Rule, to Captain Morgan, to Catherine herself. "We should all tumble to pieces if the race was made up of people like Catherine Vernon and you," the Captain laughs, and though Hester "passionately" retorts that there is "no likeness, none at all," the novel continually invites its readers to consider how these two female expressions of the "old stock" will contribute to the progress of the "race," defined narrowly as the Vernons and their firm and more broadly as British society (88).

In terms of the first, the family business, the novel's representation of these two anomalous women makes a strong case that "old stock"—talent and character—must be looked for in new places: a wider scope is necessary to locate the aptitude necessary for continued commercial success. The novel may reject the notion that a particular, inherited trait (the "head for business") can offer any guarantee, as I have argued, and it may insist on a complex, psychologized mode of character that demonstrates the difficulty of interpreting character in commercial life. Nonetheless, it does underscore the way resources of intelligence, energy, and readiness, wrapped around with moral firmness—elements of a more generalized model of business character—are potentially untapped because they appear in women.

Hester is quite self-consciously organized around a pattern of repetition: two bank crises, two absconding male heads of business, two initially overlooked talented women. One significant difference in the second iteration of the bank crisis highlights the novel's interest in establishing feminine capacity. When Catherine saves the bank at the opening of the novel, she does so with both her maternal property and her personal skill. Mr. Rule highlights the latter as he tells the story to Hester: "Her money was a great deal: but it was not the money alone. It was the heart and courage she had. We had nobody to tell us what to do—but after she came, all went well. She had such

a head for business" (297). Catherine herself is far more aware of the role her
maternal property played. When the young Hester expresses her yearning
to act—and work—as heroically as Catherine, the older woman dismisses
her with a laugh derived from her understanding of the great difference her
wealth made. Not knowing "that it was not only Catherine Vernon's personal
force and genius, but Catherine Vernon's money, which had saved the bank,"
Hester interprets this laugh as a slight to her own character and personal
capacities (73).

But in the second crisis, after Edward's betrayal, when Hester gets the
opportunity she has longed for, it is precisely her personal qualities that are
emphasized, offering far more clarity on the distinction between property
and talent than the first case. Hester sets to work with Catherine and Harry
to clarify the bank's position, buoyed up by Catherine's familial urging: "You
are young, and you are a Vernon too. Bend your mind to it. Think of nothing
but the business in hand" (442). Hester questions and investigates, analyzes
and records, contributing her energy and her acumen. And, significantly, in
the aftermath of the crisis no mention is made of one item of maternal property that Hester could contribute: a strand of pearls that is an inheritance
from her mother's family. The absence is surprising. These pearls had been
a growing source of controversy in the tense relations between the two, as
Catherine asserts openly and increasingly shrilly to all who will listen that
Hester had no right to them because, belonging to the wife of the absconding
John Vernon, they should have been absorbed as Vernon property and made
available for the bank's needs during the crisis he provoked. For the novel
to mark this particular difference in such a self-consciously structured plot
repetition—to drop an element of maternal property that has taken on nearly
hysterical significance for the two characters—focuses attention squarely on
the personal: in the end, Hester, a young woman, is the one character who
is able to absolutely untangle talent and property—the confusing mixture of
the "business abilities" of a person of family wealth and "the influence of that
wealth itself" that the Bankers' Magazine had noted in its obituary of Lionel de Rothschild. When Catherine and Hester's likeness is asserted at the
novel's close, as they come together "like mother and daughter" in conflict
and then mutual comfort (409), Hester's manifestation of talent authenti-
cates its expression in her maternal surrogate.

The link forged between Hester and Catherine in the novel's final pages
most obviously hinges on their shared Vernonness, and thus these mother-
and-child images might seem to confirm that character and talents are, fundamentally, familial traits. But, as I have discussed, another figure in the
novel has laid claim to Hester: Captain Morgan, who suggests on more than

one occasion (and with the independent acquiescence of his wife) that he fancies her his descendant "in the spirit," the grandchild of his lost daughter, Mary (87). The Morgans are the novel's primary philosophers of heredity, ruminating directly on the meaning of blood from perspectives that run the gamut from skeptical, to scientific and materialist, to emotional. At certain moments the captain voices a radical resistance to blood, announcing that he feels no claims of familial affection or responsibility for his other daughter's offspring, the stockbroker Roland Ashton and his sister Emma, in part because their "up-bringing" by a ne'er-do-well father would trump any contribution to their characters attributable to being "poor Katie's" children (157). Mrs. Morgan expresses the "materialist" standpoint, assuming the contribution that her husband rejects as she wonders, in lay biologist's terms, if Emma's shallowness is a sign that "the blood gets thin in a race when it runs too long" (353). At other moments both Morgans make the blood connection acutely significant, discovering its meaning through their emotional responses: the grandmother thrilling to the arrival of her grandson, her husband finding deeper pleasure in Roland's intelligence because he is "a young fellow of his own blood, his descendant," and sharper pain when it appears that this same "flesh and blood" has been the instrument of Edward's temptation and the bank's downfall (194, 432). In the reflections of these thoughtful characters, then, the meaning of blood is left undetermined as biological ties are rejected and reincorporated, generating emotions but also *re*generated by them, so that priority is difficult to discern.

In light of this spectrum, the fanciful, spiritual kinship that Captain Morgan senses with Hester may be just as substantial as a consanguineous one. And because we can therefore imagine that Hester is as much an "heir" to this adoptive grandfather as to any of the Vernons to whom she is biologically related, we can also imagine that her tie to Catherine, who is related to the Morgans on her mother's side, derives from a spiritual connection rather than a biological one. In other words, one *could* trace Hester's connection to Catherine through the paternal, hereditary lineage of the Vernons—with Hester as the next heir to the great Vernon grandfathers and their skills, talents, and temperaments. But she may also be connected to Catherine through a fictive kinship with her maternal relations, the Morgans, grounded in their shared qualities as thoughtful, ethical individuals. She may equally be Catherine's heir through a bloodline and through a chosen, affiliative relation. In designating Hester as heir, then, the novel calls into question the terms that make the designation apparent. Hereditary connection passes from biological mechanism to metaphorical trope to deliberate choice, and with all three elements in play Hester finally becomes a type of a new model of character, neither determined nor determinable by any one of biological nature, nurture, or self-making alone, but actively, nimbly, combining them. She cannot be understood as merely the latest Vernon business genius; she is, instead, Hester herself, a model of character with the potential to renovate the family firm with her own combination of talents, independent judgment, and developed moral sensibilities.

Despite the novel's forceful argument that business talent and character are distributed more broadly than Victorian gender conventions acknowledged, its ending has disappointed many feminist critics, as Hester, with her fresh character type and her clearly demonstrated ability, is left out of the world of work to which she has aspired.[53] The "new blood" that is brought in to renew the Vernon firm is that of an "enterprising"—presumably male—"manager," not a young, talented Vernon woman (447). Hester herself is left with "a possibility of choice" between suitors, the loyal, unspectacular Harry and the more dashing but ultimately solid Roland. But this is, in the novel's own bittersweet words, "all that can be said for her" (456). The ironic question "What can a young woman desire more?" that closes Hester's story asks readers to consider whether new narrative possibilities need to open up to her—and by extension to the family business (456).

Although the force of this disappointment certainly remains, focusing solely on the narrowing that occurs in this ending misses some of the openness that is built into it. Hester is, after all, pointedly left in a position to exercise "choice" and just as pointedly left with the choice unmade and perhaps even refused, given her professed disinclination to marry just a page or two earlier. If the close doesn't satisfy our desire to see a particular new narrative established, one based on the flourishing of female potential in the world of paid work, its lack of resolution makes for a far from conventional love-plot ending.

Furthermore, considered in light of the novel's engagement with the issue of hereditary character, the final emphasis on romantic choice may carry a greater disruptive charge than at first appears. The Darwinian overtones in the language of feminine choice between competing suitors cast a biological shadow over Hester's decision, which has, from Harry's first expression of interest, been subject to such arguments. Catherine's objections to the prospect of their marriage, for instance, are tinged with the rationalism of Galton's "judicious mating."[54] Harry and Hester would be a "ridiculous combination" because of the mismatch between her "Vernon" temper and quickness and his "stolid and heavy" nature: "If the world had been ransacked for two who ought not to come together, these two would be that pair" (124, 124–25, 124). By the end, however, all the grounds for this analysis have been unsettled. Harry's "nature" has shown unexpected capabilities, drawn out by circumstances that have also revalued stolidity and heaviness into a more estimable steadiness. Hester's essential Vernonness is no certainty. Roland, the alternative choice, has also demonstrated how difficult it is to define nature: with his familial character shown to be assigned through judgment and emotion, rather than determined by essential inheritance, and with our initial impression of slickness transformed by his emergence as a responsible counsel, Roland's character, too—and our understanding of it—is forged through a combination of circumstances and choices. Hester's final decision, therefore, faces thoroughly changed terms, all of which highlight the way character cannot be reduced to particular hereditary traits to be sought out and bred, but rather must be understood as a continuously constructed process.

The "new blood" that finally enters the Vernon family firm is not only the "enterprising manager" who helps instruct Harry, in other words, but the renovated Harry himself. The incorporation of family—Harry, and Ellen's husband Algernon Merridew—in the final incarnation of Vernon's bank occurs without reference to nature. There is no hereditary business genius to seek out and to maintain in the Vernon generations, or at least none that can be treated as the magical-scientific key to business character. There is only learning and labor to be performed by individuals for whom family history is most crucially a source of psychological complexity and ethical training. Readers may root for Catherine to keep Vernon's in the family, but the novel gives us to understand that the drive to continue the family identity of the firm arises from social, material, and emotional interests rather than any sense of innate fitness or even organizational superiority.

Hester transforms blood into a feature whose power is primarily metaphorical and social, rather than natural and essential, undermining the notion of hereditary character with which it begins. It accomplishes this and constructs its new vision of character largely through placing women into the story of the family business in the vibrant figures of Catherine and Hester. Oliphant's achievement lies in recognizing the need for a new narrative to expand the understanding of the operations of character in business. The novel's claim to authority in representing commercial life, in other words, is not limited to its insistence that a holistic, experiential, and psychological model of character—what her realist novel tracks and constructs—is necessary to understand economic agents. It also asserts its authority as an imaginatively expansive form that can incorporate new characters to see how their inclusion may challenge or reshape interpretive conventions. If Hester is finally more powerful as a figure whose story exemplifies and conveys a new model of character, without managing to establish a real commercial role for herself, the questions raised in telling her story and Catherine's press for a further expansion still of the notion of business character, to include without reservation the women who have been written out.

Conclusion

Merdle, Melmotte and Madoff. It sounds like a phony literary hedge fund.
—THOMAS MALLON

"SHOULD C.E.O.'S READ NOVELS?" THE *NEW YORK TIMES* OPINION
writer David Brooks wondered in a column in May 2009. "The question
seems to answer itself. After all, C.E.O.'s work with people all day. Novel-
reading should give them greater psychological insight, a feel for human
relationships, a greater sensitivity toward their own emotional chords." But
Brooks went on to suggest that this apparently self-evident confidence in the
benefits of novel reading for developing an "ideal personality type" for corporate leadership was misguided. Instead, he argued, "recent research" had
demonstrated that doggedness and organization were more important to
business success than the human insights that novel reading develops. "People skills" were less significant predictors of success than "attention to detail,
persistence, efficiency, analytic thoroughness, and the ability to work long
hours." "While it's important to be a sensitive, well-rounded person for the
sake of your inner fulfillment," he concluded, "the market doesn't really care.
The market wants you to fill an organizational role."[1]

One of the more striking aspects of Brooks's question about the role novels might play in developing C.E.O. character is that he asks it at all, let alone
that he frames the column around the notion that the obvious answer is that
novels will help. Conditioned as humanities scholars are to eyebrows-raised
skepticism about the practicality and career utility of our disciplines, who
would have thought to assume that novel reading and its lessons in human
character and relationships would be considered an essential step for every
aspiring C.E.O.? In fact, Brooks's conclusion—being "well-rounded" is nice,
but it won't help you get a job—is much more likely to feel intuitive.

In the intricacies of his framing, however, Brooks provides a useful reminder of two claims that have underpinned the argument of this book. The
first is that the commercial realm is not wholly captured by the theories of
professional economists and the equations and spreadsheets of analysts; it is

a sphere of social life in which participants as often as not "work with people all day." This activity, and the personal relationships, character transactions, and interpretations that it fosters, is crucial in the practice of business, from small family firms to large and complex organizations, in relationships with customers and coworkers, suppliers and contractors, bosses and subordinates, and so forth. These personal relationships, transactions, and interpretive situations form an important ground on which the relationship between literature and business has been negotiated. The second is that the history of that relationship remains more complex than accounts emphasizing simple inutility, opposition, or complicity can capture. Sometimes direct questions are asked about what literature and the various interpretive practices it has involved can do for business. Sometimes literary writing and business writing exhibit shared preoccupations with the forms and interpretive strategies used to represent and understand character. And sometimes those shared preoccupations lead businesspeople, business writers, and literary writers in very different directions.

Victorian representations of business character could be grounded in realist assumptions and narrative and interpretive norms or those of romance and adventure; they could be presented in the language of science or enchantment; they encompassed full-length biographical or fictional treatments, notes in a company ledger, and official legal documents with slight narrative content. This list is by no means exhaustive; the place of working-class character in the field of personal business, for instance, would likely prove a rich subject for future scholars. But the representations I have explored helped to shape the personal as both a means to enable everyday relations of business and a privatized way to regulate it. The tension between these two functions produced varying degrees of enthusiasm and anxiety among those who generated and used character representations, and because the same category—personal character—could serve antagonistic ends, it never managed to achieve the task it was most prominently charged with: ensuring an orderly and morally regulated commercial culture with a clear epistemological foundation.

Though business has changed dramatically from its conduct in Victorian Britain, versions of personal business and transactional character are with us today, shaped, as ever, by distinct national and local cultures. It would be a mistake to minimize the differences: that a technical vocabulary exists through which our personal connections can be branded "networks," with self-help books and courses devoted to "networking," for instance, means that even similar kinds of activities—club memberships, churchgoing, paying social calls—might be experienced in radically different ways in Victorian commercial contexts and in today's business culture. Charismatic C.E.O.s and financial gurus—figures such as Apple's Steve Jobs or Berkshire Hathaway's Warren Buffett—develop their celebrity in a thoroughly altered media environment. That same media conditions how scandalous figures are represented—how characters such as Bernie Madoff, Enron's Ken Lay, or the tawdry parade of owners of personal jets and $6,000 shower curtains that marched through the news during the early and mid-2000s embody the values of the market.[2] Despite these differences, however, it is also important to recognize the way the personal remains useful and often crucial to business, whether as staging ground, market opportunity, or trope. Management theorists have shown that by exploiting the personal connections of scientists, engineers, and middlemen of various stripes, high-technology firms are able to stay ahead in a cutthroat, globalized economy.[3] But references to the personal need not reflect actual personal relationships. They frequently constitute little more than a marketing device.

Take, for example, the opening to a column by the investment director of "The Oxford Club," an investment society which promises "Great Profits in the Company of Good Friends," in its for-members-only newsletter: "Karen and I celebrated our anniversary in Miami Beach. I promised there would be absolutely no work on this trip. My plan went awry when I discovered there were two Quiksilver (NYSE: ZQK) outlets within walking distance of the hotel."[4] The sharing of domestic confidences operates in a markedly different way from Melmotte's staging of grand balls and dinners in his opulent homes; the display of domestic wealth plays a role, but not a sufficient one. Instead, conjuring comfortable leisure, this passage seeks to consolidate its relationship with readers/investors/Good Friends through jocular gestures of intimacy, teasing with its suggestions of sex (an anniversary in Miami!) and marital bickering (the distracted husband; the nagging wife; "Honey, you *promised*..."). Offering glimpses of personal life as a way to forge a friendly connection, the column furthers the clubby marketing strategy:

> *The Oxford Club* is a private, international network of trustworthy and knowledgeable investors and entrepreneurs. We've quietly bonded in order to acquire wealth and provide for our families.... The Oxford Club keeps a low profile. We don't seek publicity and we shun that which comes our way. Our reason? The best investment tips are, by their very nature, exclusive. To ensure exclusivity, we keep our communications private and for members only. Furthermore, we do not advertise our organization, and we do not rent our members' names to the public, as most financial publishers do. Except for membership

drives, which are sent only to investors whom we believe share our interests and value privacy, we try to remain discreet.[5]

The Oxford Club newsletter has a decades-long history. That history features different names (its first incarnation, "The Royal Society of Liechtenstein," ran afoul of the local Better Business Bureau for being neither royal nor Liechtensteinian); different multimillion-dollar publishing and direct mail enterprise owners; and different authorial personae, at least one of whom did not exist (but sported the plummy, bankerish name Alexander Ross-Barclay).[6] But discretion, exclusivity, and a personal appeal from a companionable, in-the-know adviser are its hallmark. This isn't a *financial* transaction, but a personal one, the above passage seems to suggest: you are not someone whose name can be bought and sold. We know you, and we know you're our kind of person. The personal appeal softens or (the club would have it) bypasses the cold, hard market, and it promises to be a factor that promotes profits as it brings together all these knowledgeable, trustworthy, discreet friends to share their exclusive tips. In fact, an image of the Victorian era becomes part of the promotional allure: "The Oxford Club is modeled after the old English gentleman's clubs, especially those that flourished around Oxford and Cambridge in the 19th Century. The 150-year-old mansion that houses our world headquarters in Baltimore is in the English Club tradition." Not merely a virtual association produced by an Internet newsletter, the society proposes to concretize its personal connections, rebuilding the "English Club tradition" every year, with better weather, as "Oxfordians from all over the world meet for Investment U at locations including San Diego and the Florida coast."[7]

Victorian businessmen and investors, buffeted by the apparently regular rhythms of boom and crisis, might be surprised at having their era used as a touchstone of stability. But the appearance of the Victorian club is but one way in which the specific legacies of Victorian personal business—and its various representational forms—have been carried through and translated today. In a journalistic piece written in 1880, for instance, Anthony Trollope described something like the personal mode of the Oxford Club newsletter when he deplored the way the new coal and wine merchants polluted the conventions of social calls and communication, advertising themselves with fake visiting cards and circulars disguised to look like real letters. The tradesman's advertisement "used two or three years ago to make its appearance in the shape of a loose slip" that was "easily consigned to your basket." Then they came in "fastened envelopes" marked with the word "coal." "But of late,"

Trollope remarks, "the tell-tale word has been dropped, and the notices come up to us with our regular letters. They are even sent by the post, at what must surely be a great cost, because it has come to be understood that they will not otherwise be opened."[8] Not only does the coal merchant ("Messrs. Black and Sparkles") affect a personal relationship, but he also approaches potential customers in the grandiose manner of a commercial celebrity. He

> begins by giving his wished-for customers to understand that, having obtained the command of several of the most valuable collieries in England, and having devoted much personal attention to the subject, he has found himself able to supply you with coals, of which he sends you a catalogue, at certain defined prices. He sometimes informs you that the offer is only to hold good for a month. Your first impression would be one of wonder that men so great in commerce should find it worth their while to trouble themselves by writing to you upon the subject. We remember when we turned it over in our minds thinking that some one of our acquaintance had been kind enough to name us to Messrs. Black and Sparkles. But custom has quite made us used to it.[9]

We also have grown "used to" personal address, character creations, and assertions of charisma, sometimes feeling and using their power and at other moments eyeing them with skeptical savvy. We make bestsellers out of C.E.O. memoirs *and* their muckraking companions on bookstore shelves. Businesspeople and academic writers alike continue to ask whether Darwin and evolutionary science hold a key to understanding and revising commercial character. The adviser Barry Ritholtz urges investors to acknowledge the "monkey boy" within to avoid costly mistakes: "You're a monkey. It all comes down to that. You are a slightly clever, pants-wearing primate. If you forget that you're nothing more than a monkey who has been fashioned by eons on the plains, being chased by tigers, you shouldn't invest. . . . Every good financial decision I've made comes from, 'Wait a second, monkey boy, step back, don't do that.'"[10] In 2009 Scott Shane, a professor at Case Western University, trumpeted the preliminary findings of "behavioral genetics (twin) and molecular genetics (association) studies of entrepreneurship" conducted with colleagues at King's College, London, and the University of Cyprus: "the tendency to be an entrepreneur is heritable," as is "the tendency to identify new business opportunities" and to have greater "self-employment income"—all, perhaps, deriving from the genetic influence on our "personality traits." A "genome-wide association study to identify specific genes that might be associated with the tendency to become an entrepreneur" promised to further refine and biologize commercial character.[11] Galton would no doubt be interested.

Furthermore, literary writing has maintained a presence in contemporary popular business discourse. In August 2002 MSN Money's *Speculator* column listed "25 Literary Traits Every Trader Can Use," which distilled the results of a request to readers to share "trading lessons" that they had learned from literary characters. The "list of trader traits" feels not so different from the character prescriptions of Sir Arthur Helps, Samuel Smiles, and Co.: "Courageous, but prudent ... Forceful, but self-controlled ... Honest ... Loved by subordinates, colleagues." The only Victorian novelist to make the boldfaced main list is Arthur Conan Doyle (Sherlock Holmes "noticed what others missed")—though Lewis Carroll's *Alice's Adventures in Wonderland* and *Through the Looking Glass* are mentioned in an aside "for perspective on analysts." Romance and adventure stories supply the bulk of the list's trader models: D'Artagnan, Tom Sawyer, Gandalf, and Patrick O'Brian's naval captain Jack Aubrey, for instance. Still, the focus on character itself ("traits") as a crucial element forms a connection to Victorian personal business: "We think that the investor will receive 100 times more wisdom and value by reading the above books and stories than from dutifully keeping up with the endless parade of mind-numbing publications parroting has-been investment strategies."[12] The business press John Wiley and Sons published *Fictions of Business: Insights on Management from Great Literature,* by the former C.E.O. of the lingerie company Maidenform Worldwide, Inc. Noting that "literature puts us in touch with ourselves" and "encourages self scrutiny," reviewers highlighted the author's claims that literature helps businesspeople "to examine the values and personality traits that underlie the great drama that is business today" and praised the book's insights—drawn from readings of writers from Chaucer to Trollope to Arthur Miller and David Mamet—on everything from "maintaining individuality ... to handling stress and office politics" to understanding when and how to fire unproductive workers.[13] And while these texts emphasize the work literature can do for business, the more critical tradition in Victorian narrative has been kept alive as well, for instance in the *New York Times*'s bestowal of the Augustus Melmotte Memorial Prizes to noteworthy figures who exemplify commercial unsavoriness.[14]

In fact, at the moment Brooks asked "Should C.E.O.'s read novels?" his presumption that the obvious answer was "yes" was perhaps better founded than usual. As the 2008 crisis loomed and then hit, Victorian novels and their critical insights attained a remarkable prominence in popular discussions of the economy. Brooks's co-columnist, Nobel Memorial Prize–winning economist Paul Krugman, mentioned in his *New York Times* blog that the crisis had inspired him to pick up Dickens's *Little Dorrit*. An extensive discussion in the blog's comments not only endorsed novel reading but also debated which Victorian novels most aptly spoke to the current moment. *The Way We Live Now* and *Dombey and Son* joined *Little Dorrit* in Krugman's readers' imaginary syllabus. Harley Granville-Barker's little-known 1905 play *The Voysey Inheritance*, whose timely adaptation by David Mamet had been playing around the United States, made the cut. The no doubt fanciful suggestion was made that "economics grad schools should have a mandatory course in Dickens."[15] The blog discussion was sparked by the figure of Madoff, who became a one-man advertisement for Victorian literature as comparisons to Merdle, Melmotte, and Voysey popped up again and again. "Even his name is sort of Dickensian," the novelist Thomas Mallon pronounced. "Made-Off. It sounds so perfect."[16] "I default to Dickens," the economics journalist Susan Lee wrote in *Forbes.com,* quoting directly in order to establish the resemblance to Merdle as she pondered the mystery of how a "total schlub" could also be a "world-class swindler."[17] Andrew Delbanco saw something else in Madoff, a puzzle of moral consciousness whose representation would require the talents of Henry James.[18] Perhaps all the attention was effective: in the months following the Madoff scandal sales of Dickens, Trollope, and Thackeray jumped more than 15 percent, according to the London *Times.*[19] The crisis that began in late 2008 may have devastated several economies, but it was good for Victorian novelists.

Still, champions of the "read novels!" response to the business scandals of today should perhaps proceed with caution. Today's versions of the narratives of personal business may be beset by the same tension that plagued Victorian ones. Character and its narratives do not simply stand outside business, offering a ready tool through which to discipline and moralize commerce. The personal is an inherent feature of business practice, enabling both legitimate and necessary activities and successes and shady ones. What the Victorian experience suggests, in both fact and fiction, is that finer skills and forms for interpreting and representing the personal need not guarantee that the former outweigh the latter. We may learn a great deal about the operations of personal business by examining and understanding the character of a latter-day Merdle or Melmotte, as well as by examining the literary characters themselves, from the upright (if flawed) Catherine Vernon to the scheming Carker. But the impulse to treat commercial ills with "care, vigilance, and intimate knowledge of . . . character," rather than law and regulation, has been around for a long time now.[20] As part of a diversified portfolio of disciplinary tools, character and the narratives that give it shape may play useful roles—and may be unavoidable in any case. But we would be wise not to overinvest in their promise.

Notes

Introduction

1. Dickens, *Dombey and Son*, 33.
2. See, for instance, Brantlinger, *Fictions of State;* and Gagnier, *Insatiability of Human Wants.* The sense of vertiginous transformation in commercial life is, to be sure, a very real feature of Victorian culture; for an excellent discussion, see Nancy Henry and Cannon Schmitt, "Introduction: Finance, Capital, Culture."

For a reappraisal of the world of Victorian finance, see Ziegler, "City of London."
3. Speech by the chairman of the Ottoman Bank, 1956, Ottoman Bank papers, 3.
4. Speech by the chairman of the Ottoman Bank, 6.
5. For the term *personal capitalism,* see esp. Chandler, "Growth of the Transnational Industrial Firm," and *Scale and Scope.*
6. Henriques, *Wizard of Lies*, 3.
7. See, for instance, Goux, *Symbolic Economies;* and Shell, *Economy of Literature,* and *Money, Language, and Thought.*
8. The term *new economic criticism* emerged in the early 1990s, incorporating "an emerging body of literary and cultural criticism founded upon economic paradigms, models and tropes" (Osteen and Woodmansee, "Taking Account of the New Economic Criticism," 3).
9. See Poovey, *Genres of the Credit Economy.*
10. Critics, especially feminists, have long been wary of accepting the strict separation of the economic from the noneconomic. My argument joins other recent works that turn a fine-grained attention to the institutions and practices through which the crosscutting takes place; see, for instance, Corbett, *Family Likeness;* and Rappoport, *Giving Women.*
11. The concept of business might, for instance, be broken down into different specific subcategories (finance, commerce, retail trade, industry, and so forth), each of which could merit an individualized focus. But the risk in breadth is worth taking for a couple of reasons. First, though these subcategories are distinctive, the broader term *business* resonated meaningfully, if not always identically, for writers during the Victorian period, who did not necessarily feel the same compulsion to analytical precision that an economic historian would. From Scrooge's description of Marley as a "good man of business," to biographical collections with titles such as *Fortunes Made in Business,* which interspersed accounts of bankers with tales of pen makers and alpaca processors, *business* maintained a generalized conceptual power encompassing different types of competitive profit-seeking activities and

the routines, techniques, and languages they entailed. See Dickens, *Christmas Carol*, 62; see also the collection "by various writers," *Fortunes Made in Business*. Furthermore, authors themselves lived various aspects of business lives in their writing careers—at different stages (and even all at once) acting as artisans, entrepreneurial marketers, speculative investors, and so forth—such that the lived experience of a writing career might have invoked enough angles that a general term not only proved useful but might have felt necessary.

12. Carlyle, *Past and Present*, 282.

13. For a succinct account of these debates, see Levinson, "What Is New Formalism?"

14. Marx, "On the Jewish Question," 43; see also Foucault, *Discipline and Punish*, and *History of Sexuality: Volume 1*.

15. See Watt, *Rise of the Novel*; McKeon, *Origins of the English Novel*; and Armstrong, *Desire and Domestic Fiction*.

16. See Shell, *Economy of Literature*, as well as *Money, Language, and Thought*. See also Goux, *Symbolic Economies*. Jean-Christophe Agnew's work on theatricality in market relationships—focused less exclusively on print textuality—represents an important early departure from this abstracting tendency. Agnew's insights that the "transactional experience of the world," even if shaped by abstracting and depersonalizing media such as bills of exchange, should not be reduced to the effects of those media, has been influential for my study (*Worlds Apart*, 4).

17. See Michaels, *Gold Standard and the Logic of Naturalism*. The intellectual history of political economy has also been a rich vein in this body of criticism; see, for instance, Bigelow, *Fiction, Famine, and the Rise of Economics*; Gagnier, *Insatiability of Human Wants*; Gallagher, *Body Economic*; and Klaver, *A/Moral Economics*. There are noteworthy exceptions to this tendency to focus on the economy's abstractions, for example through attention to practices related to consumption—advertising, retail display, and so forth; see, for instance, A. Miller, *Novels behind Glass*; and Wicke, *Advertising Fictions*. And the literary marketplace has been studied as a site of economic practice, for instance, in Gallagher's *Nobody's Story* and in Martha Woodmansee's and Mark Rose's important work on authors and copyright. Still, the clustering of such analyses around particular foci leaves a wide range of economic activities underexamined.

18. Audrey Jaffe's *Affective Life of the Average Man* presents a compelling and subtle argument that the domain of the personal—self, identity, psychology—is intimately informed by a relationship to abstraction in the Victorian market (especially stock market) economy, for instance, as subjects come to perceive themselves as embodying a market "pulse" or feeling or to measure their identity by reference to a mathematical norm that they simultaneously participate in and stand apart from. For an older, influential approach, see Pocock, *Virtue, Commerce, and History*.

19. See, for instance, Bigelow, *Fiction, Famine, and the Rise of Economics*; Gallagher, *Body Economic*; Henry and Schmitt, *Victorian Investments*; Houston, *From Dickens to Dracula*; and O'Gorman, *Victorian Literature and Finance*.

20. See, for instance, Wagner, *Financial Speculation in Victorian Fiction*; a different approach is taken by Malton, *Forgery in Nineteenth-Century Literature and Culture*. The new economic criticism has not had a theoretical monopoly on Victorian economic subjects: for other important recent work, see, for example, Bizup, *Manufacturing Culture*; and Hack, *Material Interests of the Victorian Novel*.

21. See Hilton, *Age of Atonement*, 256; and Cottrell, *Industrial Finance 1830–1914*, 54.

22. See Whyte, *Organization Man;* and Sloan Wilson's novel *Man in the Gray Flannel Suit,* made iconic by the 1956 film of the same name.

23. R. Williams, *Country and the City,* 156.

24. See, for example, ibid., 220.

25. Christina Crosby, "Financial," in H. Tucker, *Companion to Victorian Literature and Culture,* 230, 231.

26. Herbert Sussman, "Industrial," in H. Tucker, *Companion to Victorian Literature and Culture,* 255.

27. Jennifer Wicke, "Commercial," in H. Tucker, *Companion to Victorian Literature and Culture,* 259, 261.

28. The disciplinary divergence is evidenced by the fact that a central debate among business and economic historians centers on the role played by personal capitalism in Britain's economic decline relative to other nations. See esp. Chandler, "Growth of the Transnational Industrial Firm," and *Scale and Scope.* Barry Supple provides a useful review in "Scale and Scope." Margot Finn's *Character of Credit* superbly registers the way the personal resonated in everyday economic practice. Timothy Alborn's analyses of the moral, political, and economic rhetorics and narratives through which Victorian businesses represented themselves and were represented have been enormously important to my understanding of Victorian commercial cultures. See esp. "Moral of the Failed Bank."

29. See Daunton, "Afterword," 202–20; Nenadic, "Small Family Firm in Victorian Britain"; and Mary B. Rose, "Family Firm in British Business," 61–87.

30. Mary B. Rose, "Family Firm in British Business," 68.

31. See Nicholas, "Clogs to Clogs in Three Generations?" 689.

32. See Mary B. Rose, "Family Firm in British Business," 68. Social scientists disagree on the percentage of share capital that is necessary for effective control of a company, but in a modern stock market with dispersed ownership it need not exceed 20 percent. See Zeitlin, *Large Corporation and Contemporary Classes,* 17. Compare Mary B. Rose's example of the brewing company Truman Hanbury and Company, which went public in the 1880s but remained effectively under the control of its eponymous founding families, who owned fully 67 percent of the share capital and all the company's equity ("Family Firm in British Business").

33. Lazonick, "Social Organization and Technological Leadership," 171.

34. See Chandler, "Growth of the Transnational Industrial Firm," 406.

35. Chandler, *Scale and Scope,* 286.

36. Francis, *Chronicles and Characters of the Stock Exchange,* 224–25.

37. "Testimonial to Mr. William Haig Miller," 959, 958, 958, 958.

38. "Dry Bank Statistics," 905.

39. Hirschman, "Rival Interpretations of Market Society," 1473.

40. Karl Polanyi's account of the effects of the 1834 New Poor Law in *The Great Transformation* is the classic formulation of this process. See also Perkin, *Origins of Modern English Society.* For reconsiderations of Polanyi's thesis and the concept of embeddedness, see Block, "Karl Polanyi and the Writing of *The Great Transformation,*" 276; Polanyi, "Economy as Instituted Process"; and Krippner, "Elusive Market." The concept of embeddedness is foundational to the subfield of economic sociology, which has also incorporated the analysis of intimate relationships and affect, perhaps most notably in the work of Viviana Zelizer. See, for instance, *Social Meaning of Money,* as well as *Purchase of Intimacy* and

Economic Lives. Behavioral economics, similarly, has built its insights from attention to deviations from pure rational calculation; though it remains heterodox, the subfield has received the imprimatur of a Nobel Prize (awarded to Daniel Kahneman) and has come to influence the work of orthodox scholars like Nobel laureate George Akerlof. See, for example, Akerlof and Shiller, *Animal Spirits.*

41. See also Klaver, *A/Moral Economics.*

42. Poovey, *Genres of the Credit Economy,* 28, 414.

43. Ibid., 277. The relation of the discipline of economics to reality continues to be a lively topic, especially as some prominent economists (Paul Krugman most notably) have criticized their discipline for clinging to models in the face of evidence from the 2008 economic crisis—or, put another way, for "mistaking beauty for truth" (Paul Krugman, "How Did Economists Get It So Wrong?" *New York Times Magazine,* Sept. 6, 2009, 36). The question has been taken up in an academic context by Harald Uhlig—speaking from a no less central disciplinary position than chair of the University of Chicago Department of Economics—who asks "how reality in the form of empirical evidence does or does not influence economic thinking and theory" ("Economics and Reality," 29).

44. See, for instance, Watt, *Rise of the Novel;* and Armstrong, *Desire and Domestic Fiction.* Not that commercial activity has been ignored absolutely: Watt, for instance, cites merchants' need for news as a contribution to the novel's orientation toward "formal realism" (32).

45. Lynch, *Economy of Character,* 4.

46. For more on the underspecification of the concept of the middle class, see Goodlad, "'Middle Class Cut into Two.'"

47. Poovey, *Genres of the Credit Economy,* 397.

48. Pavel, *Fictional Worlds,* 145.

49. Poovey, *Genres of the Credit Economy,* 400, 401.

50. On readers' "ordinary" responses to character, see Keen, "Readers' Temperaments and Fictional Character," 295. On the role of expectations, see Ahmed, "Willful Parts."

51. See, for instance, Pavel, *Fictional Worlds;* Ronen, "Completing the Incompleteness of Fictional Entities"; Newsom, *Likely Story;* and D. A. Miller, *Narrative and Its Discontents.* In a recent discussion, Catherine Gallagher argues that characters—ideational and suppositional though they are—tend to be textual features that make connections to our world, rather than prompting readers to create imaginary new worlds "to accommodate them" as "possible worlds" theories of fiction seem to suggest ("What Would Napoleon Do?" 332).

52. Woloch, *One vs. the Many,* 14.

53. *How to Read the Character,* 1.

54. Ibid., quoting Sir James Stevens and Ralph Waldo Emerson, 1.

55. Ibid., 20.

56. *Mercantile Letter Writer,* 1.

57. See *Business Letter Writer.*

58. [McCulloch], "Thoughts on the Improvement of the System," 425.

59. Ibid., 432.

60. [White], "Murdering Banker," 824.

61. See [McCulloch], "Thoughts on the Improvement of the System," 434, 436–37. As Poovey has suggested, well into the Victorian period accounting was frequently seen

to need the supplement of other forms of representation; it hadn't in practice established itself as the trustworthy, complete mode of analysis and representation that it claimed to be; see Poovey, "Writing about Finance in Victorian England."

62. [McCulloch], "Thoughts on the Improvement of the System," 429.

63. Ibid., 432, 434.

64. "Bankruptcy Laws," 629.

65. Alborn's "First Fund Managers" discusses such opportunities for interpersonal communication in the financial field, especially the bonus meeting, at which managers declared the bonus that policyholders would receive. These meetings, he suggests, exemplify the ambivalent significance that interpersonal encounters might hold, as they offered both an opportunity for disciplinary scrutiny and accountability and a chance for spectacle and self-promotion (59, 67).

66. See Goodlad, *Victorian Literature and the Victorian State*, chap. 1 and ix–x.

67. Gilbart, *Practical Treatise on Banking*, 12.

68. For the term *character books*, see Kynaston, *City of London*, 80.

69. *How to Read the Character*, 4–5.

70. *Business Letter Writer*, 10. See also Finn, *Character of Credit*.

71. Antony Gibbs and Sons, Ltd., Confidential Information Book on Merchant Firms (1859–). As the information books chart character, they often end up assigning it a value based on a mixture of character and property information and how "intimate" their personal "connexion" is: better or worse interest rates might be offered; someone who is "very trustworthy" meets with the response that "we should be glad to take his signature for goods for twice the value he mentions." See letter to Charles Swinburn, Santiago de Chile, Dec. 1, 1865, Antony Gibbs and Sons, Ltd., Confidential Information Book on Bank's Customers, Chiefly Foreign (1865–); entry for Geronimo Costa of Puño, Antony Gibbs and Sons, Ltd., Confidential Information Book on Merchant Firms (1859–). As a marker of the distance between Victorian personal business and the purer forms of commercial abstraction, consider the rhetorical difference between these books' assessments of creditworthiness, in which connections and assessments are traced out, and today's numerical credit scores or—even more dramatically and catastrophically—the "AAA" ratings of mortgage-backed securities assigned by ratings agencies, in which the magic of large numbers was imagined to have purged the risks implied on the individual, personal level.

72. Antony Gibbs and Sons, Ltd., Confidential Information Book on Merchant Firms (1859–).

73. See W. W. Powell, "Neither Market nor Hierarchy."

74. Antony Gibbs and Sons, Ltd., Confidential Information Book on Merchant Firms 1883–1905.

75. Antony Gibbs and Sons, Confidential Information Book on Merchant Firms (1859–).

76. Antony Gibbs and Sons, Confidential Information Book on Merchant Firms 1883–1905.

77. Antony Gibbs and Sons, Confidential Information Book on Merchant Firms (1859–).

78. See Henry's *George Eliot and the British Empire* for a related account of the connections between realist representation and the knowledge production demanded by global investment.

79. Not all novels were so fuzzy about business. Henry has done essential work, for instance, to bring to critical attention the novelist Charlotte Riddell, whose novels of the City address the business world with a directness that is rare in many better-known Victorian novels. See Henry, " 'Ladies Do It?' " 111–31.

80. Eliot, "Natural History of German Life," 51, 52.

81. Houston has noted the emergence of Gothic tropes in the face of the anxieties produced by the period's economic instability (see *From Dickens to Dracula*). Indeed, realism was far from the only generic response to economic circumstances; many accounts of the period's business practices mined "melodrama, romance, the detective story, and sensationalism" for powerful representational conventions (Poovey, introduction to *Financial System in Nineteenth-Century Britain*, 33).

82. Entry for F. et Jung Havre et Quesnelfrères Co., Aug. 17, 1864, Antony Gibbs and Sons, Ltd., Confidential Information Book on Merchant Firms (1859–).

83. Kleinwort, Sons, and Co., Cape Colonies, East Indies, China, Japan Information Book, 1875–1909, 106.

84. Ronen, "Completing the Incompleteness of Fictional Entities," 497, 498, 497.

85. Knight, *Public Guarantee and Private Suretyship*, 7, 39. At the same time that guarantee societies offered to insure business against the risks of character, it was argued that public guarantee would act as a spur to the development of character and character reading, as security became less a matter of personal connections; see 14–16. I am grateful to Tim Alborn for encouraging me to investigate guarantee societies.

1. The Trusty Agent

1. Dickens to John Forster, [June 28?, 1846], in Dickens, *Letters*, 4:573.

2. Dickens to Thomas Chapman, Lausanne, July 3, 1846, in Dickens, *Letters*, 4:575. The Dickens-Powell-Chapman episode has been discussed by several critics and biographers; see, for instance, Friedman, "Heep and Powell"; and Slater, *Charles Dickens*.

3. Dickens to Thomas Chapman, Lausanne, July 3, 1846, 575n.

4. See Slater, *Charles Dickens*, 239, which notes that Dickens's first surviving mention of his passion for Maria Beadnell was made in an 1845 letter to Powell.

5. See Dickens's letters to Thomas Powell, London, Feb. 24, 1844, and Mar. 2, 1844, and his letter to Fanny Kelly, Dec. 25, 1845, all in Dickens, *Letters*, 4:50, 61, 455.

6. Dickens to Thomas Chapman, London, Feb. 8, 1844, in Dickens, *Letters*, 4:40.

7. Dickens to Thomas Chapman, Lausanne, July 3, 1846, 575.

8. Quoted in the editors' note to Dickens to Lewis Gaylord Clark, Oct. 22, 1849, in Dickens, *Letters*, 5:631n1.

9. Dickens to Thomas Chapman, London, Oct. 20, 1849, in Dickens, *Letters*, 5:629.

10. Dickens to Thomas Chapman, London, Dec. 14, 1849, in Dickens, *Letters*, 5:671; see also Dickens to Messrs John Chapman and Co., London, Dec. 13, 1849, in Dickens, *Letters*, 5:670.

11. Dickens, *Dombey and Son*, 521; subsequent references are noted in parentheses in the text.

12. Giddens, *Modernity and Self-Identity*, 6; see also Giddens, *Consequences of Modernity*.

13. John Gibbons, *Practical Remarks on the Use of the Cinder Pig in the Puddling Fur-*

nace; and on the Management of the Forge and the Mill, quoted in Pollard, *Genesis of Modern Management,* 122.

14. Minute Books of the Bankers' Guarantee and Trust Fund, v. 1, Nov. 27, 1866.

15. Greiner, *Sympathetic Realism,* 28; see also 37.

16. See Lynch, *Economy of Character.*

17. See Ronen, "Completing the Incompleteness of Fictional Entities," 497; Frow, "Spectacle Binding," 246; and Pavel, *Fictional Worlds,* 107–12.

18. Chalmers, *Application of Christianity,* 54–55.

19. Smiles, *Self-Help,* 238.

20. Margaret Levi has suggested that *trust* has tended to act as a "holding word for a variety of phenomena that enable individuals to take risks in dealing with others, solve collective action problems, or act in ways that seem contrary to standard definitions of self-interest" ("State of Trust," 78). As Levi notes, *trust* has continued to generate a great deal of interest among "economists and political economists" who have realized the explanatory limits of models centered on "'getting the incentives right'" (77).

21. Smith, "Of Police," 538. Smith privileged openness and candor as crucial aspects of the sympathetic exchange that forged social bonds; see *Theory of Moral Sentiments,* 399–400. See also Hirschman, "Rival Interpretations of Market Society." Even without the repetition that Smith envisions here, trust enters into exchange as a factor of time. As Kaushik Basu notes, "virtually all economic exchanges entail a time-lag," which might be larger (as in Chalmers's example of exchanges between England and India) or smaller, as in the moment when a taxi driver stops the cab, before the passenger hands over payment ("On Why We Do Not Try," 2011). Trust, character, cultural norms, laws, and institutions: all these might be thought of as features addressing this time lag. I am grateful to Andrew Schrank for suggesting the reference.

22. See Hilton, *Age of Atonement,* 13. The Reverend Chalmers echoes Smith's model when he answers the question, "Why is it that he whom you have trusted acquits himself of his trust with such correctness and fidelity?" by praising a divinely ordained principle of selfishness through which the behavior of each individual, knowing that "if he forfeit the confidence of others he will also forfeit their custom," aggregates to produce a climate of commercial trust (*Application of Christianity,* 55, 58).

23. Smith, *Wealth of Nations,* 1.6.66; see also 1.10.b.122.

24. Hume, *History of England* (1778), quoted in ibid., 1.10.b.122n16.

25. Francis, *Chronicles and Characters of the Stock Exchange,* 110.

26. Evans, *Facts, Failures, and Frauds,* 3, 483. The first quotation is derived from Evans's introduction, while the second comes from the pronouncement of sentence on Redpath.

27. Ibid., 565.

28. Ibid., 483. See Robb, *White Collar Crime in Modern England.*

29. Smith, *Wealth of Nations,* 4.7.c.638–39. On the uneasy place of the manager in a large company within classical political economy, see Alborn, "Moral of the Failed Bank," 205.

30. Smith, *Wealth of Nations,* 5.1.e.741; see also 5.1.e.755.

31. In the crisis of 1825, for instance, the failure of many mining firms was blamed on mismanagement by "dishonest, absconding or alcoholic managers" (Pollard, *Genesis of Modern Management,* 21).

32. Quoted in ibid., 22.

33. See Kirby, "Big Business before 1900," 114. Earlier varieties of management include agricultural estate agents and supervisory agents in the putting-out system; see Pollard, *Genesis of Modern Management,* 26–32, 157.

34. See Pollard, *Genesis of Modern Management,* 111, 122. On family as a guarantor of trust, see Nenadic, "Small Family Firm in Victorian Britain," 88–89; Mary B. Rose, "Family Firm in British Business," 66; and Kuper, *Incest and Influence.*

35. See Pollard, *Genesis of Modern Management,* 151–52.

36. See ibid., 139, 111, 122, 138–43. François Crouzet claims that despite the tendency to look to the families and friends of partners for managers, a good proportion came from more humble backgrounds; see *First Industrialists,* 114.

37. Evans, *Facts, Failures, and Frauds,* 565, 483.

38. Review of *Claims of Labour,* 513, 513–14.

39. Ibid., 514, 515, 516.

40. Ibid., 516.

41. Advice given to George Stephenson in 1821 in the course of his work on the Stockton-Darlington railway line, quoted in Pollard, *Genesis of Modern Management,* 23.

42. Campbell, *Principles of Mercantile Law,* 133.

43. There was less protection against forgery than one might expect. For example, up until 1881 if an employer habitually paid bills containing his forged signature, it could be taken as acceptance of the agent's practice of signing, and the power of future refusal to be responsible for the bills might be jeopardized. See ibid., 129.

44. Helps, *Essays Written in the Intervals of Business,* 272. Helps's *Essays* was a popular and influential work, containing chapters such as "On the Choice and Management of Agents"; first published in 1841, it went through seven British editions by 1858 and seven more between 1870 and 1910, as well as numerous American printings. It was mentioned with approval by other business writers during the Victorian period; see, for instance, Tulloch, *Beginning Life,* and the handbook *How to Read the Character.* It was later reprinted, in part, as "The Transaction of Business" in an American volume in which it was accompanied by Dale Carnegie's "How to Win Fortune" and several other compendia of business advice. An edition was published in Tokyo in 1897. In his other works, Helps was also a proponent of rebuilding affectionate, paternalistic ties between employers and workers to heal the breach between classes (the *Edinburgh Review* piece mentioned above was a response to his work).

45. Even those who were employed in concerns that had a corporate structure, rather than individual ownership or partnership, were affected by the model of inhabiting another's role in the thought processes they were enjoined to in their daily decision making and in their relations with superiors.

46. Helps, *Essays Written in the Intervals of Business,* 263.

47. Helps, *Claims of Labour,* 156, 157, 154.

48. This tension was a topic for professionals, as well. In lectures delivered in 1848 to the Incorporated Law Society, in London, Samuel Warren proposed that because a lawyer had a duty to represent the interests of his clients, his goal in training was "the becoming capable . . . of undertaking the responsible management of the difficult affairs of other people—of becoming, in a word, their *other-selves!*" But at the same time, he needed to develop his own self so as to be able to stand apart "in order the more effectually to serve

clients blind to their own real interests" (Warren, *Moral, Social, and Professional Duties*, 47, 39). On the relation of professionalism to the market, see Robbins, "Presentism, Pastism, Professionalism," 461, and *Secular Vocations*.

49. Smiles, *Self-Help*, 315, 320.
50. Helps, *Essays Written in the Intervals of Business*, 261, 265, 260.
51. Tulloch, *Beginning Life*, 169.
52. Stowell, *Model for Men of Business*, 84; Smiles, *Self-Help*, 318.
53. Smiles, *Self-Help*, 226.
54. Ibid., 321. The emphasis on character as process raises the question of change. Most authors champion self-development, implying the potential for transformation. But when it comes to evaluating the character of others in order to determine trust, they are less likely to affirm the possibility. The wise businessman, one author suggests, "should not, on any consideration, place a person who has had anything against his character in a position of trust.... *What a man has done once, he may and probably will do again*" (*Business Life*, 43).
55. Smiles, *Self-Help*, 233. Napoleon's particular genius was for recognizing likely surrogates; he "possessed such knowledge of character as enabled him to select, almost unerringly, the best agents for the execution of his designs." Still, like a good businessman, he was appropriately wary of relying too much on others but "trusted as little as possible to agents in matters of great moment, on which important results depended" (231).
56. Helps, *Essays Written in the Intervals of Business*, 226–27.
57. Ibid., 222.
58. Ibid., 222, 223. The story produced by this self-scrutiny is not a purely psychological one; by "principle" Helps means not only the way actions fit together and what they suggest in aggregate about the nature of the individual but also the moral and religious aspects that they may be taken to reveal or violate.
59. Helps, *Claims of Labour*, 69, 65.
60. Helps, *Essays Written in the Intervals of Business*, 215.
61. Ibid., 231–32. I take "faithful outline of his history" here, in conjunction with "two or three of the most prominent actions in his life," to mean something like a résumé.
62. Ibid., 279.
63. Ibid., 230–31.
64. Ibid., 230.
65. Helps continuously emphasizes the value of attention to the feelings behind the interpersonal dynamics in business. When dealing with "suitors," for instance—job applicants or people seeking financial help—he recommends staying aware of the "natural delusions of hope" that might induce someone to "put the largest construction upon every ambiguous expression, and every term of courtesy which can be made to express anything at all in their favour," and thus being especially careful in the language one uses. Likewise, he advises concern for the mental state of employees: harsh criticism may make the employee overly "anxious" to please the employer's "fancy," rather than focusing on "the success of the undertaking" (ibid., 276, 277, 275).
66. Masson, *British Novelists and Their Styles*, 147.
67. Tulloch, *Beginning Life*, 242, 231.
68. Robson "occasionally contributed light literature to the periodicals," and his "best play," *Love and Loyalty*, enjoyed the occasional short theatrical run (Evans, *Facts, Failures, and Frauds*, 393).

69. Ibid., 393.

70. Ibid., 394.

71. Ibid., 395.

72. See Ackroyd, *Dickens,* 476–90.

73. Dickens to Messrs Bradbury and Evans, London, Nov. 3, 1845, in Dickens, *Letters,* 4:424.

74. Dickens to Bradbury and Evans, Jan. 30, 1846, in Dickens, *Letters,* 4:485.

75. Schwarzbach, *Dickens and the City,* 106.

76. See also Byrne, "Consuming the Family Economy"; Perera, "Wholesale, Retail, and for Exportation"; and Moglen, "Theorizing Fiction/Fictionalizing Theory."

77. Clark, "Riddling the Family Firm," 78; see also Byrne, "Consuming the Family Economy."

78. Woloch, *One vs. the Many,* 30, 26, 27, 29, 223.

79. For a reading that dovetails with my own, see Humpherys, *"Dombey and Son,"* 409.

80. Dickens was not alone in seeing menace in the exercise of sympathy within business settings. Evans calls the "sympathetic powers" of George Hudson, the Railway King of the mid-1840s, "remarkably strong" and describes an imaginative and performative exchange as key to Hudson's manipulation of investor affect: "He was accustomed to infuse his own confidence into others. On this occasion he went through the usual pantomime of assuming to change places with the body of shareholders. He delighted, not only to take upon himself the responsibility of a scheme—in advance of its ratification on the part of the shareholders—but to come after, in the very heigh-day of their enthusiasm and delight, and tempt them pleasingly to make back to him the bargain over which, on his assurance, he knew them all to be chuckling" (*Facts, Failures, and Frauds,* 41).

81. For accounts of Dickens's ambivalent treatment of reading, see Hadley, *Melodramatic Tactics,* chap. 3; and Brantlinger, *Reading Lesson,* chap. 4.

82. I differ here from Jeff Nunokawa's theatrical interpretation of Carker's parting shot: "the capitalist's treacherous assistant" "manages Dombey's loss of fortune not by stealing it, but by staging it" (*Afterlife of Property,* 44). Carker does not stage the loss of fortune; he writes it for Dombey to read and interpret.

83. Klaver is attentive to the novel's dynamic of surface and depth as she reads Florence's capacity for moral rejuvenation. In her account, Florence's moral depths, signified by feminine virtue (qualities of depth that she shares with other domestic female characters in the novel, notably Harriet Carker, the manager's steadfast sister), act as a stabilizing force within the business world of the novel. However, she suggests, as Florence turns into an iconic figure rather than a figure with depths, she becomes less able to sustain that moralizing function. Surface is a problem within Dickens's novel insofar as it is "false, exchangeable" (*A/Moral Economics,* 91); as Florence becomes at once surface and part of a sexual economy, she becomes a reminder of the destabilizing forces of exchangeability and masculine competition. Klaver's argument is compelling, but as a typology of character in the novel it is lacking insofar as it reduces surface to false surface. I argue, in contrast, that the novel retains a suspicion of depths, creating a model of pure surface in which, with no depths to cover, falseness is impossible. See also Duncan, *Modern Romance and Transformations of the Novel,* esp. 237–39, on Dickens's self-conscious attention to the literary genres and devices he employs.

84. See Woloch, *One vs. the Many,* chap. 2.

85. Duncan, *Modern Romance and Transformations of the Novel,* 252.

86. Evans, *Facts, Failures, and Frauds,* 1, 484.

87. Ibid., 433.

88. Ibid., 437.

89. Ibid., 484.

90. Dickens to Forster, July 25–26, 1846, and Nov. 22 and 23, 1846, all in Dickens, *Letters,* 4:593, 658.

91. See, for instance, Steven Marcus, *Dickens from Pickwick to Dombey;* and Welsh, *From Copyright to Copperfield.* See also Duncan, *Modern Romance and Transformations of the Novel,* 237.

92. Review of *Dombey and Son,* by Dickens, 1324. This was not, of course, a universal opinion. See, for instance, Trollope, *Autobiography,* 159, in which he announces that none of the characters Dickens portrayed are "human"; see also Masson, *British Novelists and Their Styles,* 248–53.

2. Routinized Charisma and the Romance of Trade

1. L. Oliphant, "Autobiography of a Joint-Stock Company (Limited)," 96, 97.

2. Ibid., 121.

3. Ibid., 98. On Grant, see Poovey, *Financial System in Nineteenth-Century Britain,* 329n; and Kynaston, *City of London,* 265–67.

4. Anderson, "Trollope's Modernity," 516. Elsewhere Anderson has discussed the routine characterological impulse in discussions of politics or ideology, genres or styles; see "Character and Ideology," 211. Sidney Laman Blanchard's "Biography of a Bad Shilling" is an earlier instance in which conceptual strain testifies to the strength of the biographical urge. See Poovey's discussion of this piece in *Genres of the Credit Economy.* On other varieties of nineteenth-century it-narrative, see Price, "From *The History of a Book.*"

5. "Sir John Brown," in *Fortunes Made in Business,* 1:244. George Robb notes the existence of an "economic demonology" in contemporary journalistic accounts; see *White Collar Crime in Modern England,* 4. Some examples of the biography genre include Francis's *Chronicles and Characters of the Stock Exchange;* Evans's *City Men and City Manners;* Bourne's two-volume *English Merchants* and *Romance of Trade;* the three-volume collection *Fortunes Made in Business;* and of course the numerous lives written by Samuel Smiles.

6. Preface to *Fortunes Made in Business,* 1:iv. The public relations purpose of the biographies is undeniable and often seems to transcend the individual subject to aim at burnishing the reputation of a class. Biographies were only one of a number of ways that businesses and businessmen represented themselves. Architectural and artistic projects, philanthropy, and cultural and community activities all contributed to the businessman's public profile. See, for instance, Dianne Sachko Macleod's valuable study *Art and the Victorian Middle Class,* which analyzes art collection practices among the Victorian business classes as strategies of self-production and image management.

7. Weber, "Sociology of Charismatic Authority," in *From Max Weber,* 245.

8. Weber, "Bureaucracy," in *From Max Weber,* 215.

9. See Swedberg, *Max Weber and the Idea of Economic Sociology,* 64–66. On more recent manifestations of business charisma, see Khurana, *Searching for a Corporate Savior.*

10. Herbert, *Culture and Anomie,* 131. Herbert is here discussing how money becomes imbued with almost sacred significance, but his argument traces this tendency toward "oc-

cult" or "magical" horizons of explanation through a number of the nineteenth-century economic and social scientific discourses that are closely identified with modernity.

11. Preface (1877) to Arthur, *Successful Merchant*, xii; subsequent references are noted in parentheses in the text.

12. Arthur, preface to Author's Uniform Edition (1885), in *Successful Merchant*, xv.

13. On realism's visual registers, see, for instance, Armstrong, *Fiction in the Age of Photography*.

14. Eliot, *Adam Bede*, 221.

15. On the history of the closet, the study in which middle-class men tended to accounts, as a space of masculine privacy, see Poovey, *History of the Modern Fact*, 34–35. The claim that the novel plays a central role in locating fundamental identity in private and "inner" life is well established: Armstrong's *Desire and Domestic Fiction*, Lynch's *Economy of Character*, and A. Miller's "Subjectivity Ltd" are among the most important instances for my argument.

16. See, for instance, "Story of Isaac Holden," in *Fortunes Made in Business*, 1:37, in which a daughter is mentioned only indirectly when the author explains that this textile manufacturer resigned his parliamentary seat "in favour of his son-in-law."

17. "Salts, and the Discovery of Alpaca," in *Fortunes Made in Business*, 1:312.

18. *Successful Merchant*, ix; Smiles, *Self-Help*, 1.

19. "Romance of Invention," in *Fortunes Made in Business*, 1:192.

20. Herbert, *Culture and Anomie*, 255. Lynch points to the spread of market relations from the late eighteenth through the nineteenth centuries as the crucial correlative of the notion of depth as character truth; see Lynch, *Economy of Character*.

21. Preface to *Fortunes Made in Business*, 1:iii.

22. "Romance of Invention," 1:187, 191. The language of romance becomes particularly prominent in the later years of the nineteenth century. For instance, Bourne's rather dry collection of biographies of 1866, *English Merchants*, is followed by his more spicily entitled history, *The Romance of Trade* (1871). *Blackwood's* published "Romance in Business," attributed to Alexander Innes Shand, in 1882. Some years later the department store magnate H. Gordon Selfridge kept the theme going in *The Romance of Commerce* (1918).

23. "Romance of Invention," 1:197.

24. Ibid., 1:204.

25. "Mr. S. C. Lister and the Story of 'Silk Waste,' " in *Fortunes Made in Business*, 1:68.

26. Ibid., 1:72.

27. Ibid., 1:52.

28. "Romance of Invention," 1:231.

29. Ibid., 1:192.

30. Ibid., 1:224.

31. "Sir Josiah Mason," in *Fortunes Made in Business*, 1:143.

32. "Sir John Brown," in *Fortunes Made in Business*, 1:243.

33. Ibid., 1:245.

34. The masculine possessive pronoun is retained as the text exalts this sentimental reader's ability to keep the iron out of "his soul." But the gender implications of *sentimental*, suggesting emotion as opposed to clear-sightedness, rule by the heart as opposed to the head, seem to cast this new ideal businessman-reader in a feminine light. However, it is not so much the sentimental, feminized style of masculinity epitomized by the eighteenth-

century "man of feeling" that is most important here; rather, the "feminine" quality most salient is adeptness with the codes of stories like the romance or the sentimental novel— long associated with women's reading—that are familiar, predictable, and conventional.

35. "Convict Capitalists," 202.

36. M. Oliphant, "Ethics of Biography," 77, 77.

37. Ibid., 84.

38. Ibid., 91, 90, 90, 90.

39. Ibid., 77. For more on Victorian controversies about the ethics and proprieties of biography, see Broughton, *Men of Letters, Writing Lives.*

40. M. Oliphant, "Ethics of Biography," 84.

41. See Carlyle, *On Heroes,* 183, and "Hudson's Statue," 281–82.

42. Stephen, "Biography," 182–83, 182, 182, 183.

43. Smiles, *Self-Help,* 226.

44. When such language is used, Smiles is more likely to apply it to figures from earlier history or occasionally in his prefatory materials. See the preface to *Industrial Biography,* for instance, in which Smiles quotes "a distinguished living mechanic" as validation for his project: "There *is* a heroism of skill and toil belonging to [men of industry], worthy of as grateful record" as the heroism displayed by "kings, warriors, and statesmen"; though it may be "less perilous and romantic," it is "not less full of the results of human energy, bravery, and character" (vi).

45. Smiles, *Industrial Biography,* 283, and *Locomotive,* 56–57.

46. That Smiles did not originate the generic narrative is evidenced by Bounderby's account of his history in Dickens's 1854 novel *Hard Times;* its parodic quality suggests that exaggerated, self-made individualism had already become a template ripe for mocking.

47. [Shand], "Contemporary Literature," 485, 491.

48. Ibid., 485–86.

49. "Report from the Secret Committee on Joint Stock Banks," 8.

50. Bigelow, *Fiction, Famine, and the Rise of Economics,* 69. On Jevons, mathematics, and moral questions, see also Klaver, *A/Moral Economics;* and Schabas, *World Ruled by Number.*

51. Playford, *Practical Hints for Investing Money,* 13, 14.

52. [Beeton], *Beeton's Guide to Investing Money,* 33.

53. Ibid., 36.

54. Preface to *Fortunes Made in Business,* 1:iv.

55. "Mr. S. C. Lister and the Story of Silk Waste," 1:68, 69; "Romance of Invention," 1:206.

56. Weber, "Bureaucracy," 199, 216.

57. Weber, "Politics as a Vocation," in *From Max Weber,* 79. See the comments of Weber's translators, H. H. Gerth and C. Wright Mills, linking charisma to both nineteenth-century liberalism and Carlyle's conception of the heroic, in their introduction to *From Max Weber,* 52–53.

58. See Weber, "Politics as a Vocation," 80.

59. Evans, *Facts, Failures, and Frauds,* 2.

60. "Mr. S. C. Lister and the Story of Silk Waste," 1:76; "The Fosters of Queensbury," in *Fortunes Made in Business,* 2:13.

61. Weber, "Sociology of Charismatic Authority," 247, 248. Gerth and Mills note that

Weber elsewhere describes an economic version of charismatic authority, drawing a distinction between "charismatic capitalists"—robber barons and conquistadors, for example—and "'sober bourgeois' capitalists" (introduction, 67). In the discourse of business charisma, Weber's distinction breaks down.

62. Weber, "Politics as a Vocation," 79, and "Sociology of Charismatic Authority," 248.

63. In this respect, the charismatic mode of business biographies stands opposed to the "charismatic sincerity" that Pam Morris has suggested was a powerful nineteenth-century style through which to claim and legitimize political and social authority. See Morris, *Imagining Inclusive Society,* 102.

64. Gallagher, *Nobody's Story,* 178. See also Robert Newsom's discussion of what he calls "the antinomy of fictional probability," or the strange process by which readers make logical assessments of the probability of facts in texts that they know are demonstrably false (because fictional) (*Likely Story,* 9).

65. "Low Moor Company," in *Fortunes Made in Business,* 1:94.

66. A suggestive connection might be drawn to the model of "surface reading" proposed by Stephen Best and Sharon Marcus, who note the way critical practices seeking to de-repress hidden meanings feel "superfluous" when they confront representations whose ideological investments and untruths are brazenly overt ("Surface Reading," 2).

67. "Romance of Invention," 1:188, 189, 189–90. See McKeon's discussion in *Origins of the English Novel* of the early novel's play with fact and fiction, belief and skepticism, enchantment and secularization, as it incorporates romance and the real to generate new epistemological habits and questions for its readers. These business biographies pick up the dynamic as a generative source of meaning and value.

68. Trollope, *Way We Live Now,* 2:449; subsequent references are noted in parentheses in the text.

69. See Sutherland, introduction to *Way We Live Now,* xvi–xxi.

70. Poovey, *Genres of the Credit Economy,* 397. Poovey is here describing another Trollope novel, *The Last Chronicle of Barset,* but her point is more general.

71. For Poovey's account of the "gestural aesthetic," see ibid., 354–70.

72. See Herbert's discussion of this cynical dynamic of belief and skepticism in Trollope's *Doctor Thorne,* in *Culture and Anomie,* chap. 5.

73. "Recent Novels," review of Anthony Trollope, *The Way We Live Now, Times* (London), Aug. 24, 1875, 4.

74. British Clothing Company, Limited, Prospectus, n.p.

75. I am grateful to Tim Alborn for sharing his knowledge of the mode of circulation of investment materials.

76. Prospectus and Reports and Balance Sheets of the London and County Banking Company, Limited, 45.

77. Ibid., 71.

78. See ibid., 73.

79. "Ornamental Directors," 1412.

80. See Pavel, *Fictional Worlds,* 37; and Ronen, "Completing the Incompleteness of Fictional Entities," 501–6.

81. Business biographies, in fact, expressed a sense that novels were prime ideological opponents within a field of competing textual representations, as the names of novelists sprinkled throughout the pages of *Fortunes Made in Business* suggest. Isaac Holden's crucial

move to Cullingworth to begin his career among "the same moorland hills upon which Charlotte Brontë used to look out from the lonely Haworth parsonage when she wrote her remarkable books," for instance, not only casts him as partaking of the same inspiration and genius as the author but also implicitly suggests his story as an alternative to *Shirley* ("Story of Isaac Holden," 1:21). Even more explicitly, the biography of Sir John Brown gives his story as a counter to "Charles Reade's desperately insulting allusion" to Sheffield—which it quotes: "this infernal city, whose water is blacking and whose air is coal"—a city Brown had helped to shape into an industrial power ("Sir John Brown," 1:245).

82. See Cohn, *Transparent Minds,* and *Distinction of Fiction.*

83. Ronen, "Completing the Incompleteness of Fictional Entities," 497.

84. See Tara McGann's excellent essay "Literary Realism in the Wake of Business Cycle Theory," in *Victorian Literature and Finance,* in which she concludes that *The Way We Live Now* is "the first realist novel about finance in the British novel tradition" (156), in part because it "undermines" literary conventions such as "the individual moral agent and even human agency" in the new financial regime.

3. Reading Ruin

1. Tennyson, *Maud,* line 21; subsequent references, to line numbers, are noted in parentheses in the text.

2. Tennyson, quoted in Hill, introduction to *Maud,* 214.

3. "Actual Working of the Present Law of Bankruptcy," 588.

4. See, for instance, Weiss, *Hell of the English;* A. Miller, "Subjectivity Ltd"; and Feltes, "Community and the Limits of Liability."

5. Eliot, *Mill on the Floss,* 173; subsequent references are noted in parentheses in the text.

6. In *Hell of the English* Weiss suggests that fictional bankruptcy often becomes a metaphor for crises of identity—social, economic, and gender—and also an opportunity for moral rebirth. See chaps. 5, 6.

7. "Scientific, Educational, and Moral Progress," 110.

8. Eliot to John Blackwood, Wandsworth, May 21, 1859, in *George Eliot Letters,* 3:69.

9. Henry, *George Eliot and the British Empire,* 84. Deanna Kreisel also discusses the old-fashionedness of the Tulliver-Dodson vision of debt in "Superfluity and Suction."

10. Fane, *Bankruptcy Reform,* 6.

11. Ibid., 4.

12. "Criminal Debtors," 1176; "Money Market and City Intelligence," *Times* (London), Jan. 4, 1858, 7. During the early and middle years of the Victorian period, the laws of credit and debt were a focus of concerted advocacy for creditors on the part of business interests. By 1860, as the historian V. Markham Lester has suggested, dissatisfaction with bankruptcy laws acted as a stimulus for the formation of the Associated Chambers of Commerce of the United Kingdom, the Institute of Chartered Accountants, and the National Association for the Promotion of Social Science. How to manage failure was thus a key issue around which a self-conscious business community began to coalesce. See Lester, *Victorian Insolvency,* 5, 129.

13. For statistics on the numbers and cost of bankruptcies and insolvencies—as well as important caveats about these statistics—see Lester, *Victorian Insolvency,* 73–80, 242.

14. "Credit or Capital," 364.

15. See Hilton, *Age of Atonement,* esp. chap. 7.

16. On the desirability of a moral narrative pattern, see Henry, " 'Rushing into Eternity,' "; and McGann, "Literary Realism in the Wake of Business Cycle Theory."

17. "Credit or Capital," 364.

18. For fuller treatments of the history of creditor-debtor relations and the laws of bankruptcy and insolvency, see Lester, *Victorian Insolvency;* and Finn, *Character of Credit.*

19. See Lester, *Victorian Insolvency,* 45–59.

20. W. C. B., letter to the editor, *Times* (London), Aug. 11, 1831, 7.

21. Fane, *Bankruptcy Reform,* 18.

22. "Rival Bankruptcy Bills," 198.

23. "First and Second Reports from the Select Committee," 100–101.

24. Ibid., 25.

25. Quoted in Hazlitt and Roche, *Bankruptcy Act,* 104–5.

26. See Bankrupt Law Consolidation Act, 1849, 12 Vict., c. 3. A thorough discussion of the challenges to gender norms, legal and otherwise, prompted by credit and debt may be found in Finn, *Character of Credit.* On women's testimony, see also Shanley, *Feminism, Marriage, and the Law.*

27. See Bankrupt Law Consolidation Act, 1849, 12 Vict., c. 3.

28. See, for instance, "First and Second Reports from the Select Committee," 15.

29. Shelford, *Law of Bankruptcy and Insolvency,* 601.

30. "Bankrupt Law Consolidation," 741.

31. "First and Second Reports from the Select Committee," 41. Of course, this mode of rationalization was intended to create a sense of fairness and predictability. The hypothetical creditor imagined by one witness, who saw "fraudulent preference" in a debtor "securing his father's debt, when he knew that his assets were inadequate to the payment of all his creditors," might be revaluing (or devaluing) the relationship between parent and child. But his resistance to even this hallowed "particular" relationship was imagined to be not simply a matter of justifiable self-interest, but also a step to ensure the smooth formation of connections and credit relationships (43).

32. Ibid., 86, 87.

33. Bankrupt Law Consolidation Act, 1849, 12 Vict., Appendix X.

34. Review of *Bankrupt Law Consolidation Act, 1849,* by Edward Wise, 1058.

35. Quoted in Weiss, *Hell of the English,* 44.

36. Hazlitt and Roche, *Bankruptcy Act,* 178n.

37. "Bankruptcy Laws," 628, 628, 629.

38. "Improved Decisions in Bankruptcy," 617.

39. "Law of Bankruptcy and Insolvency," 32.

40. Ibid., 32.

41. Ibid., 32, 33.

42. "Business-Like View of the Court of Bankruptcy," 449.

43. Quoted in Lester, *Victorian Insolvency,* 148.

44. Quoted in ibid., 156.

45. My discussion of Eliot's financial experiences is drawn from Haight, *George Eliot,* 70, 125, 140, 218, 228, 305–19, 339.

46. See Daston and Galison, *Objectivity.* Daston and Galison note that scientific objectivity involves not so much a suppression of the self as the formation of a new kind of

NOTES TO PAGES 124-138

self or ethos. See also the forum on this book in *Victorian Studies* 50, no. 4 (Summer 2008), with contributions from Anderson, ("Epistemological Liberalism"), Porter, ("Objective Self"), and J. Tucker ("Objectivity, Collective Sight, and Scientific Personae"), as well as the response from Daston and Galison.

47. See, for instance, Levine, *Dying to Know;* and Anderson, *Powers of Distance.* Rae Greiner has recently complicated the conventional alignment of these terms in her very useful discussion of "sympathetic detachment" and "sympathetic abstraction" in Eliot's work; see *Sympathetic Realism,* 122, 126.

48. See, for instance, Polanyi, *Great Transformation.*

49. Tellingly, the *Westminster Review* found Bob one of the least true-to-life characters in the novel. See [Chapman], review of *The Mill on the Floss,* 32.

50. Greiner, *Sympathetic Realism,* 28.

51. Anderson, *Powers of Distance,* 15. See also Herbert, *Culture and Anomie.* William A. Cohen has addressed the question of generalization in Eliot's narrative in *Sex Scandal,* 144–48; see also Lanser, *Fictions of Authority.*

52. Greiner, *Sympathetic Realism,* 130, 139.

53. For a related argument about Eliot's construction of narrative authority, see Freedgood, *Ideas in Things.*

54. On the importance of the secret in Eliot and *The Mill on the Floss,* see Cottom, *Social Figures,* 109; and Welsh, *George Eliot and Blackmail.*

55. Jaffe, *Vanishing Points,* 12.

56. Ibid., 12.

57. Eliot to Charles Bray, Wandsworth, Sept. 26, 1859, in *George Eliot Letters,* 3:164.

58. Cohn, *Distinction of Fiction,* 16; see also Cohn, *Transparent Minds;* and Banfield, *Unspeakable Sentences.* For a useful discussion of Eliot's promotion of the authority of the artist, able to gather and reconcile all perspectives and historical conflict into a drama of individual morality and psychology, see Cottom, *Social Figures.*

59. Shaw, *Narrating Reality,* 218.

60. Poovey has noted the way the financial plot of *The Mill on the Floss* drops out in favor of what she calls the sentimental plot and suggests that the economic "ground" of the novel is left underspecified as the sentimental plot, the "figure," increases in interest; see "Writing about Finance in Victorian England," 52. I would suggest that the financial debt does lose force, but debt remains a powerful term motivating the sentimental plot in crucial ways.

61. See Hertz, "George Eliot's Life-in-Debt," for another approach to Eliot's rhetoric of debt.

62. Eliot, *Romola,* 360.

63. Levine has called Eliot's typical narrator a "constructed, selfless self" ("George Eliot's Hypothesis of Reality," 19). Critics have disagreed about its gender, with some determining it to be masculine, some feminine, and some claiming that gender is never specified. See, for instance, Cohen, *Sex Scandal,* chap. 4; Gillooly, *Smile of Discontent;* and Sadoff, review of Gillooly, *Smile of Discontent,* 311; as well as Hayles, "Anger in Different Voices," 24n3. My analysis here has affinities with Elaine Hadley's notion of "disinterested interest" as a self-concept and practice characteristic of nineteenth-century liberalism (*Living Liberalism,* 97). On character and liberalism, see also Anderson, "Character and Ideology."

64. Bankrupt Law Consolidation Act, 1849, 12 Vict., c. 10.

65. Two recent critics have discussed this scene as a key instance of the novel's depiction of economic confusion. Kreisel focuses on its treatment of paper representations of economic value, reading it as symptomatic of a mistrust of those apparently insubstantial forms; see Kreisel, "Superfluity and Suction," 88. Kathleen Blake reads the scene as an example of how the simultaneous commitment to two economic models—the gift economy and capitalist account keeping—perplexes Victorian characters; see Blake, *Pleasures of Benthamism.*

66. And in fact it was not automatic: the *Westminster Review* objected specifically to the scene, arguing that "the morality, we mean business morality, of burning a bill of exchange from sentimental motives" was a point "in which her insight . . . fails her" ([Chapman], review of *The Mill on the Floss,* 32).

67. [Dallas], review of *Silas Marner,* by George Eliot, *Times* (London), Apr. 29, 1861, 12.

4. The Heir Apparent

1. Dickens, *Hard Times,* 118.

2. Ibid., 231.

3. Ibid., 232.

4. "Does Talent Go in the Male Line?" 369.

5. Dickens, *Hard Times,* 232, 233.

6. See Kuper, *Incest and Influence,* 117–25, on the Rothschilds' strategy of cousin marriage to maintain the power of the family firm.

7. Beer, *Darwin's Plots,* 77. Of course, norms surrounding women's nonparticipation in business activity were contested throughout the Victorian period, and in practice women played roles—paid and unpaid, acknowledged and unacknowledged, as labor and as providers of capital. See, for instance, Davidoff and Hall, *Family Fortunes;* and Henry, " 'Ladies Do It?' "

8. Grove, *Address to the British Association,* 69.

9. Charles Lamb, "Hester," epigraph to M. Oliphant, *Hester;* subsequent references are in parentheses in the text.

10. [Shand], "Romance in Business," 228. Assumptions of the commercial significance of racial and national markers made their way into companies' information books, as in an 1894 entry on "Arnhold Korberg + Co." in the records of Antony Gibbs and Sons, which notes of the proprietors, "By race + nationality they are German Jews" (Confidential Information Book on Merchant Firms 1883–1905).

11. "Low Moor Company," 1:127–28; "Peases of Darlington," 1:373. For all that it seems "remarkable," the authors invoke hereditary narratives quite frequently; see also, for example, "Fosters of Queensbury," 2:55.

12. *How to Do Business,* 42, 24, and see 56.

13. See, for instance, Galton's account of his mind at work reading a railway prospectus in "Psychometric Facts," 432–33.

14. "Professor Tyndall on Science," 9.

15. Galton, "Measurement of Character," 185.

16. Galton, "Anthropometric Laboratory," 333, 334, 334, 334–35, 333, 335.

17. Galton, *Hereditary Genius,* 282.

18. Ibid., 63, 110.

19. Ibid., 73. Galton's sample includes men of science, but he hesitates to include engineers, as it seems more difficult, in his view, to separate out circumstance and opportunity

from innate talents in their case. But other writers were quite ready to accept the notion of particular hereditary talents for engineers. A review of a memoir (edited by Samuel Smiles) by James Nasmyth, inventor of the steam-hammer, suggests that his family history proves "the law of heredity in mental as in physical character," highlighting the "inventive genius" or "faculty of resourcefulness" and the trait of "mechanical and artistic ingenuity" that has been "a distinguishing feature in this branch of the Nasmyths for the last two hundred years" ("Steam-Hammer and Its Inventor," 161, 163, 161).

20. See Richards, *Darwin and the Emergence of Evolutionary Theories*, 92, 98; see also Romanes, "Darwinian Theory of Instinct." Bowler's *Mendelian Revolution* contains a useful discussion of contemporary ideas of heredity.

21. Galton, "Hereditary Talent and Character, Second Paper," 322. See also Galton, "Theory of Heredity," 94.

22. Maudsley, "Materialism and Its Lessons," 256. Walter Bagehot, too, relied on a notion of inherited habits in his account of the distinction between "present savages" and prehistoric man: the latter "had not had time to ingrain his nature so deeply with bad habits, and to impress bad beliefs so unalterably on his mind as they have. They have had ages to fix the stain on themselves, but primitive man was younger and had no such time" (*Physics and Politics*, 120).

23. "Natural Inheritance," 376.

24. "Hereditary Talent," 118.

25. Ibid., 119.

26. "Edison's Electric Light," *Times* (London), Jan. 14, 1880, 8.

27. Frederickson, "Liberalism and the Time of Instinct," 304.

28. "Mr. S. C. Lister and the Story of 'Silk Waste,'" 1:65; "Sir Josiah Mason," 1:177. However, as much as instinct could be conceived as a powerful, if mysterious, source of action and efficacy, its link to "primitive" stages of development remained. In Mark Pattison's "Industrial Shortcomings," which considered British affairs in an international context, instinct is linked into a chain of associations with inheritance, tradition, caste, superstition, and habit—which are cast in imperial terms to imply backwardness (738). The genius of the north of Britain, in his view, is the ability to blend instinct and reason, tradition and innovation, but the balance is not struck elsewhere in Britain.

29. Instinct might also saddle contemporaries with qualities that were no longer adaptive. Bagehot's account of commercial volatility blames the inheritance of aspects of "human nature" that were suited to earlier stages of existence, such as the "impulse to action" (*Physics and Politics*, 164). In his own "civilized" time, in which pressures to hunt food are diminished, this translates into "mere love of activity" (164, 168). Manias result not just from the "wish to get rich" but also from this impulse. If "operations with their own capital will only occupy four hours of the day," contemporary traders "wish to be active and to be industrious for eight hours, and so they are ruined" (168).

30. "Promoters and the Public," 142.

31. Because of its distance from predictable, willed action, instinct is associated with the shady magic of the commercial world as well. Pattison, for instance, suggests that an "instinct of craft" has created "mystery" in the Stock Exchange that puts the investing public at risk ("Industrial Shortcomings," 740).

32. E. T. Powell, *Evolution of the Money Market*, 258, 259. Powell announces his aim as "the attempted application of the biological theory of evolution" and the latest "physico-chemical research" to the operations of finance, proceeding through chapters focusing on

(among other topics) "Embryology," the "Biological Analogy," and "Natural Selection" (viii, xiii, xiv).

33. Houston's analysis of this text in *From Dickens to Dracula* is extremely suggestive; see chap. 5 for her argument about Gothic corporations.

34. Entries on W. Everitt Son Mulford Bridge Lowestoft, Mar. 22, 1870, John Hoyle, Trujillo and Lima, Dec. 28, 1863, and Ernst Niebuhr Jr., Hamburg, Apr. 11, 1877, all in Antony Gibbs and Sons, Confidential Information Book on Merchant Firms (1859–) and Confidential Information Book on Bank's Customers, Chiefly Foreign (1865–).

35. Galton, "History of Twins," 575.

36. See "Hereditary Qualities," *Times* (London), Feb. 24, 1877, 4.

37. Galton, "Hereditary Improvement," 117.

38. Letter to the editor, *Bankers' Magazine and Journal of the Money Market* (Feb. 1881): 127, 128. The specter of degeneration was not limited to family firms or "aristocratic" banks. The *Economist* worried that "parasites" on the Stock Exchange signaled evolutionary decline: "Morally, as well as physically, parasitical life is the result of degeneration, and in some senses this also seems to be true commercially" ("Parasites of the Stock Exchange," 1081).

39. L. Levi, "Scotch Banking," 555. The blood trope reached from this professional high to the sensational low. Take, for instance, the story "The Victim of the Derby," in which the firm "Bagstock, Bare, and Cunliffe's" is said to "import new blood into its veins by the absorption now and then of a promising member of its staff." That this is offered only after twenty-five years of service suggests the torpidity hindering the advancement of business and its younger generations. The protagonist's reproductive wishes (his desire to marry a partner's daughter) fall victim to this glacial pace; when he attempts to quicken it through gambling, the results are predictably catastrophic (Fall, "Victim of the Derby," 1:180).

40. "Late Baron Lionel de Rothschild," 541, 541–42.

41. Jay, *Mrs Oliphant*, 133; see also 132–33, 57. As Jay notes, the science behind these assumptions was not established. Even so, she suggests, Oliphant was preoccupied—even obsessed—by the way heredity influenced physical, mental, and moral attributes.

42. M. Oliphant, *Autobiography*, 91.

43. See, for instance, Jay, *Mrs Oliphant*, 60–61, 102; and M. Williams, *Margaret Oliphant*, 161.

44. Galton, "Hereditary Talent and Character: Part I," 160.

45. Ibid., 165.

46. Ibid., 157.

47. Review of *Hereditary Genius*, 253. At other moments, the reviews and Galton emphasize greater parity in the contributions of both sexes to the heritability of genius, even in surprising arenas: women were, for instance, thought to be much less significant sources than men of hereditary poetic ability but only "slightly inferior" in transmitting judicial talent (258).

48. Galton, *Hereditary Genius*, 51.

49. Wagner has discussed *Hester*'s rhetoric of inheritance in *Financial Speculation in Victorian Fiction* (160–62).

50. See chap. 2; Peterson also points out the way Catherine's career follows a prototypical masculine model of success. See "Female *Bildungsroman*," 79.

51. See Cleere, *Avuncularism*.

52. Herbert Gibbs to Vicary Gibbs, Feb. 29, 1884, Antony Gibbs Private Letters to Partners 1884–91, 47. See also Alban Gibbs to Vicary Gibbs, Feb. 29, 1884, 45, and Henry Gibbs to Vicary Gibbs, n.d., 11.

53. See, for instance, Peterson, "Female *Bildungsroman,*" 80; and Jay, *Mrs Oliphant,* 61.

54. Galton, *Inquiries into Human Faculty and Its Development,* 25n.

Conclusion

1. David Brooks, "In Praise of Dullness," *New York Times,* May 19, 2009.

2. For the $6,000 shower curtain, part of the extravagant (and company-supported) home renovation of the convicted C.E.O. of Tyco, Dennis Kozlowski, see Stewart, "Spend! Spend! Spend!" 147. This came to be an iconic image (one of many) of crassness and ethical bankruptcy in the upper reaches of the executive class.

3. See W. W. Powell, "Neither Market nor Hierarchy."

4. Alex Green, "The Oxford Insight," http://www.oxfordclub.com (accessed Mar. 1, 2005).

5. Ibid.

6. See Tony Hetherington, "Secret Club Breaks Law," *Sunday Times* (London), Nov. 17, 1991; Hatch, "Renaissance Man," 58.

7. Green, "Oxford Insight."

8. Trollope, *London Tradesmen,* 82–83.

9. Ibid., 84–85.

10. Serchuk, "Barry Ritholtz's Monkey Theory."

11. Scott A. Shane, "Are Entrepreneurs Born or Made?" *You're the Boss* (blog), *NYTimes.com,* Sept. 21, 2009.

12. Victor Niederhoffer and Laurel Kenner, "25 Literary Traits Every Trader Can Use," *The Speculator,* MSNMoney, Aug. 22, 2002, http://www.dailyspeculations.com/about%20us/archives/spec_duo_archives/archieve/08-22-2002.htm.

13. Harvey Schachter, "The Truths about Management Can Be Found in Great Fiction," review of *Fictions of Business: Insights on Management from Great Literature,* by Robert Brawer, *Globe and Mail* (Canada), Jan. 20, 1999. See also Brawer, *Fictions of Business.*

14. See, for instance, Gretchen Morgenson, "A Year's Debacles, From Comic to Epic," *New York Times,* Dec. 28, 2003; "The Envelopes, Please," *New York Times,* Jan. 2, 2005; and "A Year to Suspend Disbelief," *New York Times,* Dec. 31, 2006.

15. Wonks Anonymous, comment on Paul Krugman, "Madoff/Merdle," *The Conscience of a Liberal* (blog), *New York Times,* Dec. 19, 2008, http://krugman.blogs.nytimes .com/2008/12/19/madoffmerdle/.

16. Quoted in Patricia Cohen, "When Dockets Imitate Drama," *New York Times,* Dec. 26, 2008.

17. Lee, "Schlub and a Narcissist."

18. Quoted in P. Cohen, "When Dockets Imitate Drama."

19. Ben Macintyre, "The Way We Read Now as Our World Totters," *Times* (London), Mar. 12, 2009.

20. "Bankruptcy Laws," 629.

Bibliography

Archival Sources

Antony Gibbs and Sons, Ltd. Confidential Information Book on Bank's Customers, Chiefly Foreign (1865–). London Metropolitan Archives.
———. Confidential Information Book on Merchant Firms (1859–). London Metropolitan Archives.
———. Confidential Information Book on Merchant Firms 1883–1905. London Metropolitan Archives.
Antony Gibbs Private Letters to Partners 1884–91. London Metropolitan Archives.
British Clothing Company, Limited. Prospectus (London, 1865). Guildhall Library.
Kleinwort, Sons, and Co. Cape Colonies, East Indies, China, Japan Information Book, 1875–1909. London Metropolitan Archives.
Minute Books of the Bankers' Guarantee and Trust Fund. London Metropolitan Archives.
Ottoman Bank papers. London Metropolitan Archives.
Prospectus and Reports and Balance Sheets of the London and County Banking Company, Limited, from December 31st, 1837, to December 31st, 1887 (Inclusive). London, 1888. Guildhall Library.
Provisional Prospectus of the Bank of West Africa, Limited (1879). London Metropolitan Archives.

Published Sources

Ackroyd, Peter. *Dickens*. New York: HarperCollins, 1990.
"The Actual Working of the Present Law of Bankruptcy." *Economist*, June 2, 1860, 588.
Agnew, Jean-Christophe. *Worlds Apart: The Market and the Theater in Anglo-American Thought, 1550–1750*. Cambridge: Cambridge University Press, 1986.
Ahmed, Sara. "Willful Parts: Problem Characters or the Problem of Character." *New Literary History* 42, no. 2 (Spring 2011): 231–53.
Akerlof, George, and Robert J. Shiller. *Animal Spirits: How Human Psychology Drives the Economy and Why It Matters for Global Capitalism*. Princeton, N.J.: Princeton University Press, 2009.
Alborn, Timothy L. *Conceiving Companies: Joint-Stock Politics in Victorian England*. New York: Routledge, 1998.

———. "The First Fund Managers: Life Insurance Bonuses in Victorian Britain." In Henry and Schmitt, *Victorian Investments,* 58–78.

———. "The Moral of the Failed Bank: Professional Plots in the Victorian Money Market." *Victorian Studies* 38, no. 2 (Winter 1995): 199–226.

———. *Regulated Lives: Life Insurance and British Society, 1800–1914.* Toronto: University of Toronto Press, 2009.

Anderson, Amanda. "Character and Ideology: The Case of Cold War Liberalism." *New Literary History* 42, no. 2 (Spring 2011): 209–29.

———. "Epistemological Liberalism." *Victorian Studies* 50, no. 4 (Summer 2008): 658–65.

———. *The Powers of Distance: Cosmopolitanism and the Cultivation of Detachment.* Princeton, N.J.: Princeton University Press, 2001.

———. "Trollope's Modernity." *ELH* 74, no. 3 (Fall 2007): 509–34.

Armstrong, Nancy. *Desire and Domestic Fiction: A Political History of the Novel.* New York: Oxford University Press, 1987.

———. *Fiction in the Age of Photography: The Legacy of British Realism.* Cambridge, Mass.: Harvard University Press, 1999.

Arthur, William. *The Successful Merchant: Sketches of the Life of Mr. Samuel Budgett, Late of Kingswood Hill.* Author's Uniform Edition. London, 1885.

Bagehot, Walter. *Physics and Politics; or, Thoughts on the Application of the Principles of "Natural Selection" and "Inheritance" to Political Society.* Edited by Roger Kimball. 1872. Chicago: Ivan R. Dee, 1999.

Banfield, Ann. *Unspeakable Sentences: Narration and Representation in the Language of Fiction.* Boston: Routledge and Kegan Paul, 1982.

"The Bankruptcy Laws." *Economist,* June 9, 1849, 628–29.

"Bankrupt Law Consolidation." *Economist,* July 7, 1849, 740–41.

Basu, Kaushik. "On Why We Do Not Try to Walk Off without Paying after a Taxi Ride." *Economic and Political Weekly,* November 26, 1983, 2011–12.

Beer, Gillian. *Darwin's Plots: Evolutionary Narrative in Darwin, George Eliot and Nineteenth-Century Fiction.* London: Ark, 1983.

[Beeton, Samuel Orchard]. *Beeton's Guide to Investing Money with Safety and Profit.* London, 1870.

Best, Stephen, and Sharon Marcus. "Surface Reading: An Introduction." *Representations* 108, no. 1 (Fall 2009): 1–21.

Bigelow, Gordon. *Fiction, Famine, and the Rise of Economics in Victorian Britain and Ireland.* Cambridge: Cambridge University Press, 2003.

Bizup, Joseph. *Manufacturing Culture: Vindications of Early Victorian Industry.* Charlottesville: University of Virginia Press, 2003.

Blake, Kathleen. *The Pleasures of Benthamism: Victorian Literature, Utility, Political Economy.* Oxford: Oxford University Press, 2009.

Blanchard, Sidney Laman. "A Biography of a Bad Shilling." *Household Words* 2 (January 1851): 420–26.

Block, Fred. "Karl Polanyi and the Writing of *The Great Transformation.*" *Theory and Society* 32, no. 3 (June 2003): 275–306.

Bourne, H. R. Fox. *English Merchants: Memoirs in Illustration of the Progress of British Commerce.* 2 vols. London, 1866.

————. *The Romance of Trade*. London, 1871.

Bowler, Peter J. *The Mendelian Revolution: The Emergence of Hereditarian Concepts in Modern Science and Society*. Baltimore, Md.: Johns Hopkins University Press, 1989.

Brantlinger, Patrick. *Fictions of State: Culture and Credit in Britain, 1694–1994*. Ithaca, N.Y.: Cornell University Press, 1996.

————. *The Reading Lesson: The Threat of Mass Literacy in Nineteenth-Century British Fiction*. Bloomington: Indiana University Press, 1998.

Brawer, Robert A. *Fictions of Business: Insights on Management from Great Literature*. New York: John Wiley and Sons, 1998.

Broughton, Trev Lynn. *Men of Letters, Writing Lives: Masculinity and Literary Auto/Biography in the Late Victorian Period*. London: Routledge, 1999.

The Business Letter Writer: A Complete Guide to Mercantile Correspondence, with the Addition of Numerous Commercial Forms. London, n.d., ca. 1880.

Business Life: The Experiences of a London Tradesman with Practical Advice and Directions for Avoiding Many of the Evils Connected with Our Present Commercial System and State of Society. London, 1861.

"A Business-Like View of the Court of Bankruptcy." *Economist*, April 28, 1860, 449–50.

Byrne, Kathleen. "Consuming the Family Economy: Tuberculosis and Capitalism in Charles Dickens's *Dombey and Son*." *Nineteenth Century Contexts* 29, no. 1 (March 2007): 1–16.

Campbell, Richard Vary. *Principles of Mercantile Law, in the Subjects of Bankruptcy, Cautionary Obligations, Securities over Moveables, Principal and Agent, Partnership, and the Companies Acts*. Edinburgh, 1881.

Carlyle, Thomas. "Hudson's Statue." In *Latter-Day Pamphlets*, 254–92. London: Chapman and Hall, 1907.

————. *On Heroes, Hero-Worship, and the Heroic in History*. Edited by Carl Niemeyer. 1840. Lincoln: University of Nebraska Press, 1966.

————. *Past and Present*. 1843. Edited by Richard D. Altick. New York: New York University Press, 1965.

Celebrities at Home: Reprinted from "The World." 3 vols. London, [1877?]–79.

Chalmers, Thomas. *The Application of Christianity to the Commercial and Ordinary Affairs of Life, in a Series of Discourses*. New York, 1821.

Chandler, Alfred D., Jr. "The Growth of the Transnational Industrial Firm in the United States and the United Kingdom: A Comparative Analysis." *Economic History Review* 33, no. 3 (August 1980): 396–410.

————. *Scale and Scope: The Dynamics of Industrial Capitalism*. Cambridge, Mass.: Belknap Press, 1990.

[Chapman, John]. Review of *The Mill on the Floss*, by George Eliot. *Westminster Review*, 18, no. 1 (July 1860): 24–33.

Clark, Robert. "Riddling the Family Firm: The Sexual Economy in *Dombey and Son*." *ELH* 51, no. 1 (Spring 1984): 69–84.

Cleere, Eileen. *Avuncularism: Capitalism, Patriarchy, and Nineteenth-Century English Culture*. Stanford, Calif.: Stanford University Press, 2004.

Cohen, William A. *Sex Scandal: The Private Parts of Victorian Fiction*. Durham, N.C.: Duke University Press, 1996.

Cohn, Dorrit. *The Distinction of Fiction*. Baltimore, Md.: Johns Hopkins University Press, 1999.

———. *Transparent Minds: Narrative Modes for Presenting Consciousness in Fiction*. Princeton, N.J.: Princeton University Press, 1978.

"Convict Capitalists." *All the Year Round*, June 9, 1860, 201–4.

Corbett, Mary Jean. *Family Likeness: Sex, Marriage, and Incest from Jane Austen to Virginia Woolf*. Ithaca, N.Y.: Cornell University Press, 2008.

Cottom, Daniel. *Social Figures: George Eliot, Social History, and Literary Representation*. Minneapolis: University of Minnesota Press, 1987.

Cottrell, P. L. *Industrial Finance 1830–1914: The Finance and Organization of the English Manufacturing Industry*. 1980. London: Routledge, 2006.

"Credit or Capital." *Economist*, April 3, 1858, 363–65.

A Creditor. *County Courts; or, A Letter to Bailey Cochrane, Esq*. London, 1848.

"Criminal Debtors." *Economist*, October 22, 1859, 1176–77.

Crouzet, François. *The First Industrialists: The Problem of Origins*. Cambridge: Cambridge University Press, 1985.

Daston, Lorraine, and Peter Galison. *Objectivity*. Brooklyn, N.Y.: Zone Books, 2007.

———. "Response: *Objectivity* and Its Critics." *Victorian Studies* 50, no. 4 (Summer 2008): 666–77.

Daunton, Martin. "Afterword." In Henry and Schmitt, *Victorian Investments*, 202–20.

Davidoff, Lenore, and Catherine Hall. *Family Fortunes: Men and Women of the English Middle Class, 1780–1850*. Chicago: University of Chicago Press, 1987.

Dickens, Charles. *A Christmas Carol*. In *The Christmas Books, Vol. 1: A Christmas Carol/ The Chimes*, edited by Michael Slater. 1843. Harmondsworth: Penguin, 1971.

———. *Dealings with the Firm of Dombey and Son, Wholesale, Retail, and for Exportation*. Edited by Alan Horsman. 1848. Oxford: Oxford University Press, 1982.

———. *Hard Times*. Edited by Jeff Nunokawa and Gage McWeeny. 1854. New York: Longman, 2004.

———. *The Letters of Charles Dickens, Volume Four, 1844–1846*. Edited by Kathleen Tillotson and Nina Burgis. Oxford: Clarendon Press, 1977.

———. *The Letters of Charles Dickens, Volume Five, 1847–1949*. Edited by Graham Storey and K. J. Fielding. Oxford: Clarendon Press, 1981.

"Does Talent Go in the Male Line?" *Chambers' Edinburgh Journal*, December 13, 1845, 369–71.

"Dry Bank Statistics." *Bankers' Magazine and Journal of the Money Market* (November 1881): 905–9.

Duncan, Ian. *Modern Romance and Transformations of the Novel: The Gothic, Scott, Dickens*. Cambridge: Cambridge University Press, 1992.

Eliot, George. *Adam Bede*. Edited by Stephen Gill. 1859. Harmondsworth: Penguin, 1980.

———. *The George Eliot Letters*. 9 vols. Edited by Gordon S. Haight. New Haven, Conn.: Yale University Press, 1954–78.

———. *The Mill on the Floss*. Edited by Gordon S. Haight. 1860. Boston, Mass.: Houghton Mifflin, 1961.

———. "The Natural History of German Life." *Westminster Review* 66, no. 129 (July 1856): 51–79.

———. *Romola*. Edited by Dorothea Barrett. 1862–63. Harmondsworth: Penguin, 1996.

Evans, David Morier. *City Men and City Manners: The City or the Physiology of London Business.* London, 1845.
———. *Facts, Failures, and Frauds: Revelations Financial, Mercantile, Criminal.* 1859. Newton Abbot: David and Charles, 1968.
Fall, Marcus. "The Victim of the Derby." In *London Town: Sketches of London Life and Character,* 1: 179–89. London, 1880.
Fane, C. *Bankruptcy Reform: In a Series of Letters Addressed to William Hawes, Esq.* London, 1848.
Feltes, N. N. "Community and the Limits of Liability in Two Mid-Victorian Novels." *Victorian Studies* 17, no. 4 (June 1974): 355–69.
———. *Modes of Production of Victorian Novels.* Chicago: University of Chicago Press, 1989.
Finn, Margot. *The Character of Credit: Personal Debt in English Culture, 1740–1914.* Cambridge: Cambridge University Press, 2003.
"First and Second Reports from the Select Committee of the House of Lords on Bankruptcy and Insolvency." *Parliamentary Papers* 1849 (372).
Fortunes Made in Business: Series of Original Sketches, Biographical and Anecdotic, from the Recent History of Industry and Commerce, by Various Writers. 3 vols. London, 1884–87.
Foucault, Michel. *Discipline and Punish: The Birth of the Prison.* Translated by Alan Sheridan. 1977. New York: Vintage, 1979.
———. *The History of Sexuality: Volume 1: An Introduction.* Translated by Robert Hurley. 1978. New York: Vintage, 1990.
Francis, John. *Chronicles and Characters of the Stock Exchange.* 2nd edition. London, 1851.
Frederickson, Kathleen. "Liberalism and the Time of Instinct." *Victorian Studies* 49, no. 2 (Winter 2007): 302–12.
Freedgood, Elaine. *The Ideas in Things: Fugitive Meaning in the Victorian Novel.* Chicago: University of Chicago Press, 2006.
Friedman, Stanley. "Heep and Powell: Dickensian Revenge." *Dickensian* 90 (Spring 1994): 36–43.
Frow, John. "Spectacle Binding: On Character." *Poetics Today* 7, no. 2 (1986): 227–50.
Gagnier, Regenia. *The Insatiability of Human Wants: Economics and Aesthetics in Market Society.* Chicago: University of Chicago Press, 2000.
Gallagher, Catherine. *The Body Economic: Life, Death, and Sensation in Political Economy and the Victorian Novel.* Princeton, N.J.: Princeton University Press, 2006.
———. *Nobody's Story: The Vanishing Acts of Women Writers in the Marketplace, 1670–1820.* Berkeley: University of California Press, 1994.
———. "What Would Napoleon Do? Historical, Fictional, and Counterfactual Characters." *New Literary History* 42, no. 2 (Spring 2011): 315–36.
Galton, Francis. "The Anthropometric Laboratory." *Fortnightly Review* 31, no. 183 (March 1882): 332–38.
———. *Hereditary Genius.* Rev. ed. 1869. New York, 1891.
———. "Hereditary Improvement." *Fraser's Magazine* 7, no. 37 (January 1873): 116–30.
———. "Hereditary Talent and Character: Part 1." *Macmillan's Magazine* 12, no. 68 (June 1865): 157–66.
———. "Hereditary Talent and Character, Second Paper." *Macmillan's Magazine* 12, no. 70 (August 1865): 318–27.

———. "The History of Twins, as a Criterion of the Relative Powers of Nature and Nurture." *Fraser's Magazine* 12, no. 71 (November 1875): 566–76.

———. *Inquiries into Human Faculty and Its Development.* London, 1883.

———. "Measurement of Character." *Fortnightly Review* 36, no. 212 (August 1884): 179–185.

———. "Psychometric Facts." *Nineteenth Century* 5, no. 25 (March 1879): 425–33.

———. "A Theory of Heredity." *Contemporary Review* 27 (December 1875): 80–95.

Gerth, H. H., and C. Wright Mills. Introduction to *From Max Weber: Essays in Sociology*, by Max Weber, 3–74. Translated and edited by H. H. Gerth and C. Wright Mills. New York: Oxford University Press, 1946.

Giddens, Anthony. *The Consequences of Modernity.* Cambridge: Polity Press, 1990.

———. *Modernity and Self-Identity: Self and Society in the Late Modern Age.* Stanford, Calif.: Stanford University Press, 1991.

Gilbart, James William. *A Practical Treatise on Banking.* London, 1836.

Gillooly, Eileen. *Smile of Discontent: Humor, Gender, and Nineteenth-Century British Fiction.* Chicago: University of Chicago Press, 1999.

Goodlad, Lauren M. E. "'A Middle Class Cut into Two': Historiography and Victorian National Character." *ELH* 67, no. 1 (Spring 2000): 143–78.

———. *Victorian Literature and the Victorian State: Character and Governance in a Liberal Society.* Baltimore, Md.: Johns Hopkins University Press, 2003.

Goux, Jean-Joseph. *Symbolic Economies: After Marx and Freud.* Translated by Jennifer Curtiss Gage. Ithaca, N.Y.: Cornell University Press, 1990.

Greiner, Rae. *Sympathetic Realism in Nineteenth-Century British Fiction.* Baltimore, Md.: Johns Hopkins University Press. 2012.

Grove, W. R. *Address to the British Association for the Advancement of Science, Delivered by the President, W. R. Grove, Esq., Q.C., M.A. F.R.S., at Nottingham, August 22, 1866.* 2d ed. London, 1867.

Hack, Daniel. *The Material Interests of the Victorian Novel.* Charlottesville: University of Virginia Press, 2005.

Hadley, Elaine. *Living Liberalism: Practical Citizenship in Mid-Victorian Britain.* Chicago: University of Chicago Press, 2010.

———. *Melodramatic Tactics: Theatricalized Dissent in the English Marketplace, 1800–1885.* Stanford, Calif.: Stanford University Press, 1995.

Haight, Gordon S. *George Eliot: A Biography.* New York: Oxford University Press, 1968.

Hatch, Denny. "Renaissance Man." *Target Marketing* 20, no. 10 (October 1997): 58–60, 64.

Hayles, N. Katherine. "Anger in Different Voices: Carol Gilligan and *The Mill on the Floss.*" *Signs* 12, no. 1 (Autumn 1986): 23–39.

Hazlitt, William, and Henry Philip Roche. *The Bankruptcy Act, 1861, Incorporating So Much as Remains in Force of the Bankrupt Law Consolidation Act, 1849, and of the Bankruptcy Act, 1854.* London, 1861.

Helps, Sir Arthur. *The Claims of Labour: An Essay on the Duties of the Employers to the Employed.* 2nd edition. London, 1845.

———. *Essays Written in the Intervals of Business.* 1841. In *"Companions of My Solitude"; "Essays Written in the Intervals of Business"; and "An Essay on Organization in Daily Life,"* 209–97. London, 1879.

Henriques, Diana B. *The Wizard of Lies: Bernie Madoff and the Death of Trust*. New York: Times Books, 2011.

Henry, Nancy. *George Eliot and the British Empire*. Cambridge: Cambridge University Press, 2002.

——. "'Ladies Do It?': Victorian Women Investors in Fact and Fiction." In O'Gorman, *Victorian Literature and Finance*, 111–31.

——. "'Rushing into Eternity': Suicide and Finance in Victorian Fiction." In Henry and Schmitt, *Victorian Investments*, 161–81.

Henry, Nancy, and Cannon Schmitt. "Introduction: Finance, Capital, Culture." In Henry and Schmitt, *Victorian Investments*, 1–12.

——, eds. *Victorian Investments: New Perspectives on Finance and Culture*. Bloomington: Indiana University Press, 2009.

Herbert, Christopher. *Culture and Anomie: Ethnographic Imagination in the Nineteenth Century*. Chicago: University of Chicago Press, 1991.

"Hereditary Talent." Review of *Hereditary Genius*, by Francis Galton. *Chambers's Journal of Popular Literature, Science, and Arts*, February 19, 1870, 118–22.

Hertz, Neil. "George Eliot's Life-in-Debt." *diacritics* 25, no. 4 (Winter 1995): 59–70.

Hill, Robert W., Jr. Introduction to *Maud; A Monodrama*. In *Tennyson's Poetry*, 213–14.

Hilton, Boyd. *The Age of Atonement: The Influence of Evangelicalism on Social and Economic Thought, 1785–1865*. Oxford: Clarendon Press, 1988.

Hirschman, Albert O. "Rival Interpretations of Market Society: Civilizing, Destructive, or Feeble?" *Journal of Economic Literature* 20, no. 4 (December 1982): 1463–84.

Houston, Gail. *From Dickens to Dracula: Gothic, Economics, and Victorian Fiction*. Cambridge: Cambridge University Press, 2005.

How to Do Business: A Pocket Manual of Practical Affairs and Guide to Success in Life. New York, 1857.

How to Read the Character by the Actions, Manner, and Speech, According to the Observations and Maxims of the Most Eminent Philosophers, Poets, Statesmen, Men of Business, Etc. Brighton, 1876.

Humpherys, Anne. "*Dombey and Son:* Carker the Manager." *Nineteenth-Century Fiction* 34, no. 4 (March 1980): 397–413.

"Improved Decisions in Bankruptcy." *Economist*, June 6, 1857: 617.

Jaffe, Audrey. *The Affective Life of the Average Man: The Victorian Novel and the Stock-Market Graph*. Columbus: Ohio State University Press, 2010.

——. *Vanishing Points: Dickens, Narrative, and the Subject of Omniscience*. Berkeley: University of California Press, 1991.

Jay, Elisabeth. *Mrs Oliphant: "A Fiction to Herself"; A Literary Life*. Oxford: Clarendon Press, 1995.

Johnes, Arthur James. *Should the Law of Imprisonment for Debt in the Superior Courts Be Abolished or Amended? In a Letter to the Right Hon. Lord Brougham and Vaux*. London, 1868.

Keen, Suzanne. "Readers' Temperaments and Fictional Character." *New Literary History* 42, no. 2 (Spring 2011): 295–314.

Khurana, Rakesh. *Searching for a Corporate Savior: The Irrational Quest for Charismatic CEOs*. Princeton, N.J.: Princeton University Press, 2002.

Kirby, Maurice W. "Big Business before 1900." In Kirby and Rose, *Business Enterprise in Modern Britain*, 113–38.

Kirby, Maurice W., and Mary B. Rose, eds. *Business Enterprise in Modern Britain: From the Eighteenth to the Twentieth Century*. London: Routledge, 1994.

Klaver, Claudia C. *A/Moral Economics: Classical Political Economy and Cultural Authority in Nineteenth-Century England*. Columbus: Ohio State University Press, 2003.

Knight, James. *Public Guarantee and Private Suretyship*. London, 1849.

Kreisel, Deanna. "Superfluity and Suction: The Problem of Saving in *The Mill on the Floss*." *NOVEL: A Forum on Fiction* 35, no. 1 (Autumn 2001): 69–103.

Krippner, Greta R. "The Elusive Market: Embeddedness and the Paradigm of Economic Sociology." *Theory and Society* 30, no. 6 (December 2001): 775–810.

Kuper, Adam. *Incest and Influence: The Private Life of Bourgeois England*. Cambridge, Mass.: Harvard University Press, 2009.

Kynaston, David. *The City of London, Volume 1: A World of Its Own, 1815–1890*. London: Chatto and Windus, 1994.

Lanser, Susan Sniader. *Fictions of Authority: Women Writers and Narrative Voice*. Ithaca, N.Y.: Cornell University Press, 1992.

"The Late Baron Lionel de Rothschild." *Bankers' Magazine and Journal of the Money Market* 39 (July 1879): 541–42.

"The Law of Bankruptcy and Insolvency." *Economist*, January 9, 1858, 32–33.

Lawson, William John. *The History of Banking*. London, 1855.

[Lawson, W. R.]. "A Black Year for Investors." *Blackwood's Edinburgh Magazine* 137 (February 1885): 269–84.

Lazonick, William. "Social Organization and Technological Leadership." In *Convergence of Productivity: Cross-National Studies and Historical Evidence*, edited by William J. Baumol, Richard R. Nelson, and Edward N. Wolff. 164–93. New York: Oxford University Press, 1994.

Lee, Susan. "A Schlub and a Narcissist." *Forbes.com*, March 27, 2009. http://www.forbes.com/2009/03/26/narcissist-schlub-dickens-dorrit-merdle-opinions-columnists-madoff.html.

Lester, V. Markham. *Victorian Insolvency: Bankruptcy, Imprisonment for Debt, and Company Winding-Up in Nineteenth-Century England*. Oxford: Clarendon Press, 1995.

Levi, Leone. "Scotch Banking.—Lessons from the Bankruptcy of the City of Glasgow Bank." *Bankers' Magazine and Journal of the Money Market* 39 (July 1879): 542–56.

Levi, Margaret. "A State of Trust." In *Trust and Governance*, edited by Margaret Levi and Valerie Braithwaite, 77–101. New York: Russell Sage Foundation, 1998.

Levine, George. *Dying to Know: Scientific Epistemology and Narrative in Victorian Novels*. Chicago: University of Chicago Press, 2002.

———. "George Eliot's Hypothesis of Reality." *Nineteenth Century Fiction* 35, no. 1 (June 1980): 1–28.

Levinson, Marjorie. "What Is New Formalism?" *PMLA* 122, no. 2 (March 2007): 558–69.

Lynch, Deidre Shauna. *The Economy of Character: Novels, Market Culture, and the Business of Inner Meaning*. Chicago: University of Chicago Press, 1998.

Macleod, Dianne Sachko. *Art and the Victorian Middle Class: Money and the Making of Cultural Identity*. Cambridge: Cambridge University Press, 1996.

Malton, Sara. *Forgery in Nineteenth-Century Literature and Culture: Fictions of Finance from Dickens to Wilde.* New York: Palgrave, 2009.

Marcus, Steven. *Dickens from Pickwick to Dombey.* New York: Norton, 1965.

Marsh, Joss Lutz. "Good Mrs. Brown's Connections: Sexuality and Story-Telling in *Dealings with the Firm of Dombey and Son*," *ELH* 58, no. 2 (Summer 1991): 405–26.

Marx, Karl. "On the Jewish Question." In *The Marx-Engels Reader,* edited by Robert C. Tucker, 2nd edition, 26–52. New York: Norton, 1978.

Masson, David. *British Novelists and Their Styles: Being a Sketch of the History of British Prose Fiction.* 1859. Darby, Pa.: Darby Books, 1969.

Maudsley, Henry. "Materialism and Its Lessons." *Fortnightly Review* 26, no. 152 (August 1879): 244–60.

[McCulloch, J. R.]. "Thoughts on the Improvement of the System of Country Banking." *Edinburgh Review* 63, no. 128 (July 1836): 419–41.

McGann, Tara. "Literary Realism in the Wake of Business Cycle Theory." In O'Gorman, *Victorian Literature and Finance,* 133–56.

McKeon, Michael. *The Origins of the English Novel 1600–1740.* 1987. Baltimore, Md.: Johns Hopkins University Press, 2002.

The Mercantile Letter Writer; or, Guide to Business Correspondence in the Warehouse, Shop, or Counting-House. Glasgow, n.d., ca. 1855.

Michaels, Walter Benn. *The Gold Standard and the Logic of Naturalism: American Literature at the Turn of the Century.* Berkeley: University of California Press, 1988.

Miller, Andrew H. *Novels behind Glass: Commodity Culture and Victorian Narrative.* Cambridge: Cambridge University Press, 1995.

———. "Subjectivity Ltd: The Discourse of Liability in the Joint Stock Companies Act of 1856 and Gaskell's *Cranford*." *ELH* 61, no. 1 (Spring 1994): 139–57.

Miller, D. A. *Narrative and Its Discontents: Problems of Closure in the Traditional Novel.* Princeton, N.J.: Princeton University Press, 1981.

Moglen, Helene. "Theorizing Fiction/Fictionalizing Theory: The Case of *Dombey and Son*." *Victorian Studies* 35, no. 2 (Winter 1992): 159–84.

Morris, Pam. *Imagining Inclusive Society in Nineteenth-Century Novels: The Code of Sincerity in the Public Sphere.* Baltimore, Md.: Johns Hopkins University Press, 2004.

"Natural Inheritance." *Bow Bells,* May 12, 1869, 376.

Nenadic, Stana. "The Small Family Firm in Victorian Britain." *Business History* 35, no. 4 (October 1993): 86–114.

Newsom, Robert. *A Likely Story: Probability and Play in Fiction.* New Brunswick, N.J.: Rutgers University Press, 1988.

Nicholas, Tom. "Clogs to Clogs in Three Generations? Explaining Entrepreneurial Performance in Britain since 1850." *Journal of Economic History* 59, no. 3 (September 1999): 688–713.

Nunokawa, Jeff. *The Afterlife of Property: Domestic Security and the Victorian Novel.* Princeton, N.J.: Princeton University Press, 1994.

O'Gorman, Francis, ed. *Victorian Literature and Finance.* Oxford: Oxford University Press, 2007.

Oliphant, Laurence. "The Autobiography of a Joint-Stock Company (Limited)." *Blackwood's Edinburgh Magazine* 120, no. 729 (July 1876): 96–122.

Oliphant, Margaret. *The Autobiography of Margaret Oliphant: The Complete Text.* Edited by Elisabeth Jay. New York: Oxford University Press, 1990.

———. "The Ethics of Biography." *Contemporary Review* 44 (July 1883): 76–93.

———. *Hester.* Edited by Philip Davis and Brian Nellist. 1883. Oxford: Oxford University Press, 2003.

"Ornamental Directors." *Economist*, November 22, 1884, 1411–12.

Osteen, Mark, and Martha Woodmansee. "Taking Account of the New Economic Criticism: An Historical Introduction." In *The New Economic Criticism: Studies at the Intersection of Literature and Economics,* edited by Martha Woodmansee and Mark Osteen, 3–50. New York: Routledge, 1999.

"Parasites of the Stock Exchange." *Economist*, September 6, 1884, 1081–82.

Pattison, Mark. "Industrial Shortcomings: An Address." *Fortnightly Review* 28, no. 168 (December 1880): 737–51.

Pavel, Thomas G. *Fictional Worlds.* Cambridge, Mass.: Harvard University Press, 1986.

Perera, Suvendrini. "Wholesale, Retail, and for Exportation: Empire and the Family Business in *Dombey and Son.*" *Victorian Studies* 33, no. 4 (Summer 1990): 603–20.

Peterson, Linda. "The Female *Bildungsroman:* Tradition and Revision in Margaret Oliphant's Fiction." In *Margaret Oliphant: Critical Essays on a Gentle Subversive,* edited by D. J. Trela, 66–89. Selinsgrove, Pa.: Susquehanna University Press, 1995.

Perkin, Harold. *Origins of Modern English Society.* London: Routledge, 1969.

Phillips, Joseph D. "The Theory of Small Enterprise: Smith, Mill, Marshall, and Marx." *Explorations in Economic History* 16, no. 3 (June 1979): 331–40.

Playford, Francis. *Practical Hints for Investing Money: With an Explanation of the Mode of Transacting Business on the Stock Exchange.* 2nd edition. London, 1856.

Pocock, J. G. A. *Virtue, Commerce, and History.* Cambridge: Cambridge University Press, 1985.

Polanyi, Karl. "The Economy as Instituted Process." In *Trade and Market in Early Empires,* edited by Karl Polanyi, Conrad M. Arensberg, and Harry W. Pearson, 243–70. Glencoe, Ill.: Free Press, 1957.

———. *The Great Transformation: The Political and Economic Origins of Our Time.* Boston, Mass.: Beacon Press, 1957.

Pollard, Sidney. *The Genesis of Modern Management: A Study of the Industrial Revolution in Great Britain.* Cambridge, Mass.: Harvard University Press, 1965.

Poovey, Mary, ed. *The Financial System in Nineteenth-Century Britain.* New York: Oxford University Press, 2003.

———. *Genres of the Credit Economy: Mediating Value in Eighteenth- and Nineteenth-Century Britain.* Chicago: University of Chicago Press, 2008.

———. *A History of the Modern Fact: Problems of Knowledge in the Sciences of Wealth and Society.* Chicago: University of Chicago Press, 1998.

———. "Writing about Finance in Victorian England: Disclosure and Secrecy in the Culture of Investment." In Henry and Schmitt, *Victorian Investments,* 39–57.

Porter, Theodore M. "The Objective Self." *Victorian Studies* 50, no. 4 (Summer 2008): 641–47.

Powell, Ellis T. *The Evolution of the Money Market, 1385–1915: An Historical and Analytical Study of the Rise and Development of Finance as a Centralised, Co-ordinated Force.* London: Financial News, 1916.

Powell, Walter W. "Neither Market nor Hierarchy: Network Forms of Organization." *Research in Organizational Behavior* 12 (1990): 295–336.

Pressnell, L. S. *Country Banking in the Industrial Revolution*. Oxford: Oxford University Press, 1956.

Price, Leah. "From *The History of a Book* to a 'History of the Book.'" *Representations* 108 (Fall 2009): 120–38.

"Professor Tyndall on Science." *Times* (London), October 2, 1877, 8–9.

"Promoters and the Public." *Saturday Review*, July 29, 1871, 141–42.

Rappoport, Jill. *Giving Women: Alliance and Exchange in Victorian Culture*. New York: Oxford University Press, 2011.

"Recent Novels." *Times* (London), August 24, 1875, 4.

"Report from the Secret Committee on Joint Stock Banks; Together with the Minutes of Evidence, and Appendix." *Parliamentary Papers* 1836 (591).

Review of *The Bankrupt Law Consolidation Act, 1849*, by Edward Wise. *Economist*, September 22, 1849, 1058.

Review of *The Claims of Labour: An Essay on the Duties of the Employers to the Employed*, by Sir Arthur Helps. *Edinburgh Review* 81, no. 164 (April 1845): 498–525.

Review of *Dombey and Son*, by Charles Dickens. *Economist*, October 10, 1846, 1324.

Review of *Hereditary Genius*, by Francis Galton. *Fraser's Magazine* 2, no. 8 (August 1870): 251–65.

Richards, Robert J. *Darwin and the Emergence of Evolutionary Theories of Mind and Behavior*. Chicago: University of Chicago Press, 1989.

"The Rival Bankruptcy Bills." *Economist*, February 19, 1859, 198–99.

Robb, George. *White Collar Crime in Modern England: Financial Fraud and Business Morality, 1845–1929*. Cambridge: Cambridge University Press, 1992.

Robbins, Bruce. "Presentism, Pastism, Professionalism." *Victorian Literature and Culture* 27, no. 2 (1999): 457–63.

———. *Secular Vocations: Intellectuals, Professionalism, Culture*. New York: Verso, 1993.

Romanes, G. J. "The Darwinian Theory of Instinct." *Nineteenth Century* 16, no. 91 (September 1884): 434–50.

Ronen, Ruth. "Completing the Incompleteness of Fictional Entities." *Poetics Today* 9, no. 3 (1988): 497–513.

Rose, Mark. *Authors and Owners: The Invention of Copyright*. Cambridge, Mass.: Harvard University Press, 1995.

Rose, Mary B. "The Family Firm in British Business, 1780–1914." In Kirby and Rose, *Business Enterprise in Modern Britain*, 61–87.

Sadoff, Diane. Review of *Smile of Discontent: Humor, Gender, and Nineteenth-Century British Fiction*, by Eileen Gillooly. *Victorian Studies* 43, no. 2 (Winter 2001): 309–11.

Schabas, Margaret. *A World Ruled by Number: William Stanley Jevons and the Rise of Mathematical Economics*. Princeton, N.J.: Princeton University Press, 1990.

"Scientific, Educational, and Moral Progress of the Last Fifty Years," *Economist*, February 1, 1851, 109–11.

Schwarzbach, F. S. *Dickens and the City*. London: Athlone Press, 1979.

Selfridge, H. Gordon. *The Romance of Commerce*. London: John Lane, 1918.

Serchuk, David. "Barry Ritholtz's Monkey Theory." *Forbes.com*, March 13, 2009. http://

www.forbes.com/2009/03/12/barry-ritholtz-interview-intelligent-investing-ritholtz
.html#.

[Shand, Alexander Innes]. "Contemporary Literature: Biography, Travel, and Sport."
Blackwood's Edinburgh Magazine 125, no. 762 (April 1879): 482–506.

———. "Romance in Business." *Blackwood's Edinburgh Magazine* 131, no. 796 (February
1882): 221–45.

Shanley, Mary Lyndon. *Feminism, Marriage, and the Law in Victorian England.* Princeton,
N.J.: Princeton University Press, 1989.

Shaw, Harry E. *Narrating Reality: Austen, Scott, Eliot.* Ithaca, N.Y.: Cornell University
Press, 1999.

Shelford, Leonard. *The Law of Bankruptcy and Insolvency, Comprising the Statutes Now in
Force on Those Subjects, Methodically Arranged, and the Reported Cases Thereon to the
Present Time.* 3rd ed. London, 1862.

Shell, Marc. *The Economy of Literature.* Baltimore, Md.: Johns Hopkins University Press,
1978.

———. *Money, Language, and Thought: Literary and Philosophical Economies from the
Medieval to the Modern Era.* Berkeley: University of California Press, 1982.

Slater, Michael. *Charles Dickens.* New Haven, Conn.: Yale University Press, 2009.

Smiles, Samuel. *Industrial Biography: Iron-Workers and Tool-Makers.* Boston, 1864.

———. *The Locomotive: George and Robert Stevenson.* Vol. 5 of *Lives of the Engineers.* 1857.
London, 1874.

———. *Self-Help: With Illustrations of Character, Conduct, and Perseverance.* Edited by
Peter W. Sinnema. 1859. Oxford: Oxford University Press, 2002.

Smith, Adam. *An Inquiry into the Nature and Causes of the Wealth of Nations.* 1776. Edited
by R. H. Campbell, A. S. Skinner, and W. B. Todd. 2 vols. Indianapolis: Liberty Fund,
1981.

———. "Of Police." 1766. In *Lectures on Jurisprudence,* edited by R. L. Meek, D. D. Ra-
phael, and P. G. Stein, 486–531. Indianapolis: Liberty Fund, 1982.

———. *The Theory of Moral Sentiments.* 1759. Edited by Knud Haakonssen. Cambridge:
Cambridge University Press, 2002.

"The Steam-Hammer and Its Inventor." *Chambers's Journal of Popular Literature, Science,
and Art,* March 17, 1883, 161–65.

Stephen, Leslie. "Biography." *National Review* 22, no. 128 (October 1893): 171–83.

Stewart, James B. "Spend! Spend! Spend!" *New Yorker,* February 17, 2003, 132–47.

Stowell, Hugh. *A Model for Men of Business; or, Lectures on the Character of Nehemiah.*
1854. 4th edition. London, 1872.

Supple, Barry. "Scale and Scope: Alfred Chandler and the Dynamics of Industrial Capitalism." *Economic History Review* 44, no. 3 (1991): 500–514.

Sutherland, John. Introduction to *The Way We Live Now* (1875), by Anthony Trollope,
edited by John Sutherland, vii–xxviii. Oxford: Oxford University Press, 1982.

———. *Victorian Novelists and Publishers.* London: Athlone Press, 1976.

Swedberg, Richard. *Max Weber and the Idea of Economic Sociology.* 2nd edition. Princeton,
N.J.: Princeton University Press, 2000.

Tennyson, Lord Alfred. *Maud; A Monodrama.* 1855. In *Tennyson's Poetry,* edited by Robert W. Hill Jr., 213–48. New York: Norton, 1971.

———. *Tennyson's Poetry.* Edited by Robert W. Hill Jr. New York: Norton, 1971.

"Testimonial to Mr. William Haig Miller." *Bankers' Magazine and Journal of the Money Market* (November 1879): 958–59.

Tracy, Robert. *Trollope's Later Novels*. Berkeley: University of California Press, 1978.

Trollope, Anthony. *An Autobiography*. 1883. Edited by David Skilton. Harmondsworth: Penguin, 1996.

———. *London Tradesmen*. London: Elkin Mathews and Marrot, 1927.

———. *The Way We Live Now*. 1875. Edited by John Sutherland. 2 vols. Oxford: Oxford University Press, 1982.

Tucker, Herbert F. *A Companion to Victorian Literature and Culture*. Oxford: Blackwell, 1999.

Tucker, Jennifer. "Objectivity, Collective Sight, and Scientific Personae." *Victorian Studies* 50, no. 4 (Summer 2008): 648–57.

Tulloch, John. *Beginning Life: Chapters for Young Men on Religion, Study, and Business*. London, 1864.

Uhlig, Harald. "Economics and Reality." *Journal of Macroeconomics* 34, no. 1 (2010): 29–41.

Urwick L., and E. F. L. Brech. *The Making of Scientific Management*. 2 vols. 1957. Bristol: Thoemmes Press, 1994.

Wagner, Tamara S. *Financial Speculation in Victorian Fiction: Plotting Money and the Novel Genre, 1815–1901*. Columbus: Ohio State University Press, 2010.

Warren, Samuel. *The Moral, Social, and Professional Duties of Attorneys and Solicitors*. 1848. Albany, N.Y., 1870.

Watt, Ian. *The Rise of the Novel: Studies in Defoe, Richardson, and Fielding*. 1957. Berkeley: University of California Press, 2001.

Weber, Max. *From Max Weber: Essays in Sociology*. Translated and edited by H. H. Gerth and C. Wright Mills. New York: Oxford University Press, 1946.

Weiss, Barbara. *The Hell of the English: Bankruptcy and the Victorian Novel*. Lewisburg, Pa.: Bucknell University Press, 1986.

Welsh, Alexander. *From Copyright to Copperfield: The Identity of Dickens*. Cambridge, Mass.: Harvard University Press, 1987.

———. *George Eliot and Blackmail*. Cambridge, Mass.: Harvard University Press, 1985.

[White, James]. "The Murdering Banker." *Blackwood's Magazine* 44, no. 278 (December 1838): 823–32.

Whyte, William H. *The Organization Man*. 1956. Philadelphia: University of Pennsylvania Press, 2002.

Wicke, Jennifer. *Advertising Fictions: Literature, Advertising, and Social Reading*. New York: Columbia University Press, 1988.

Wiener, Martin J. *English Culture and the Decline of the Industrial Spirit, 1850–1980*. Cambridge: Cambridge University Press, 1981.

Williams, Merryn. *Margaret Oliphant: A Critical Biography*. London: Macmillan, 1986.

Williams, Raymond. *The Country and the City*. Oxford: Oxford University Press, 1973.

Wilson, Sloan. *The Man in the Gray Flannel Suit*. 1955. New York: Four Walls Eight Windows, 2002.

Woloch, Alex. *The One vs. the Many: Minor Characters and the Space of the Protagonist in the Novel*. Princeton, N.J.: Princeton University Press, 2003.

Woodmansee, Martha. *The Author, Art, and the Market: Rereading the History of Aesthetics*. New York: Columbia University Press, 1996.

Woodmansee, Martha, and Peter Jaszi, eds. *The Construction of Authorship: Textual Appropriation in Law and Literature.* Durham, N.C.: Duke University Press, 1994.

Zeitlin, Maurice. *The Large Corporation and Contemporary Classes.* New Brunswick, N.J.: Rutgers University Press, 1989.

Zelizer, Viviana A. *Economic Lives: How Culture Shapes the Economy.* Princeton, N.J.: Princeton University Press, 2011.

———. *The Purchase of Intimacy.* Princeton, N.J.: Princeton University Press, 2005.

———. *The Social Meaning of Money: Pin Money, Paychecks, Poor Relief, and Other Currencies.* Princeton, N.J.: Princeton University Press, 1997.

Ziegler, Garrett. "The City of London, Real and Unreal." *Victorian Studies* 49, no. 3 (Spring 2007): 431–55.

Index

Italicized page numbers refer to illustrations.

Bigelow, Gordon, 87
biography, 83–84, 85, 193n39. *See also*
    business biographies
"Biography of a Bad Shilling" (Blanchard),
    191n4
Blackwood's, 21, 69, 147–48
Blake, Kathleen, 198n65
Blanchard, Sidney Laman, 191n4
blood: in *Hester*, 160, 164, 168, 169–70;
    and property, 162; and talent, 148,
    155–56, 200n39
board meetings, 22
boards of directors, 3
bonus meetings, 185n65
bosses. *See* employer(s)
Bourne, H. R. Fox, 191n5, 192n22
Bradbury and Evans, 54
British Clothing Company, Limited, 98;
    prospectus, *98*
Brontë, Charlotte, 160, 195n81; *Shirley*,
    195n81
Brontë, Emily, 160
Brooks, David, 173, 178, 179
Brown, John, 81, 195n81
Budgett, Samuel, 72–73, 74, 75, 76, 85
Buffett, Warren, 175
bureaucracy, 22, 89
bureaucratization, 10
business, 6, 7, 16–17, 173–74, 181n11,
    186n79; associations of, 195n12; and
    character, 4, 5–6, 8, 18–19, 20–23, 25–28,
    40, 48–52, 55, 66–68, 70–72, 74–78, 82,
    86–88, 102, 118, 122–23, 140, 145, 146,
    150, 165, 166, 169–71, 186n85; and cha-
    risma, 71, 89–94, 95, 104, 193–94n61;
    and fiction, 78, 91–94, 95, 153; and
    gender, 192–93n34; and heredity, 143,
    144, 146, 148, 151, 152–54, 165, 177–78;
    and impersonality, 6, 9–12; and instinct,
    145, 148; and literature, 74, 76, 140–41,
    174, 178–80; and psychology, 127–28;
    and public relations, 191n6; and reading,
    49–53, 55, 62, 70, 81–82; and realism,
    24–26, 74, 81, 83, 84, 86; reform of, 5–6,
    20–22, 24, 26, 70, 120, 174; and repre-
    sentation, 5, 7, 14–16, 24–28, 86–88,

140–41, 183n28, 186n81; and romance,
    71, 74, 78–79, 81, 84–86, 88, 192n22; and
    self-interest, 127–28, 132; as social activ-
    ity, 6, 14, 16–17, 24–25, 39, 87, 142–43;
    talent for, 143, 144, 146, 148, 152, 156, 157,
    160–61, 163, 166–67, 169–70, 177–78;
    transformations in, 1–3, 55, 174–77.
    See also big business; corporation(s);
    family firm(s); personal business; small
    business; women in business
business biographies, 7, 28, 70, 73–74,
    88, 177, 191n5, 199n19; and character,
    70–72, 74, 77–78, 80, 82–86; and
    charisma, 71, 89–94, 97; and cliché, 84,
    96; detail in, 77, 82, 84, 85; Dickens on,
    82; and family, 77, 192n16; and fiction,
    72, 92; and gender, 143, 192–93n34; and
    heredity, 148, 198n11; and inner life, 77,
    80; and market discipline, 69, 82–84, 92;
    as models for emulation, 70, 75, 89; and
    novels, 194n81; and private life, 76–77,
    80, 83–84, 102; and public relations,
    191n6; and realism, 74, 81, 83, 84; and
    romance, 71, 74, 78–79, 81, 84, 192n22;
    in *The Way We Live Now*, 94, 95, 102
business handbooks/manuals. *See* advice
    manuals

capital, 97, 112, 144; sources of, 42, 45, 54,
    77
capitalism, 5, 6, 8, 9, 14, 65, 84; and calcu-
    lation, 153; and character, 71, 72, 84; and
    charisma, 71, 72; and credit, 112; and
    enchantment, 72, 104; and impersonal-
    ity, 89; industrial vs. mercantile, 55; and
    the novel, 16; and trust, 40; in Victorian
    Britain, 1, 2, 3, 9, 12, 28, 55, 65. *See also*
    business; finance; market; personal
    capitalism
Carlyle, Thomas, 84, 193n57; *Past and
    Present*, 6
Carroll, Lewis, 178
certificate of conformity, 108, 109, 113,
    116–18, 120, 122, 133. *See also* bank-
    ruptcy; character
Chalmers, Thomas, 41

91–94, 95, 153; and fact, 15, 71, 95; and
  probability, 194n64
Fictions of Business (Brawer), 178
finance, 2, 3, 9
Finn, Margot, 183n28, 196n18
Forbes.com, 179
forgery, 34, 43, 47, 66, 188n43
formalism, 15, 140–41; and character, 18,
  141; and economics, 15; and literature,
  15, 95. *See also* new formalism
Fortunes Made in Business, 78–82, 83, 85,
  89, 90, 191n5, 192n16; and charisma, 90,
  91, 92–94; and heredity, 148, 198n11;
  and novels, 194n81; and romance, 79,
  93–94
Foucault, Michel, 8, 22
Francis, John, 13, 191n5
Fraser's, 160
fraud, 25, 82, 117, 120; and managers, 37,
  43, 66
Frederickson, Kathleen, 153

Galison, Peter, 196n46
Gallagher, Catherine, 91–92, 184n51
Galton, Francis, 178, 198n13; and character
  measurement, 149–51; and eugenics,
  146, 155, 159–60, 169; and gender, 158–
  60, 200n47; *Hereditary Genius,* 147,
  150, 158, 198n19; —, Yorke family tree in,
  *159; Inquiries into Human Faculty and
  Its Development,* 146; and statistics, 155;
  and talent, 147, 150–51, 152, 155, 158–60,
  198n19
Gaskell, Elizabeth, *North and South,* 108
genius, 147. *See also* talent
genre, 7, 15, 16, 17, 186n81; and business
  biography, 74; and interdisciplinarity,
  7–8, 15
Gerth, H. H., 193n57, 193n61
Giddens, Anthony, 36
Goodlad, Lauren, 22
Gothic, 154, 186n81, 200n33
Goux, Jean-Joseph, 8
Grant, Albert, 69, 94, 95
Granville-Barker, Harley, 179
Greiner, Rae, 39, 130, 197n47

Grove, W. R., 145
guarantee societies, 27, 186n85; and
  managers, 37

Hadley, Elaine, 197n63
Hawes, William, 116–17
Helps, Sir Arthur, 19, 47–52, 178; *Essays
  Written in the Intervals of Business,*
  47–48, 188n44, 189n58, 189n61, 189n65
Henry, Nancy, 111, 185n78, 186n79
Herbert, Christopher, 72, 78, 191n10
heredity, 143, 144, 198n11; and behaviors,
  151–52; and character, 144–45, 153,
  155, 156, 162; and gender, 143, 157–61,
  200n47; Lamarckian view of, 151; and
  morality, 151; and statistics, 155; and
  talent, 143, 144, 177–78
Hirschman, Albert, 14
Holden, Isaac, 194–95n81
Houston, Gail, 154, 186n81, 200n33
How to Read the Character, 19–20, 188n44
Hudson, George, 90, 94, 95, 190n80
humanities, 173
Hume, David, 43

impersonality, 2, 3, 9, 13, 28; and charisma,
  91; and corporate forms, 6, 10, 69–70;
  and market, 11, 14, 27, 65, 88–89; and
  modernity, 89. *See also* abstraction;
  embeddedness
Industrial Biography (Smiles), 193n44
industry, 1, 3
information books, 7, 23–25, 27, 86, 185n71,
  198n10
insolvency, 111, 195n13. *See also* bankruptcy; ruin
instinct, 143, 148, 152–53, 199nn28–29,
  199n31
investment, 28, 72, 194n75; manuals,
  87–88
investors, 22
it-narratives, 69, 191n4

Jaffe, Audrey, 132–33, 182n18
James, Henry, 179
Jay, Elisabeth, 200n41

Jevons, William Stanley, 87, 193n50
Jobs, Steve, 175
joint-stock companies, 1, 6, 69, 70; and
managers, 43–44, 45, 47; and trust,
43–44, 45
joint-stock ownership, 10, 20–21

kinship, 14, 36; in *Hester,* 162–63, 168
Kleinwort, Sons, and Co., 27
Kozlowski, Dennis, 201n2
Kreisel, Deanna, 195n9, 198n65
Krugman, Paul, 179, 184n43

Law Magazine, 123
Lay, Ken, 175
Lee, Susan, 179
lenders. *See* creditors
Lester, V. Markham, 195nn12–13, 196n18
Levi, Margaret, 187n20
Levine, George, 124, 197n63
Lewes, George Henry, 123
liberalism, 193n57, 197n63
limited liability, 1, 3, 6, 12, 70; introduction
of, 10, 12, 22, 112, 120
lineage, 144, 157, 158
Lister, S. C., 79–80, 153
London and County Bank, 99–100
Lynch, Deidre, 16–17, 78, 192n15, 192n20

Macleod, Dianne Sachko, 191n6
Madoff, Bernie, 3, 173, 175, 179
magic, 71, 89, 90, 91, 102. *See also*
enchantment
Mallon, Thomas, 173, 179
Mamet, David, 178, 179
manager(s), 13, 22, 36–40, 54, 55, 188n33;
and character, 38, 46, 66; and character
interpretation, 36–37, 38–40, 48–52;
compensation of, 42–43, 44–45; Dickens as, 54; and employers, 46–48, 58–
60, 188n43; and family, 44–45, 188n36;
and fraud, 37, 43, 66; independence of,
48, 55–58; and large companies, 187n29,
188n45; and partnership, 37; and personal business, 36; in political economy,
42–44, 47, 187n29; and reading, 36–37,

38–40, 58–59; and self-interest, 37, 38,
45, 46, 58; and sympathy, 39; terminology for, 37; and trust, 37–38, 42–44
Marcus, Sharon, 194n66
market, 5, 17, 83, 92; as abstract system, 6,
12, 13, 14, 24, 108, 109, 113, 173; discipline
for, 20, 22, 26, 28, 86, 104, 109; as economic force, 27, 37, 42, 43, 46, 82; for
labor, 55; and literary writing, 40, 104,
109; rationalization of, 108, 109, 113, 114;
and subjectivity, 9, 65
Marx, Karl, 8, 10
Mason, Sir Josiah, 81, 153
Masson, David, 52
Maudslay, Henry, 85
Maudsley, Henry, 151
McCulloch, J. R., 20–21, 22
McGann, Tara, 195n84
McKeon, Michael, 8, 194n67
melodrama, 186n81
middle class, 17, 184n46
Miller, Arthur, 178
Mills, C. Wright, 193n57, 193n61
modernity, 4, 8, 11, 12, 16, 55, 89, 192n10
modernization, 10, 55
money, 5, 8–9, 191n10
Morris, Pam, 194n63

names, 2, 7, 21, 95; in annual reports, 99–
100; on prospectuses, 96–99, 100–102
Napoleon, 49, 189n55
narration, 123; and free indirect discourse,
103, 129, 130; and omniscience, 26, 103,
129–33
networks, 3, 18, 24, 58, 174
new economic criticism, 4, 5, 8–9, 181n8,
182n20
new formalism, 7
new historicism, 7, 15
Newsom, Robert, 194n64
New York Times, 173, 178, 179
novels, 5, 9, 52, 57–58, 66, 179; and capitalism, 8, 16–17, 78 184n44, 194n81;
and character, 78, 102–4, 140, 146, 173;
detail in, 77; and enchantment, 194n67;
and formalism, 15; history of, 4, 5, 8,

Romance of Commerce, The (Selfridge),
192n22
Romance of Trade, The (Bourne), 191n5,
192n22
Ronen, Ruth, 27
Rothschild, Baron Lionel de, 156
Rothschild, Nathan Meyer, 156
Rothschild family, 145, 148
routinized charisma, 71, 91–92, 95, 102
ruin, 107; and character, 110; and character
knowledge, 107; and family, 114–16;
literary examples of, 108; in *The Mill on
the Floss*, 109–10, 139. *See also* bankruptcy; insolvency

Sadleir, John, 94, 95, 99–100
Salt, Titus, 77
Saturday Review, 153
Secret Committee on Joint-Stock Banks
(1836), 86
Select Committee of the House of Lords
on Bankruptcy and Insolvency (1849),
114, 116–17
self-interest, 22, 37, 51; and character
interpretation, 125–28; of creditors, 114,
118, 122, 124–25, 140, 196n31; and trust,
41–42, 43, 44, 45, 46, 187n20
Selfridge, H. Gordon, 192n22
sensationalism, 186n81
sentimentalism, 192–93n34
Shand, Alexander Innes, 192n22
Shane, Scott, 177
Shaw, Harry, 135
Shell, Marc, 8, 9
small business, 1, 2, 145
Smiles, Samuel, 70, 73, 77, 90, 178, 191n5,
193n44, 193n46, 199n19; and character,
48, 49, 85–86; and romance, 193n44;
Self-Help, 48, 49, 77, 82, 85, 189n55; and
trust, 41
Smith, Adam, 21, 42, 43, 47, 187n21
Spencer, Herbert, 153
state, 28, 122, 134
Stephen, Leslie, 84
Stephenson, George, 85, 188n41
Stephenson, Robert, 85

stereotype, 78, 97, 102
stock exchange, 10, 11, 199n31, 200n38;
character in, 87
stock market, 9, 182n18
subjectivity, 8, 9, 16, 132–33; and depth, 8,
16, 17, 40, 49–52, 65–66
Successful Merchant, The (Arthur), 72–77,
78
succession, 145, 153–55; in *Hester*, 158, 161
surety, 27, 37
surface reading, 194n66
Sutherland, John, 94
sympathy, 187n21; and abstraction, 130,
197n47; and business character, 39,
49, 51–52; and debtors, 124; and Eliot,
123–24, 130, 134–35; and knowledge,
123–25, 130; threat in, 190n80

talent, 143, 144, 147; for business, 143, 144,
146, 148, 152, 156, 157, 177–78; for engineering, 198–99n19; in *Hester*, 160–61,
163, 166–67, 169–70; for law, 150, 152;
for science, 152, 198–99n19
Tennyson, Alfred Lord, 107; *Maud*, 107,
108
Thackeray, William Makepeace, 77, 179;
The Newcomes, 108
Times (London), 97, 113–14, 155, 179
Tipperary Bank, 99
traits, 148, 150–51, 152, 163, 178
transactional character, 4, 5, 7, 14, 16, 21, 71,
174; and trust, 35
Trollope, Anthony, 100, 176–77; on Dickens, 191n92. *Works: The Last Chronicle
of Barset*, 17, 18; *London Tradesmen*,
176–77; *The Way We Live Now*, 10, 28;
94–97, 101–4, 179, 195n84; —, Augustus
Melmotte in, 94–97, 101–4, 173, 175, 179
trust, 3, 28, 35, 40–43; and attachment,
44–46; and character, 22, 35, 46, 65, 66;
and character reading, 40, 53, 55, 62, 65;
and family, 44–45; and joint-stock companies, 44; in literary character, 18, 40;
in network, 24; price of, 27, 42–43; and
property, 21, 22; and self-interest, 41–42,
43, 44, 45, 187nn20–22

Recent Books in the Victorian Literature and Culture Series